CROSS-CULTURAL ESSENTIALS   3

LIVING IN GOD'S NARRATIVE

ROMANS, 1ST AND 2ND THESSALONIANS

Living in God's Narrative
Romans, 1st and 2nd Thessalonians
Biblical Foundations, Module 3 of the Cross-Cultural Essentials Curriculum

Copyright © 2019 AccessTruth

Version 1.1

978-0-6484151-2-1

All Rights Reserved. Except as may be permitted by the Copyright Act, no part of this publication may be reproduced in any form or by any means without prior permission from the publisher. Requests for permission should be made to info@accesstruth.com

Unless mentioned Scripture quotations are taken from the New American Standard Bible® (NASB), Copyright © 1960, 1962, 1963, 1968, 1971, 1972, 1973, 1975, 1977, 1995 by The Lockman Foundation. Used by permission. www.Lockman.org

Scripture quotations marked NLT are taken from the Holy Bible, New Living Translation, copyright © 1996, 2004. Used by permission of Tyndale House Publishers, Inc., Wheaton, Illinois 60189. All rights reserved.

Scripture quotations marked NCV are taken from the New Century Version®. Copyright © 2005 by Thomas Nelson. Used by permission. All rights reserved.

Published by AccessTruth
PO Box 8087
Baulkham Hills NSW 2153
Australia

Email: info@accesstruth.com
Web: accesstruth.com

Cover and interior design by Matthew Hillier
Edited by Simon Glover

Table of Contents

About the Cross-Cultural Essentials Curriculum 5

TUTORIAL 3.1 7
Introducing Romans

TUTORIAL 3.2 13
A powerful message for all

TUTORIAL 3.3 19
Finding ourselves condemned

TUTORIAL 3.4 23
Finding ourselves judged

TUTORIAL 3.5 29
Answering Jewish objections

TUTORIAL 3.6 35
Hopeless before a holy God

TUTORIAL 3.7 41
The basis for justification

TUTORIAL 3.8 47
The results of justification

TUTORIAL 3.9 53
From justification to life

TUTORIAL 3.10 59
Living a new life

TUTORIAL 3.11 65
Brought to despair

TUTORIAL 3.12 69
Deliverance now and in the future

TUTORIAL 3.13 75
God's faithfulness to Israel

TUTORIAL 3.14 81
An unfathomable plan

TUTORIAL 3.15 87
Righteousness practiced

TUTORIAL 3.16 93
Relating to authority

TUTORIAL 3.17 99
Christian liberty

TUTORIAL 3.18 105
Paul's ministry plans

TUTORIAL 3.19 111
The Church in Thessalonica

TUTORIAL 3.20 117
A call to persevere

TUTORIAL 3.21 123
A reason to continue

TUTORIAL 3.22 129
Blameless at the judgment seat

TUTORIAL 3.23 135
Living in light of our hope

TUTORIAL 3.24 141
The day of the Lord

TUTORIAL 3.25 147
God will bring rest

TUTORIAL 3.26 153
Don't forget the truth

TUTORIAL 3.27 153
Focus on Christ

About the Cross-Cultural Essentials Curriculum

It's no secret that there are still millions of people in the world living in "unreached" or "least-reached" areas. If you look at the maps, the stats, and the lists of people group names, it's almost overwhelming. The people represented by those numbers can't find out about God, or who Jesus Christ is, or what He did for them because there's no Bible in their language or church in their area – they have *no access* to Truth.

So you could pack a suitcase and jump on a plane, but then what? How would you spend your first day? How would you start learning language? When would you tell them about Jesus? Where would you start? The truth is that a mature, grounded fellowship of God's children doesn't just "happen" in an unreached area or even in your neighborhood. When we speak the Truth, we need to have the confidence that it is still the same Truth when it gets through our hearer's language, culture and worldview grid.

The *Cross-Cultural Essentials* curriculum, made up of 10 individual modules, forms a comprehensive cross-cultural training course. Its main goal is to help equip believers to be effective in providing people access to God's Truth through evangelism and discipleship. The *Cross-Cultural Essentials* curriculum makes it easy to be better equipped for teaching the whole narrative of the Bible, for learning about culture and worldview and for planting a church and seeing it grow.

More information on the curriculum can be found at *accesstruth.com*

Introduction to Module 3: Living in God's Narrative

Module 3 is the final Biblical Foundations section of the *Cross-Cultural Essentials* curriculum. Bible teacher and pastor Scot Keen walks us through Romans and 1st and 2nd Thessalonians giving us a quick overview of how these significant letters fit into God's Narrative. Scot digs into what the Apostle Paul wanted to convey to these new churches about who He is, His plans, His purposes and how the very same truths relate to us today.

ABOUT THE CROSS-CULTURAL ESSENTIALS CURRICULUM

How to use this module

Read / watch / listen: Read through the tutorial. If you have an online account at *accesstruth.com*, or the DVD associated with this module you can watch the video or listen to the audio of the tutorial.

Discussion Points: At the end of some tutorials there are discussion points. It may be helpful to write down your answers so you can process your thoughts. If you are doing the tutorials in a group, these points should prove helpful in guiding the discussion.

Activities: Some tutorials have activities that involve practical tasks, worksheets that need to be completed, or may just ask for a written answer.

Primary Contributor

Scot Keen has been teaching the Bible for many years. He serves as Interim Pastor at Skiff Lake Bible Church and is a professor and the Dean of Education at Ethnos360 Bible Institute, Jackson. Scot teaches several Bible and Theology courses, his favorite being Acts, Romans, Bibliology, and Soteriology. Scot is married to April and they have three kids. In his spare time, he goes hiking and deer hunting.

3.1 Introducing Romans

 OBJECTIVES OF THIS TUTORIAL

Bible Teacher Scot Keen introduces the themes of the book of Romans and explores why Paul wrote it. Then he delves into the implications which Romans has for our lives as believers and for the Church as a whole.

Introduction

We are calling this module Living in God's Narrative because we are dealing with the book of Romans and 1 and 2 Thessalonians which help us to live inside the story that God is writing in history. The letters of Thessalonians are written by a church planter to a church plant, so they are relevant for someone who wants to spend their life involved in reaching the unreached with the Gospel and seeing churches established that honor the Lord. We believe that you are going to be built up in the faith and encouraged through these books.

How Romans is significant

We will begin this module with the book of Romans. The major theme that Paul covers in Romans is the righteousness of God. The book of Romans is significant in terms of its content and also its potential life impact. The content of the book of Romans is unique in that Paul covers several heavy theological topics that are very relevant for the Christian life.

We will call this "potential life impact" because it is not a given that a believer is going to read the book of Romans and then automatically be impacted. It is a potential life impact, and it comes down to the question, "Are we going to choose to respond in faith and obedience to God's word?" If we do, then the potential life impact is almost immeasurable.

For example, if we come to grips with the message of Romans, then we are going to stop looking for righteousness in ourselves because we are going to realize there is none. We will stop trying to give God a reason to love us because we will realize that we never gave Him a reason to love us in the first place. We will stop worrying about whether or not we have done enough to be accepted by a holy God because we will be convinced that it is not about what we have done; rather, we are saved because Christ satisfied God's wrath when He died on the cross.

We will not worry about security and whether or not we will make it into heaven when we die because we are going to find that, through Christ, we are secure and our salvation is a settled matter. We are going to find that we can walk in newness of life, empowered by the Spirit of God and liberated from indwelling sin, because of the fact that we died with Christ and that we rose again to walk in newness of life.

Furthermore, we are going to find that it is possible to live in fellowship with other believers who come from different theological backgrounds, although they have different convictions about issues of Christian liberty. All of that is addressed in the book of Romans, so it truly is life changing. We encourage you to be asking God to challenge you throughout this module. Ask God to help you respond in a way that is pleasing to Him so that his word can have maximum impact in your life.

Historically the significance of the book of Romans has been huge. For example, in the fourth century, it was the book of Romans that challenged Augustine. Then during the Reformation, it was the book of Romans that lit a fire under Martin Luther with the statement the just shall live by faith. It was also the book of Romans (through the influence of the Moravians) that challenged John Wesley and caused him to trust in Christ alone. Romans has had a profound impact throughout church history, and it is not because Romans is more inspired than other books, but rather because of the content that God has placed in this book.

We find that the book of Romans is unique for several reasons. First of all, it is the most theological of all of Paul's letters. It deals with theological topics like the lost-ness of humanity, justification by faith, redemption, propitiation (all terms that we will unfold later on in the module). It also deals with Christian life principles; being dead to sin and alive under God. It deals with Christian liberty and with God's plan and purpose for Israel as a nation, including Israel's future.

It is also the largest of Paul's letters. The book of Romans has more quotes from the Old Testament than any other letter that Paul writes. In fact, Paul eludes to the Old Testament more than fifty-seven times in the book of Romans.

And finally, it is the most formal of Paul's letters. It is written in a logical way and, in that sense, it is formal because Paul is not necessarily singling out problems until he gets towards the end of the book.

Authorship and Audience

Paul is the author of the book of Romans and in chapter sixteen we find that Tertius is his scribe. We also find in chapter sixteen that Paul commends Phoebe to the church in Rome. Phoebe was a servant of the church in Cenchrea, which is about nine miles away from Corinth, which was where Paul was when he wrote this letter. Evidently after Paul wrote the letter, he placed it in the hands of Phoebe who carried it to the church in Rome.

That is some of the background on the authorship of Romans. As far as the audience goes, Romans 1:7 reveals that Paul is writing to the believers in Rome. Now it is possible- and in fact likely- that the church in Rome was made up of several house churches. In chapter sixteen Paul identifies unique groups of believers in Rome. These house churches would have collectively made up the church in Rome.

We don't know how the church in Rome began. We have no record of an apostle going there before the church existed. One possible and informed guess would be that Jews who were present at Pentecost from Rome heard the Gospel, as proclaimed by Peter, and took it with them on their return to Rome. You can read about the visitors present at Pentecost from Rome in Acts chapter two.

Now that is just a possibility so we cannot be confident about that. However, what we can be confident about is that the church in Rome was made up of believers from both Jewish and Gentile backgrounds. This is going to be very important, as it relates to the purpose of the book. There are several things accomplished by the writing of the book of Romans that are not necessarily the main purpose.

Why Paul wrote the book of Romans

For example, Paul introduces himself to the church in Rome by way of explaining his theological positions to them. They had never met Paul personally, and yet in chapter fifteen, Paul says he wants to be aided by them in an outreach to Spain. He wants them to be a partnering church, so Paul introduces himself to them.

It is also a letter of edification. In Romans 15:14 Paul says that he is convinced that the church in Rome is full of goodness, full of knowledge and able to admonish one another. So they were a maturing church, but he says, "I have written very boldly to remind you, again, because of the grace that was given to me from God to be a minister of Jesus Christ to the Gentiles, ministering as a priest the gospel of God, so that my offering of the Gentiles may be acceptable, sanctified by the Holy Spirit."

What Paul is saying there is that he pictures his ministry in the terms of a priest, and he wants to see the church in Rome sanctified by the power of God's Spirit, a maturing church, so that when this church stands before Christ at His judgment seat, He will be pleased with them. In other words, Paul wants them to grow so that they are pleasing to God and he wants to see this ministry of building up the Church as ultimately an act of worship to God. He wants to edify them, or in other words, to build them up.

There is also an aspect of protection here. Romans 16:17 says, "Keep your eye on those who cause dissensions and hindrances contrary to the teaching which you learned, and turn away from them." That would be Apostolic Doctrine. If anyone teaches contrary to Apostolic Doctrine, watch out for those people. Paul is trying to protect them. They were probably being targeted by legalistic Judaizers, and Paul is going to give them this letter of true doctrine to protect them from false doctrine.

The theme of unification

We believe that is the major reason why Paul wrote the book of Romans was for unification. Let's go back to what we just saw a few minutes ago. The church was comprised of Jews and Gentiles. We have to think like a first century Jew or a first century Gentile to really appreciate this. These believers came from very different backgrounds, and with their different backgrounds came different convictions and different liberties that they would either enjoy or refrain from.

Here is a personal illustration. I grew up in the south-eastern United States, and it is not uncommon there for believers to chew tobacco and to smoke. In World War 2 people from the southern US moved to the northern US to find jobs in factories. As these southerners moved to the north, they were appalled that the believers there would sometimes have alcoholic beverages, and the believers in the north were appalled that the believers from the south would chew tobacco. These were just different convictions based on culture.

Now the Jews would abstain from meat and would recognize certain holy days, even though they were not under the law. The Gentiles had no regard for any of those things and yet they are going to be unified together as God's people. Paul writes the book of Romans to unify them so that they can function together in a way that honors Christ. Paul is going to specifically deal with these issues of Christian liberty in chapters fourteen and fifteen.

As you go through the book of Romans, you will notice the unification theme. In chapter one Paul says, "I am not ashamed of the gospel. It is the power of God for salvation for everyone who believes, to the Jew first, and also the Gentile." Right out of the gate Paul is showing that the Gospel is the answer for mankind's sin, whether Jew or Gentile.

He is going to show us in chapter 3:9 that they both need a savior. "What then? Are we better than they? Not at all; for we have already charged that both Jews and Greeks are all under sin." Both need a Savior. Both are justified by faith.

Paul is going to say that God justifies the Gentiles by faith and that He justifies the Jews by faith. Both are saved in the same way. In chapter ten Paul will say that God is rich in mercy towards both Jew and Gentile, and finally, in chapters fourteen and fifteen that they can live together in unity because of who they are in Christ.

Implications of unification

Now this is an important to see that this is Paul's purpose because it is going to impact the way we read the book. Consider how you are going to serve the Lord in your ministry. The chances are you are going to be serving with people from different backgrounds and you need to be convinced that God's word is able to unify believers, and that God is able to work in us so that we can function together as a healthy body and reach the world with the Gospel. Romans is going to get us there.

Before we move on, remember that Romans is the most theological of all of Paul's letters. Sometimes people say, "Don't talk about doctrine, because doctrine divides," but we want you to catch what Paul is saying. Paul is writing a doctrinal book, and he's doing it for the purpose of unification.

Doctrine does not have to divide. In fact, doctrine can unite us around the person of Christ, and that is exactly what Paul does in this book. It also shows us that doctrine is very practical. Paul uses doctrine to unify believers, so it has a practical purpose there.

Finally as far as the theme of the book of Romans, Paul is going to show us that God's righteousness is lacking in unsaved man. It is imputed to believing sinners. It is imparted as we walk by faith. It is vindicated, or shown to be true, through God's dealing with Israel. And finally, it is lived out in practical application. This is the skeleton of the book of Romans that we'll be following throughout this module.

Worldviews present in Rome

Paul is writing to the believers located in Rome, which was approximately thirteen miles in circumference. The people in Rome were divided as far as the socioeconomic classes. The rich lived in villas and the poor lived in apartments. As far as the socioeconomic conditions, approximately fifty percent of the population in the city of Rome were slaves. It was basically the top five percent who controlled everything in Rome, so there was a huge gap between the rich and the poor.

In Rome and in the Greco-Roman world everyone believed in many gods. They were polytheistic. Some of the religions were licensed by Rome and others were not, but nevertheless, there were many religions.

For example, there might be gods that would be seen as the gods of Asia. There were also hometown deities, or civic deities, and these were the deities that would be worshiped in specific locations. If you read the book of Acts, you're going to hear about Zeus and Hermes. Their territory is larger than some of the other gods.

Then you have Diana of the Ephesians. You also have people who worship gods in their own home. People had both civic deities (large geographical deities) and they also had deities in their home. As Acts chapter seventeen will show us, sometimes they would even have an alter to an unknown god just in case they missed someone.

So the Romans were very polytheistic. They believed in many gods. In fact it has been said about the Greco Roman world, they were comfortable with many gods, as long as no god claimed to have a corner on the market. In other words, they were comfortable with many gods as long as no one god claimed to be the exclusive god. That is going to be a problem, as you know, when we look at the New Testament.

Athenagoras of Athens

There is a quote from Athenagoras, which is second century, but it shows the culture that was already there, present in the first century. I want you to catch this. It says that, "As regards, first of all, the allegation that we are atheists ... most of those who charge with atheism ... charge us with not acknowledging the same gods as the cities." What we are pointing out here is that in the Greco Roman world, if you only believed in one god, you were as good as an atheist to those around you.

Here is another quote from the same author, "As to the other complaint that we do not pray to and believe in the same gods as the cities, the very men who charge us with atheism for not admitting the same gods as they acknowledge are not agreed among themselves concerning the gods." You get this picture in the Greco Roman world that many gods are worshiped. If someone only believes in one god then they are seen as an atheist, and that is going to be a major issue, because Paul is going to say that Jesus Christ is Lord.

One inscription that was found on a coin of Caesar Nero in Corinth says, "Nero, Lord of the Entire World." This is a claim of being the absolute Lord, or the Supreme Lord. Nero was the Caesar when Paul wrote the book of Romans, and Caesar's presence was felt throughout the Roman Empire.

Athenagoras of Athens

It was common in Greco Roman culture for people to be called "lord". So a wife could call her husband "lord," or a servant would call his master "lord," and someone in a chain of command would call their superior "lord". There was no problem with that as long as someone did not claim to be the supreme lord. Only Caesar Nero could make that claim, and he in fact claimed to be lord of the entire world.

It was this world that the first century Christians went into, and they said that there is one Lord, one Faith, one Baptism. The reason we are bringing that out is because Paul states in Romans 1:16 that he is not ashamed of the Gospel. Paul is counter cultural in his claims. He is going against the flow by proclaiming that Christ alone is Lord, regardless of what Rome and Nero claimed.

Let's be challenged by the same mindset: we are going into a world that can be hostile to our faith, and yet we are not ashamed of the Gospel of Christ.

INTRODUCING ROMANS

? DISCUSSION POINTS

1. How do we know that the Church in Rome was comprised of believers from both Jewish and Gentile backgrounds?

2. What was the occasion for the book? i.e. Why did Paul want to write them?

3. What is the theme of the book?

4. Approximately how many Jews were living in Rome during the first century?

5. How does our culture compare with 1st century Rome?

➡ ACTIVITIES

1. In half a page describe the religion of the Roman Empire.

3.2 A Powerful Message for All

 OBJECTIVES OF THIS TUTORIAL

We explore the roots of the Gospel message in the Old Testament. We find that the Gospel is relevant to both believers and unbelievers, powerfully bringing about salvation and sanctification. This module was developed from lessons presented by Bible Teacher Scot Keen.

Introduction

We will begin this tutorial with an introduction to the book of Romans by zooming in on Romans chapter one, verses 1-17. We will start by ascertaining the author and the audience of the book of Romans. We have already looked at this briefly but this time we will dig deeper into the details.

Paul's credentials

In Romans 1:1 we find Paul's credentials which tell us more about him as an author. Paul is a bond servant of Christ Jesus called as an apostle and is set apart for the Gospel of God. Notice that the first thing off Paul's pen is a description of himself as a slave of Christ. Someone with a Greco-Roman worldview would picture a man or a woman on an auction block being sold to the highest bidder. When Paul claims this of himself he actually sees it as a positive thing. He thinks of himself first and foremost as a slave of Jesus Christ. Often when we introduce ourselves we speak about ourselves positively so that people will value us. Paul's primary form of identification is that he is someone who is bought by Another. He is the property of the Lord Jesus.

Now that is amazing in and of itself, but it is even more amazing when you consider who Paul used to be. His life's work was previously dedicated to stamping out Christianity. This man who hated Christ and Christians is now gladly owning himself as a slave of Christ. Obviously it is only the grace of God that can do that in a person's life.

Notice that Paul says he is an apostle set apart for the Gospel of God. Calling himself a slave involves who he belongs to. But calling himself an apostle of Christ involves the role that he has been given. In calling himself an apostle he is informing the Romans right out of the gate that he is writing, not as a gifted teacher or as someone with an opinion, but rather he is writing with apostolic authority in order to establish doctrine. What Paul writes is God's Word and he wants it to be seen as such.

Let me give you a personal analogy. When I think about being set apart for the Gospel, I think about the cast iron skillets that my family used for cooking food. We had different skillets and cookers for different purposes. We had one that we called the cornbread skillet, and you could not cook anything else on it because it might mess it up. It was set apart for a purpose. Likewise Paul saw himself as set apart for a purpose, and that purpose was for the Gospel of God. God set him apart from his mother's womb, as he says in Galatians, for a specific ministry- the ministry of the Gospel of God's grace.

Paul's message

Notice that Paul elaborates on this further. He calls the message the Gospel of God, and highlights it further by describing it as God's Good News. This Gospel is a message that God has, and because it is Good News, he wants it to go to the nations.

This Good News is rooted in the Old Testament. Paul says it was promised beforehand through God's prophets in the Holy Scriptures. Paul wants his audience to see that the Gospel is not something new, making it somehow detached from the Old Testament. It was actually promised in the Old Testament. You would have noticed this if you completed modules one and two of the AccessTruth Curriculum. We are following God's Narrative throughout history. We find Paul saying that the Gospel is in fact part of the Narrative and it was promised long ago.

Missionaries Bob Kennel and George Walker planted a church in Papua New Guinea in the Basotho Tribe. They taught the Bible chronologically when they presented the Gospel. The new believers told them, "We believed your message because our stories are like logs. They abruptly begin and they abruptly end. They have no continuity. When you gave us God's word, you started from the beginning and so we saw that God's message has roots. It's rooted in history, and it develops fully in the New Testament." Well that is the message that Paul proclaimed, "The gospel of God, which he promised beforehand through his prophets in the holy Scriptures, concerning his Son." This Good News in centered on the person of Christ.

Jesus was a descendant of David. That also shows the Old Testament roots of the Gospel. The prophets foretold that the Messiah would be a descendant of David. David had the kingship, and because Jesus is a descendant of David, Jesus can ultimately reign over Israel and over the world.

"[Jesus] was declared the son of God with power by the resurrection from the dead, according to the Spirit of holiness, Jesus Christ our Lord" (Romans 1:4). Jesus Christ was declared to be the son of God with the resurrection. This is significant because the fact that Christ rose from the dead declares him to be the promised Messiah.

Paul explains that the Gospel message is sent to the nations. "Through whom we have received grace and apostleship to bring about the obedience of faith among all the Gentiles for his name's sake," (Romans 1:5). It is beautiful how Paul begins this book. Paul describes God's Gospel, promised in the Scriptures and inspired through God's prophets. It is the Gospel of God's son, and it is God who is using it to reach out to the world.

Paul's audience

Right at the beginning of the book of Romans we have the global focus of the Gospel. Paul says, "Through whom we have received grace and apostleship to bring about the obedience of faith among all the Gentiles". Let's ponder that for just a second. When he says through whom, he is talking about Jesus. Jesus is active in church history. He is the One who gave Paul his apostolic ministry for a purpose. The purpose was that Paul would be sent to the nations. So Paul went to the nations seeking to bring about the obedience of faith. He wanted them to not only believe the Gospel, but also to walk in obedience to God's Word. Paul did all this for his namesake, Christ Jesus.

Paul describes his audience as, "all who are beloved of God in Rome called saints." Just as Paul was set apart for the Gospel, so are the believers in Rome. They too are set apart as saints to belong to God.

A prayer for the church

Let's look into the author and audience further here. Paul gives his desire to visit the Romans in verses eight through ten. He says, "First, I thank my God through Jesus Christ for you all, because your faith is being proclaimed throughout the whole world. For God... is my witness as to how unceasingly I make mention of you."

Paul is incessantly praying for the believers in Rome, and he specifically lays out his prayer. Paul prays that God would make it possible for him to go to Rome. He has had a desire for many years to go there. His desire is to impart a spiritual gift to the church there.

If all we had was that phrase, we could conclude that Paul plans to hand out spiritual gifts from a big gift bag or something like that. He explains what he means further in the chapter. When Paul says he wants to give them a spiritual gift, he is speaking about discipleship. He wants them to be encouraged by one another's faith. Paul wants to go to Rome and build them up in the faith, and that in itself would be a spiritual gift. It would be a gift of discipleship that would build them up spiritually in the Lord. In turn, Paul also believed that he would benefit from interacting with the believers there.

Paul goes on to speak of his desire to visit them. He says, "I do not want you to be unaware, brethren, that often I have planned to come to you (and have been prevented so far) so that I may obtain some fruit among you also, even as among the rest of the Gentiles." Paul has traveled throughout the Roman world, and he has seen the fruit of the Gospel as people have to come faith in Christ. Paul has seen people become mature and churches become established. He wants to come to Rome to see that same type of fruit there.

Paul explains that he is obligated both to Greeks and the Barbarians. Now technically both these categories are Gentiles, but Paul is picking opposite ends of the spectrum. Paul doesn't care whether they are refined Greeks or rough Barbarians living on the fringes of the Roman empire. He doesn't care whether they own a three-piece suit or if they are dressed in simple clothing found from a jungle setting. He sees them as souls for whom Christ died and himself as obligated to take the Gospel message to them.

Catch this amazing statement in verse fifteen, "I am eager to preach the gospel to you also who are in Rome." Paul says he is eager to preach the Gospel to those in Rome. Who is Paul talking to? He is talking to believers in Rome. Now there is no doubt that Paul wanted to reach out to unbelievers in Rome, but Paul says here that he wants to preach the Gospel also to believers.

This is going to be significant as we move through the book of Romans. Paul is going to use the Gospel with some elasticity. The Gospel is a message to unsaved people, but it is also for believers. Paul says in chapter sixteen that believers are established by the Gospel message. Paul has confidence in the Gospel message ("I am not ashamed of the gospel") and so wants to share it in Rome.

Thesis Statement

In fact, this is Paul's thesis statement for the book, and he is going to elaborate on this the rest of the way through. "I am not ashamed of the gospel. It is the power of God for salvation to everyone who believes. To the Jew first and also to the Greek."

There are a few things worth noticing here. First of all, Paul says the Gospel is the power of God for salvation. It is not a power of God, meaning one of many, it is the exclusive message by which men can be saved (men and women obviously). It is the only message, and that is true for Jews as well as Gentiles. The reason it is the power of God for salvation is that it speaks about the righteousness of God. In it (meaning in the Gospel message) the righteousness of God is revealed.

The Gospel message reveals how we receive God's attribute of righteousness. The Message also reveals that Christ died for our sins, and that He rose again the third day. In Romans chapter two Paul says the righteous man shall live by faith. So Paul is not ashamed of the Gospel and is ready to preach it in Rome. He knows the power of the Message. It brings salvation to unbelievers, and it brings sanctification to those who have already believed.

? DISCUSSION POINTS

1. Paul states that he is called an Apostle. What kind of authority does this give him?

2. Paul said that through Christ he received grace and apostleship. This is a reference to...?

3. For what purpose did Paul receive grace and apostleship?

4. What did Paul mean when he said that he wanted to impart to them some spiritual gift?

5. In 1:15 Paul said he was eager to preach the gospel to the Romans. Why would he be eager to preach the gospel to people that were already saved?

6. Paul says that the righteousness of God is revealed in the gospel. What does he mean by that statement?

3.3 Finding Ourselves Condemned

 OBJECTIVES OF THIS TUTORIAL

We see that all mankind is under God's wrath, both Jews and Gentiles. We have all rejected God's Truth, which is evident in creation. This module was developed from lessons presented by Bible Teacher Scot Keen.

Introduction

In the previous tutorials we discussed Paul's thesis, "For I am not ashamed of the gospel, for it is the power of God for salvation to everyone who believes, to the Jew first and also to the Greek" (Romans 1:16-17). Paul unifies the church in Rome by showing that both Jews and Gentiles are in need of a Savior and that the Gospel is the answer to the needs of both.

Righteousness needed

So far Paul has introduced the letter of Romans and given his thesis statement. Now he goes into a large section on righteousness and condemnation. Paul says, "We have already charged (or given allegations, given proof) that both Jews and Gentiles are all under sin."

This is significant because when Paul gets to chapter three he says, we have been proving this. That means that everything Paul says up until this point is his proof. So we need to read Romans 1:18- 3:20 as Paul's evidence that all of humanity is under sin and needs a Savior.

Paul will break it down for us. He will look first at God's wrath towards Gentiles and then show us the impartiality of God's wrath towards Jews and Gentiles. He will then specifically focus on the Jew and God's wrath and afterwards will conclude with a section has implications for all humanity. We will follow this sequence in the following tutorials.

Revelation of God's wrath towards Gentiles

Look at Romans 1:18-32. We see the revelation of God's wrath towards the Gentiles. We are talking about those who have no written witness of God's Word. It is important to catch that upfront. In Romans chapter one Paul says, "People have rejected the knowledge of God through creation." He goes on to say in verse twenty, "For since the creation of the world his invisible attributes, his eternal power and divine nature, have been clearly seen, being understood through what has been made."

We are telling you this upfront so that you see that the Gentiles are condemned even though they do not have God's Word. All they have is God's testimony through creation. The destiny of the heathen (those who have never heard the Gospel) is a big theological topic. Paul is talking about these people and he shows us that they too are condemned and without excuse.

We challenge you in this tutorial to let God's word speak more loudly than your cultural beliefs. This will challenge your worldview about those who have never heard the Gospel.

Wrath revealed

Let's zero in on verse eighteen in Romans chapter one. Paul says, "For the wrath of God is revealed from heaven against all ungodliness and unrighteousness of men who suppress the truth in unrighteousness." God's wrath is revealed and what it reveals is ungodliness. This does not necessarily refer to someone who is living in dramatic wickedness. It refers to anyone who does not care that God's wrath is against them, even though it has been revealed to them. Paul is talking specifically about people who suppress the Truth in unrighteousness.

We see that God's Truth, through creation, reaches the conscience of mankind, and mankind in turn suppresses it for the sake of unrighteousness. To give you a personal example, growing up there were times I wanted to enjoy my sin, but the presence of God's Word interfered with my enjoyment of it. So I would ignore God's Truth in order to enjoy unrighteousness.

Well, that is the idea here. Mankind holds back, or suppresses, the Truth for the sake of unrighteousness. And wrath is revealed from heaven against all the unrighteousness and ungodliness of mankind.

Truth revealed

But not only wrath is revealed, but also truth is revealed. Look at verse nineteen in Romans chapter one. Paul says, "Because that which is known about God is evident within them; for God made it evident to them." When he says evident within them, he is referring to the fact that God made human beings in His image with a capacity to perceive the revelation of God, whether through creation or through His written Word.

But how did God make His Truth evident to the nations? They do not have God's Word, so how did God make it evident to them? Verse twenty tells us. Paul says, "Since the creation of the world his invisible attributes, his eternal power and divine nature, have been clearly seen."

Listen to this language. Invisible and yet clearly seen. God's invisible attributes are clearly seen and they have been seen since creation. The idea is that since God said, "Let there be light," there has been an ongoing testimony to God's existence in creation. Creation demands the existence of a Creator.

Let me give you a personal example. Years ago I took my family to a zoo in Fort Wayne, Indiana. As we walked into the zoo, my five-year-old son suddenly stopped in his tracks when he spotted some vines in the shape of a horse. He stood there for the longest time and finally said, "They had to do that." He realized that this was not the way that vines and tall grasses naturally grow. He knew that Someone with intelligence had created it. It was not just an accident.

If that is true of vines and grasses fashioned in the shape of a horse, how much truer is it in the case of all of God's creation! Since the creation of the world, God's invisible attributes have been clearly seen, being understood through what has been made. So Paul says, "They are without excuse." Since the time God spoke the world into existence, there has been testimony of His existence. Psalm nineteen confirms this by saying, "The heavens declare the glory of God and the firmament shows his handiwork and day after day reveal speech and knowledge." Creation is God's silent, ongoing testimony to His existence.

Here is another personal example. When I was growing up in South-East Kentucky, my friends and I frequently explored the mountains. On one occasion, we found a rock which we decided to camp under. We soon discovered pieces of flint in the rock. It occurred to us that there must have been life there before us. Perhaps Indians had camped under that rock many decades or centuries before. It is the same with God's creation. You see evidence of His presence everywhere and, for that reason, Paul says, "They are without an excuse."

So far we have seen wrath revealed from heaven, truth revealed in God's creation, and now we see that God's Truth has been rejected. Look closely at verse twenty. Paul says, "Because God's testimony is clear and constant, man is without an excuse." When Paul says without an excuse, he uses the Greek word anapologetos. This is the same word that is used in 1 Peter referring to the fact that we should always be ready to give an answer for our faith. In other words, we should be ready to give an apology.

Truth rejected

Being ready to give an apology means being ready to give a reason or a defense. Because of God's creation and the testimony to His existence, men are anapologetos. They are without a reason or defense. There is nothing that they can say in their defense because God's creation testifies to the fact that God exists. They had truth but they rejected that truth and, for that reason, they stand condemned. Look at verse twenty-one. "Even though they knew God, they did not honor him as God or give thanks."

Paul is speaking historically of a time when the nations had a knowledge of God. Most likely this refers to the time when Noah's three sons came off the ark, and the nations that follow them, leading up to the time of Babel. They exchanged the knowledge of God for a lie.

Paul says, "For even though they knew God, they did not honor Him as God or give thanks, but they became futile in their speculations, and their foolish heart was darkened. Professing to be wise, they became fools and exchanged the glory of the incorruptible God for an image." And again, he says, "They exchanged the truth." To exchange the Truth means that at one point in their history they must have been in possession of the Truth.

Given over to impurity

No one returns an item to a store and opens up an empty bag and says they want to exchange it. You cannot exchange something if you do not have something to begin with. They exchanged both the Truth of God and the glory of God. And so, we have seen that Truth was revealed and then rejected. Because of that, God gave mankind over to impurity.

Look at verse twenty-four. Paul says, "Therefore God gave them over in the lusts of their hearts to impurity, so that their bodies would be dishonored among them. For they exchanged the truth of God for a lie, and worshiped and served the creature rather than the Creator, who is blessed forever." As a result of rejecting the God's knowledge, God gave man over to his darkened heart.

Given over to degradation

Mankind came to a place of believing a lie over truth, and so became undiscerning. In verse twenty-six Paul says, "For this reason God gave them over to degrading passions; for their women exchanged the natural function for that which is unnatural, and in the same way also the men abandoned the natural function of the woman and burned in their desire toward one another."

Now we have homosexuality coming out of this rejection of God's knowledge, pulling mankind into a moral, downward spiral. Paul begins to talk about what they did and what God did. In terms of what they did, Paul says, "They exchanged the glory of God. They exchanged the truth of God, they did not see fit to retain God in their knowledge." God is responding to the nation's rejection of His Truth by giving them over to the lusts of their hearts. He gave them over to degrading passions and a depraved mind.

Note that God did not make them have a depraved mind. God turned them over to go the direction that their hearts had already chosen. If you have ever stood on a riverbank holding onto a boat with a rope, all you have to do is just let go of the rope and the current will carry the boat away. That in essence is what God did. He allowed mankind to go their own way, the way of their wicked hearts. In doing so God gave them over to the impurities that were already in their hearts.

Given over to a depraved mind

So far we have seen truth revealed, truth rejected, and mankind given over to impurity, degradation and a depraved mind which is incapable of discernment. Look at what Paul says in verse twenty-eight. He says, "And just as they did not see fit to acknowledge God any longer, God gave them over to a depraved mind." They have a mind that can actually believe something that makes no sense whatsoever.

You see this happening throughout history. Let's look at some examples of this happening. There is a tribal group in Papua New Guinea that had a practice of mummifying elders. The tribal people there came to the conclusion that their elders could work magic on them and could bring either sickness or blessing. After the elders die, the people mummify them and bring them sacrifices daily. They bring food on a plate and leave it there for the elders. Now you could ask them, "If they're eating the food, how come the food is still there?" They would say, "The spirit of the ancestor takes the spirit of the food." It is obvious to us that have become futile in their speculations, given over to a reprobated mind. We look at this in disbelief from the standpoint of our civilized culture and wonder how could anyone believe a lie such as that.

An example from Western culture

But flip it around and look at western culture. Charles Darwin came up with the Theory of Evolution and made arguments claiming that advanced lifeforms came from primitive lifeforms. People from third-world and majority-world countries look at the western world and wonder how anyone could be foolish enough to believe that. You get in essence is what Paul is saying in Romans one professing to be wise, they became fools.

Think of it this way. If mankind rejects truth then the only alternative is to walk in lies. That is exactly what has happened throughout the world. Notice verse thirty-two. Paul says, "And although they know the ordinance of God, that those who practice such things are worthy of death, they not only do the same, but also give hearty approval to those who practice them." And the reason we are calling attention to this verse is because, so far, Paul has been using past tense. They knew God, they did not honor God, God gave them over. It is all in past tense. But now Paul uses present tense. "Although they know (present tense) that those who do such things are worthy of death." Paul is highlighting that the state the Gentile world was in was the result of rejecting the knowledge of God. And because truth has been revealed mankind is now without excuse.

Think of Richard Dawkins, an avowed atheist and an opponent of Christianity. When debating John Lennox he said, "When we go into a garden, and we see how beautiful it is and we see colored flowers, of course it is natural to think that there must be a gardener. Any fool is likely to think there must be a gardener. The huge achievement of Darwin was to show that that didn't have to be true." Listen to what he says here, "Of course it's difficult, of course it would have to wait until the mid-nineteenth century before anybody thought of it." He is in fact saying, "It seems so obvious that if you have a garden then there must be a gardener who created it. What Darwin did was show us the staggering, counter-intuitive fact that this can be explained by an undirected process."

What we are calling attention to in Dawkin's quote is that he himself admits that it is only natural to conclude that when there is a garden, there must be a gardener. He is saying that it is counter-intuitive to think otherwise. How did mankind get to the place it is in? It is because we rejected the knowledge of God. When you reject the knowledge of God the only alternative is to walk in lies.

However the book of Romans does not leave us there. We will soon see that God has provided salvation for all mankind, including those who are in the remotest parts of the earth living in the darkest depravity. Were it not for God, who has sent out the Gospel of His Son (as we saw earlier in chapter one), those nations would still be there, perishing without any hope whatsoever.

TUTORIAL 3.3

❓ DISCUSSION POINTS

1. God's wrath is revealed from heaven against those who are doing what?

2. In order to suppress the truth, what do people have to possess in the first place?

3. How is this truth revealed? Through what means?

4. What is being revealed about God through this means?

5. From your text, what phrases describe how well God has revealed Himself through creation?

6. According to the text, what did these people do with what they knew about God?

7. These people suppressed the truth, etc. What did God do in response to their sin?

8. How is God's wrath manifested in Romans 1?

9. How do we know from this passage that Paul is talking

➡ ACTIVITIES

1. What are some possible objections one might hear when teaching about the lost state of those who have never heard? Write down any examples of interaction you have had with other believers and what their response has been.

3.4 Finding Ourselves Judged

 OBJECTIVES OF THIS TUTORIAL

We discover that God's judgment is not partial. It is not biased, and so is inescapable. Paul explains these truths to a self-righteous audience who think that they can bypass God's judgment. This module was developed from lessons presented by Bible Teacher Scot Keen.

Introduction
Last time we explored the revelation of God's wrath towards the Gentiles as we saw in Romans 1:18-32. Paul said that mankind is without excuse because of God's clear and constant testimony through creation. Now Paul moves onto the impartiality of God's wrath towards Jews and Gentiles. In this tutorial we will be focusing on Romans 2:1-16.

Impartiality of God's wrath
Paul will not single out the Jews until verse seventeen in chapter two. But we can see Paul tiptoeing up on the Jews, saying things that refer to them, although he does not identify his audience until later on. We know that because Paul is addressing people who think they are better than the Gentiles, commonly referred to as barbarians. They assume that they will escape God's wrath because of their ethnicity. Paul is going to show them that they are basing their hopes on something that will not hold. He will show them that God's wrath is impartiality towards both Jews and Gentiles.

God's Judgment is inescapable
Paul begins chapter two by highlighting that God's judgment is inescapable. In verse one of chapter two Paul says, "Therefore, you have no excuse." Now that should strike us as an odd statement because, when Paul originally wrote Romans, there were no chapter divisions, and he only mentions the Gentiles. Let's go back to verse thirty-two in chapter one, "And although they know the ordinance of God, that those who practice such things are worthy of death, they not only do the same, but also give hearty approval to those who practice them." He is talking about the Jews and he says, "Therefore, you are without an excuse." That really seems odd. How come they are accountable and with an excuse when we are talking about what someone else did? Paul will explain that.

Paul says, "You have no excuse, everyone of you who passes judgment, for in that which you judge another, you condemn yourself; for you who judge practice the same things." We believe that Paul is addressing the Jews here. Paul says, "When you judge the Gentiles and say they shouldn't do that and you do the same thing, then by your own confession you are saying, 'I, too, deserve God's judgment'".

Let's use the story of King David and the prophet Nathan (in Samuel chapter two) as an example. David committed adultery with Bathsheba. God sent Nathan the Prophet to expose David's sin. Nathan tells a parable. He told a story about a poor man who owned a lamb, which happened to be precious to his family. Nathan also speaks of a rich man who, although having everything he wanted, stole the poor man's lamb for himself. David was so angry that he said, "That person deserves to die," to which Nathan responded, "You are that man because you took the wife of your Hittite to make her your own."

When David said that rich man deserved to die he was actually condemning himself. That is what the Jews are doing here in chapter two. They are pointing at the Gentiles and saying, "Those people deserve God's judgment," but they themselves are doing the same things. By their own admission, they too deserve God's judgment. In verse two Paul says, "And we know that the judgment of God rightly falls upon those who practice such things." He is getting them to agree with him here. He says, "We know. You and I know this. We know that God's judgment rightly falls on people who do these bad things." These self-righteous Jews are not connecting the dots that they too deserve God's wrath.

To give you another personal example, I had a mentor who worked with a tribal group in the Philippines called the Kalanguya Tribe. When my mentor was working with this group he asked, "Can you tell me what a good Kalanguya is like?" He wanted to find out about their standards of righteousness. They said, "Well, a good Kalanguya is good to his wife and he provides for his family. He's a hard worker. He helps other people. He shares." They gave their list of things a good Kalanguya would do. Then, he asked, "Can you show me somebody who's like that?" I kid you not, they said, "We don't have anybody like that in our village."

It is easy for mankind to describe what a good person should be like, but Paul is not concerned about Jews' ability to describe a good person. He wants them to see that they do not live up to the standard that they describe. In verse three Paul says, "Do you suppose this, O man, when you pass judgment, and you do the same thing, do you suppose that you will escape the judgment of God?" Of course they did. They assumed that they would escape God's judgment because they were Jews and not Gentiles. They assumed that even though they did the same things that others were doing, that they were somehow sheltered from God's wrath by simply having Abraham's DNA. Paul shows them that that simply is not the case.

In verse four Paul says, "Or do you think lightly of the riches of His kindness and tolerance and patience, not knowing that the kindness of God leads you to repentance?" Because God is not executing judgment on the Jews in that moment, they assumed that all was well between them and God. Paul says, "No, the reason God is not judging you is in order to give you opportunity to repent." God holding back judgment does not equal God giving approval. God is giving the Jews an opportunity to come to faith in Christ.

God's judgment is unbiased

We are coming to what may be the most difficult, but perhaps also the most important, portion of Romans. In verse five Paul says, "But because of your stubbornness and unrepentant heart you are storing up wrath for yourself in the day of wrath and revelation of the righteous judgment of God." The Jews were unwilling to repent. Every day that went by wrath was building up. They would face that wrath on the day of God's judgment. Paul wants them to recognize that God's wrath is unbiased. He explains this further.

Now coming up is what is called, in literary terms, a chiasm. It is a literary device that was used by authors in the Greco-Roman world. These authors would frame a statement for the sake of emphasis. Some people call it a truth sandwich. Paul makes certain statements that seem to make no sense until we see them in our context.

In verse six Paul says that God will render to each person according to his deeds. He says in verse seven, "To those who by perseverance in doing good seek for glory and honor and immortality, eternal life; but to those who are selfishly ambitious and do not obey the truth, but obey unrighteousness, wrath and indignation."

Can you see the problem with that? It sounds like Paul is saying that if you do good, you get immortality and eternal life. If you do good, then you will receive honor, peace and glory. It sounds like Paul is saying that you get eternal life by doing good works, but remember that Paul is talking to the self-righteous Jews, and he wants to shut the door on their self-righteous claims. Paul in essence is saying, "Okay. If you do good and only good, you'll get eternal life." He is saying, "Let's test your theory. If you think you can be good enough to earn God's salvation go ahead and try it, but be warned that if you cannot be good enough then there will be distress for every man who does evil and God will judge the Jew first."

Paul mirrors these statements in the chiasm. God judges all men equitably. All men will be judged impartially. Those who do good get eternal life. But those who do evil will suffer God's wrath. Paul wants to make it empathically clear to the Jews that everyone who does evil, whether they are Jews or Gentiles, will face the wrath of God.

The Jews thought that they would be treated with preference. Paul says yes, they will be treated with preference. The Jews will be judged first and the Gentiles after. Everyone will get exactly what they deserve. If the Jews have done evil, then they will be the first to be judged. He is taking away their hope of self-righteousness and he uses a literary device called a chiasm to do that.

God's judgment is based on deeds

Listen to Paul's next argument. He explains that God's judgment is based on deeds. The Jews had a problem with this. They thought that simply being Jews (possessing a higher moral standard than non-Jews) made them right with God. Paul is going to say, "No, it is not what you know or possess, but rather, what you do that will be judged."

Paul explains this in Romans 1:12-16. Notice that he says in verse twelve, "For all who have sinned without the law will also perish without the law, and all who have sinned under the law will be judged by the law." Those who sin without the Law are Gentiles. They do not have God's Word and will perish without the Law. In contrast, those who sin under the Law will be judged by the Law.

To give a personal illustration, years ago when I was studying Romans, I used a marker to cross out every additional phrase in the book of Romans in order to get the gist of what Paul was saying. I discovered something that I think is profound. Taking away the supporting phrases, without the law and under the law gave me, "All who have sinned will perish. All who have sinned will be judged." Paul communicated the exact same thing in the chiasm. There will be wrath for every person who does evil, to the Jews first, and also to the Gentiles.

Impartiality of God's wrath

Paul's point is that everyone who sins will be judged. That is something that the Jews had a problem with. Paul explains that God's wrath is impartial. In verse fourteen Paul says, "For when Gentiles who do not have the Law do instinctively the things of the law, these, not having the law, are a law to themselves, in that they show the work of the law written in their hearts, their conscience bearing witness and their thoughts alternately accusing or else defending them."

This is a difficult section, but it is worth taking the time to understand. Paul says that the Gentiles instinctively follow the Law. Some read that and take it to mean that there must be groups of people out there who actually live up to God's standard. That is not what Paul is saying. When Paul says that they follow the Law and have it written on their hearts, he is simply saying that all mankind has standards.

That was an issue for the Jews. They had a standard, the Law, and they thought that possessing it made them right with God. Paul said, :No, it is not your possession of the standard that justifies you before God. The question is, do you live up to that standard?" Paul says that, in fact, everyone has a standard. The Gentiles instinctively have a standard. They show that the Law is written on their hearts. Possession of a standard is not what makes one right with God. The only way to be good enough is to actually live up to that standard. If not, Paul says that there is wrath for every person who does evil.

Paul is not saying here that people are justified by their deeds. He is trying to bring the Jews to the end of themselves by recognizing that there is nothing they can do. He is trying to show them the futility of trying to become right with God through good works. It is not a possession of a standard, or even an attempt at a standard, that makes you right with God. People can only be good enough if they live up to that standard. Paul says that God will judge the secrets of men through Jesus Christ. He ends with a note of seriousness that God, who looks at the heart and judges the secrets of men, will be the One to evaluate. This means that the Jew is left wanting before a Holy God.

❓ DISCUSSION POINTS

1. Who is Paul focusing on in this section?

2. How do we know (from what Paul will later say in Romans) that Paul isn't teaching that men can actually be saved by doing good in verses 7-10?

3. What is Paul's point in verses 7-10?

4. What does Paul mean when he says that the Gentiles do instinctively the things in the law?

3.5 Answering Jewish Objections

 OBJECTIVES OF THIS TUTORIAL

Paul continues to explain that the Jews are under God's wrath, as are the Gentiles. He brings to light an inconsistency between the Jews' claims and their conduct. This module was developed from lessons presented by Bible Teacher Scot Keen.

Introduction

We have seen so far that God's wrath is revealed towards the Gentiles and that God's testimony is clear and constant, which means that mankind is without excuse.

Paul acts like a prosecuting attorney in this section of Romans. He targets different groups of people. He begins with the Gentiles and then sneaks up on the Jews. He is talking to self-righteous people who think they are good enough to earn God's salvation. Paul lets them know that if they do good, then they will get good in return. However, he never holds this out as an actual option. He is saying, in essence ,if people think they can go down that road, then they had better do it perfectly because if not, they are going to face God's wrath. It is not the possession of a standard that makes people right with God. The only way people can claim to be righteous is if they can actually live up to a perfect standard. And Paul knew that the Jews couldn't live up to their rules.

Inconsistency of claim and conduct

Paul pointedly calls attention to the Jews and God's wrath (Romans 2:17-3:18). Paul is going to firstly show the inconsistency of their claim and conduct. The Jews claimed to be right with God because of their identity as Jews. But their conduct did not measure up to their claims so Paul says in Romans 2:17-19, "But if you bear the name 'Jew' and rely upon the law and boast in God, and know his will and approve the things that are essential, being instructed out of the law and are confident that you yourself are a guide to the blind, a light to those who are in darkness." When Paul says 'but', they may have had a ray of hope. "Wait a minute. We are Jews and we do teach other people and we are instructed out of the Law and we do love the word of God and we are correctors of the immature." Maybe they thought, "Wow, there's hope for us. Maybe the fact that we're Jews will shelter us from God's wrath."

But Paul turns the tables very quickly. He says in Romans 3:21, "But now apart from the law the righteousness of God has been manifested, being witnessed by the law and the prophets." Paul is planning to highlight that although the Jews had possession of the Law and were trusting in it to make them right with God, it was the very thing that they were trusting in (the Law) that actually condemned them before a holy God.

It is stated elsewhere that the Jews were trusting in the Law to make them right with God. In John chapter five Jesus said, "Don't think that I will accuse you before the Father; the one who accuses you is Moses, in whom you have set your hope." They were trusting in their Law observance to make them right with God. So Paul is going to show that possession of the Law does not make people right with the Lord.

Paul then goes through a list of things that the Jews were known to brag about. He says that they rely on the Law and boast in God. They approve God's will and the things that are essential, and not only that, they are also instructed by the Law. They are confident that they are a guide to the blind and a light to those in darkness, a teacher to the foolish and a teacher of the immature. Because of this possession of the Law, they were confident that they were a guide to the blind. Jesus actually reversed that and said, yes they are guides, but they are blind ones! Obviously if a blind guide leads the blind, then the guide is not leading properly because he or she can't see.

The Jews were confident that they were a light to those in darkness, meanwhile being in darkness themselves. They were confident that they could teach others. In fact Jesus said that the scribes and Pharisees would "travel around on sea and land to make one proselyte." They were teaching other people, but in their very efforts they were making someone twice the child of hell than they were to begin with. Not only was the individual still lost, but now they thought they were right with God because they followed the message that was given to them by the Jews.

So Paul is going to demonstrate that both Jews and Gentiles are under God's wrath. He says that the scribes and Pharisees placed themselves "in the chair of Moses." Jesus said, "They say things" but "do not do them." They were teaching others, but they were not teaching themselves. And Paul was not the first one to make that statement- Jesus made it first.

Paul is showing an inconsistency between the Jew's claim and conduct. Notice the terminology here, you who say, you who teach, you who preach. These are all things that came out of their mouths, not actions that they manifested with their bodies. In the book of Matthew Jesus said, "These people honor me with their lips, but their hearts are far away from me."

The Jews brought shame on God by failing to live for him while at the same time claiming to be his people. Look at Romans 2:23. Paul says, "You who boast in the Law, through your breaking the Law, do you dishonor God? For the name of God is blasphemed among the Gentiles because of you, just as it is written." In this verse Paul is quoting from Isaiah chapter fifty-two and Ezekiel chapter thirty-six. "Those who rule over them," continually "howl." They are laughing and mocking the Jews and God's name was being "blasphemed all day long." Look at Ezekiel chapter thirty-six, "When they came to the nations where they were scattered, they profaned God's holy name." So they were supposed to live for the honor of God and instead brought shame to him everywhere they went because, again, of the inconsistency of their claim and conduct.

This reminds me of the 1980s and the televangelist scandals that took place in the United States. Many people who were confronted with the gospel would point at the televangelists and say, "If this is what Christianity is all about, I don't want anything to do with it." That is what the Jews were causing by their failure.

I saw a news story recently about a young man who broke into a fitness center. As soon as he made it into the building he grabbed a security camera and turned it away from him, or so he thought, but actually what he did was turn it to face himself! He thought he was hiding from something that would condemn him, but in fact was condemning himself. That is what the Jews were doing. When they claim to be justified by the Law and they fail to live up to it, they were trusting in the very thing that condemned them.

Insufficiency of Jewish Externalism

Paul goes on to talk about the insufficiency of Jewish Externalism. This refers to the rite of circumcision and things of that nature. Look at Romans 3:25. Paul says, "For indeed circumcision is of value if you practice the Law; but if you are a transgressor of the Law, your circumcision has become uncircumcision." This goes all the way back to Genesis chapter seventeen when circumcision was the sign of the Abrahamic covenant. It was a sign that the Jews were members of this covenant nation and therefore were God's people. That is what circumcision was supposed to signify. It was also intended to signify that they were separated from the rest of the world, separated for God.

But Paul states that if they do not live accordingly, then this sign becomes uncircumcision. Think of it like a wedding ring. A wedding ring is a symbol that one spouse is committed to the other. It is a statement that the husband is committed to his wife and the wife is committed to her husband. If one spouse cheats on the other, even if they're wearing the ring, it is like their wedding band becomes an un-wedding band. It signifies an inconsistency. It is not living up to what it is supposed to communicate. The external sign does not match the reality and that is the point Paul is trying to make regarding circumcision.

Paul says, "If the uncircumcised man keeps the requirement of the law will not his uncircumcision be regarded as circumcision? And he who is physically uncircumcised if he keeps the law, will he not judge you even though you have the law, but you don't keep it?" In essence Paul is saying, "What do you think really matters the most? The sign or the reality that goes with it? What if someone is not circumcised but is living to the standard of the Law? Is that better or worse than being circumcised and yet not living up to the standard?" Paul wants the Jews to realize that their Jewish externalism does not make them right with God.

The Jews were very quick to throw this back. Paul had traveled much of the known world by the time that he wrote the book of Romans. He knows Jewish excuses and so knows that the first thing out of their mouth would be, "Yeah, but we have the Law." Paul says, "Yeah, I know you have the Law, but you don't keep it". "Yeah, but we're circumcised," they would reply. And Paul would say, "Yeah, but it doesn't match any corresponding reality."

Douglas Moo in his commentary on Romans says, "Judaism claimed that no person who is circumcised will go down to Gehenna." In other words, the Jews were trusting that if they were circumcised then they would be spared God's wrath. Paul is removing the blinkers from the Jews so they can see things from God's perspective.

The Jews were claiming to be spared from God's wrath because of their Jewishness: "I call myself a Jew. I have the Law". They claimed that their circumcision would shelter them from God's wrath and Paul takes that argument off the table. Now that he has dealt with those arguments he deals with the loose ends, the wild statements that they will make in desperation.

Think of it this way. You may have noticed that when people on TV are being interrogated for a crime they often start throwing out wild excuses, especially when the truth comes out. That is what the Jews are doing here. In Romans 3:1, here are some questions that they ask, "What advantage has the Jew? What is the benefit of circumcision?" They are saying, "Paul, okay, if you're telling us that circumcision doesn't make us right with God, what's the point of being circumcised anyway? What's the point of being a Jew? What's the value in that?" Paul answers back, "Great in every respect."

There were advantages of being Jewish. Jews grew up with access to the Word of God. They could hear about the salvation that God had promised to provide, but that didn't automatically make them right with God. It just gave

 them access to the Truth. So, Paul agreed with them that there were advantages to being a Jew, just not in the way that they thought.

Answers to Jewish Objections

Their next excuse in is Romans 3:3, "What then? If some did not believe, their unbelief will not nullify the faithfulness of God, will it? May it never be! Rather, let God be found true, though every man be found a liar." The next objection is, "Well, what if some Jews don't believe? God will not break his promises to the Jews if some don't believe." Paul replies, "Of course not. God will be true even when every man is found to be a liar." He quotes Psalm ninety-five which says, "God will be justified in his words."

Now this is a cryptic statement that Paul is going to unfold further in Romans chapters nine through eleven although he alludes to it here. If you think about this from the first century perspective, the Jews were asking, "Well, what advantage do Jews have if the Gospel is going to Gentiles and if being a Jew doesn't automatically shelter one from God's wrath?" Paul says, "There are advantages." What if some Jews don't believe? Is God is still going to keep His promises? Yes, he will keep His Word even if every man is proven to be a liar.

Paul goes on to the next argument that the Jews would give in Romans 3:5. He says, "But if our unrighteousness demonstrates the righteousness of God, what shall we say? The God who inflicts wrath is not unrighteous, is he? (I am speaking in human terms)." Paul is using an argument that he heard when interacting with the Jews. In essence they would say if their sinfulness makes God look more righteousness then why does He find fault with them, because after all they are making God look good? That is basically their argument. Paul says, "May it never be. Otherwise, how will God judge the world?"

Imagine a Jew were to say, "Okay, if God accuses me and if he holds me guilty, why would He do that? My sin makes Him look better." Paul would reply, "Well, would you want God to apply that logic to the Gentiles?" The Gentiles could use the same argument and insist that their sin makes God look better too. If God can't judge someone who is a sinner, then he can't judge the world. Of course, no Jew was going to agree with that. Paul is saying, "Yes, God is going to judge the world and He is going to judge the Jews as well."

Their final argument comes in Romans 3:7-8, "But if through my lie the truth of God abounded to his glory, why am I also still being judged as a sinner? And why not say (as we are slanderously reported and as some claim that we say), 'Let us do evil that good may come'?" Notice how Paul doesn't even enter into that discussion. He says in Romans 3:8, "Their condemnation is just." In other words, he says they deserve God's wrath. Paul is not even going to take their bait. He refuses to go down that road.

So far Paul has shown an inconsistency in the Jews' claim and conduct. They claim to be right with God because of their possession of the Law and yet do not keep that standard. There is clearly an insufficiency in Jewish externalism. They had circumcision and trusted in that as their salvation, but Paul took that away from them. Then he finally answered their objection that their sin made God look better. So why would God judge them? Paul explained that they deserve God's judgment. Paul has taken away every hope that the Jews would have, and in doing that, he silences them so that they can see that their only hope is in God's grace.

❓ DISCUSSION POINTS

1. Who is Paul focusing on in this section?

2. These people are placing their confidence in what three things?

3. What did the Jew's wrongly assume about being a descendant of Abraham?

3.6 Hopeless Before a Holy God

 OBJECTIVES OF THIS TUTORIAL

Paul explains that mankind is helpless before a holy God. He concludes with the implications this truth has for believers. This module was developed from lessons presented by Bible Teacher Scot Keen.

Introduction

In this tutorial, we will cover the conclusion to Paul description of the judgment of God. So far Paul has been like a prosecuting attorney. He first brings allegations against the Gentiles. They have exchanged the truth of God for a lie, and as they have the testimony of creation, they are without an excuse. He then explains that God's wrath is impartial towards Jews and Gentiles.

Arguments Rebuffed

Paul confronts the self-righteous Jews by showing them that simply having a standard will not make them right with God; what is important is living up to that standard. Then Paul specifically calls out the Jews, claiming that they trust in the possession of the Law. They trust in the fact that they are Jews. They trust in the fact that they are circumcised. Paul pulls each of these props out from under them showing them that they have no legs to stand on. They have no hope before a holy God.

In the conclusion of Romans 3:9-20, I like to picture a fisherman who has thrown out a net and in it is all of humanity. Paul pulls the net in and inside he sees both the Gentiles and the Jews. He hangs the net up on a hook, and stands back and looks at it, saying, "There is none righteous. Not even one. There is none who does good. There's none who seeks after God. They've all become unprofitable." What Paul says about one, he says about all. Listen to Paul repeat himself here. He says twice, "There is none who does good, not even one. There is none who seeks after God. Not even one." What is true of one is true of all. And this sums up what we have heard so far.

Now look at Romans 3:9, "What then, are we better than they?" The Jews are asking whether they as Jews are better than the Gentiles. Paul says, "No, we have already charged," or proved, "that both Jews and Greeks are under sin." This theme will be significant as we move through the rest of Romans. Notice that when Paul says, "Under sin," it's like he is personifying sin as an evil dictator who reigns over humanity.

Paul gives several reasons to back his argument. He bases his reasoning on several Old Testament quotes. In Romans 3:10 Paul says, "As it is written, there is none righteous. Not even one." No one is righteous before a holy God in and of themselves. Paul anticipates some pushback, and so he says that there is no one righteous, not even one. Just in case we were wondering. Not even one. There is no one who deserves God's salvation. We are all sinners.

In a previous tutorial, we looked at the theme of condemnation. In Romans 1:18, Paul says, "God's wrath is revealed against all unrighteousness," so God's wrath is targeted towards unrighteousness. That is a problem because he says there is no one who is righteous. Not even one. Everyone is an object of the God's wrath. Paul goes on to say that there is no one who understands (Romans 3:11). There is no one who seeks God. This is similar to what Paul said in Corinthians, "The world through its wisdom did not come to know God." No one is going to reason their way into heaven. Apart from a response to God's divine revelation, no one can be saved. There is no one who understands. There is no one who seeks God.

Often people have trouble with this verse because it does seem like there are some who seek God. It is safe to say that people seek answers to nagging questions like "Where did we come from, and why are we here, and what happens after we die?" People seek answers to questions. People seek to lay their fears to rest. We want to have a sense of well-being because we recognize that something is wrong. We have already seen in Romans that our conscience tells us something is wrong, that we are not living up to even to our own standards. We do seek to allay our fears, but we are not (based on the authority of God's word) seeking God. We are not seeking Him, although ironically God is the One who seeks those who are not seeking him.

Look at Romans 3:12, "All have turned aside, together they have become useless; there is none who does good, there is not even one." When Paul says, "They have turned aside," he is referring to humanity going its own way. Think about Isaiah chapter fifty-three, "All we, like sheep, have gone astray." This is willful departure from the will of God; this is mankind rejecting God. Paul takes it further by declaring that they have become useless or unprofitable, using terminology the Greek would use when speaking about fruit that is unripe. Mankind is like a rotten tomato, still bearing the image and likeness of God, but not living up to its purpose. Mankind has become useless.

Implications of God's Judgment

Then Paul dares to say, "There is no one who does good. Not even one." There is no one who does good. Granted, there are people who, from a human perspective, do good things, but Paul is not talking from a human perspective. Paul is talking about doing good in such a way that would commend us to God, getting us closer to heaven, and so he says, "There is no one who does good." No one. Unsurprisingly people can have difficulty with this section of Romans, and rightly so, because it humbles every one of us and it takes away any hope for self-righteousness.

When Paul says, "There's no one who does good," people ask questions like, "What about Mother Theresa, who lived in poverty so that she could reach out to the poverty stricken in India? What about people like Princess Diana who, before her death, would reach out in compassion to people with aids, back in the day when people were scared to touch people who had aids?" These were individuals who tried to do benevolent things for other human beings, seemingly because they genuinely cared for them. Remember Paul is not talking about doing good from a human perspective. He is talking about doing something that will get us closer to heaven by commending us to God, and he says, "There is no one who does good. Not even one." By making these statements, Paul is levelling the playing field and showing that we are all hopeless sinners before a holy God. If God does not graciously provide salvation, then no one can be saved. No one!

Paul continues in Romans 3:13, "Their throat is an open grave, with their tongues they keep deceiving, the poison of asps is under their lips." Paul says that humanity is defiled, similar to how a grave would defile a Jew, "With their tongues, they keep deceiving." Why is it the tongue that deceives? It is because out of the abundance of the heart, the mouth speaks. Our tongues are deceitful because our hearts are deceitful. Paul goes on to say, "Whose mouth is full of cursing and bitterness; their feet are swift to shed blood, destruction and misery are in their paths, and the path of peace they have not known. There is no fear of God before their eyes."

This is a scathing but true estimation of humanity. Again, this is humbling for all of humanity. We are in no position to declare the Gospel of God's grace until we have come to grips with it ourselves. It is humbling but also necessary to realize that our only standing before God is what Christ has done for us, and in saying so, Paul levels the playing field so that he can unify the church in Rome. Paul continues, "Destruction and misery are in their paths." I have visited areas where tornadoes have gone through the United States, and it is incredible to see the damage. Wherever the tornado goes, it leaves behind a trail of destruction, and that what humanity is like. Wherever we go, we leave wreckage in our path. We hurt other people because we are sinners and we need a Savior.

In Romans 3:19 Paul says, "We know that whatever the law says, it speaks to those who are under the law." Paul has already shown that all of humanity is under sin and now he is going to show that all of humanity is guilty before God. To come back to that phrase under sin, why is it that people hurt other people? Why is it that our feet are swift to shed blood? It is because we are sinners. We sin because we are already sinners. We do not become sinners by sinning. Paul shows our universal guilt before God in Romans 3:19-20. He says, "Whatever the law says, it says to those who are under the law."

Let's pause there for a while. Who was it under the Law? The Jews; whatever the law says, it speaks to the Jews. Notice the interesting twist in the following statement, "Whatever the law says, it says to those under the law so that every mouth may be closed and all the world guilty or accountable before God." How can the fact that the Jews did not live up to the Law make the whole world liable for judgment? Think of it this way, if a farmer is concerned whether or not his ground is good enough to raise crops, he will not sew seed in the entire field. He will first test the ground by planting some seeds in the corner of the field.

Think of it another way. In a cooking contest the judges don't eat the entire cake to give it the blue ribbon. They just eat a portion of it and make a judgment based on that. God gave his law to the Jews. He gave them prophets to warn them. He placed them in their own land and blessed them. If the Jews could not live up to the Law, then arguably no one else could. Because of their failure Paul says, "All the world is guilty before God, and every mouth is closed." He goes on to say that this is true because by the works of the law, by doing good, no flesh, no humanity will be justified in God's sight. Through the Law comes the knowledge of sin. The Law was given to show that no one can measure up to God's standard and that mankind's only hope is grace.

Mankind's Helpless Condition

I will summarize by reminding you that people will never welcome grace until they see that it is their only hope. Paul is ruthless and aggressive in showing the condemnation of all humanity, but he does it for a reason. He wants to silence every mouth so that no one is offering excuses as to why they are right with God apart from grace. God silences every mouth. People will never welcome grace until they see that grace is their only hope. Paul takes the Jews there. When sharing God's Truth with others, it is a wonderful thing for us to consider that the Good News is good news precisely because the bad news is very bad.

Secondly, not only do people do bad things, but they are bad. Paul shows that people are under sin by the things that they do. People who do not have God's Word, Gentiles, do not become sinners by rejecting the testimony of creation. People reject creation's testimony because they love darkness better than light. They are already sinners. The Jews do not claim self-righteousness under the Law and then somehow become condemned because they cannot measure up. They cannot keep the Law because they are under sin.

They are sinners. As humans we not only do bad things, we are bad. We are desperately wicked. We are a race of helpless sinners under sin, and so we deserve condemnation.

Think of it this way, we are not just sinners, we are helpless, hopeless sinners away from Christ. Don't take this the wrong way. We are helpless sinners because there are none of us from Adam's race who can fix our own problem. We are sinners and we cannot get out of this mess. We are hopeless in the sense that no other human being can get us out of this, as far as Adam's race goes. It is going to take help from outside. It is going to take a Savior. We are helpless, hopeless sinners. We are under God's wrath, and rightfully so. The wrath of God is against all unrighteousness of men, and there are none righteous. Every avenue of escape has been closed. The Gentile cannot hide by saying, "I didn't know." Paul said, "No, you had the testimony of creation." The Jews cannot hide beneath the Law of Moses, beneath their Jewishness, or beneath their circumcision. Paul has eradicated every avenue of escape.

Every hope that people have has been taken away. Do you see what Paul has done here? He has literally silenced every mouth and shown all the world guilty before God. Mankind in and of itself is hopelessly, helplessly lost. What are we to do? Apart from God's intervention, there is nothing that we can do. We have no claim on God, and God is under no obligation whatsoever towards us. God does not owe us anything, yet if anyone acts, it must be God. This is the most desperate situation seen in Scripture. When I think about desperate situations in Scripture, I usually think about Israel on the banks of the Red Sea with Pharaoh's army behind them. Unless God intervenes, they have no chance. This is even worse than Israel on the banks of the Red Sea.

Speaking to Believers

Consider this: why does Paul say these things to believers? We might forget that Paul is talking to believers here. Why does he say all this to them? Paul is laying a theological basis for his later appeal for unity among the believers. Now the Jews cannot see themselves as superior to Gentile believers because, after all, they were all helplessly lost before God until God intervened through Christ.

You might be asking, "What does this have to do with me?" Firstly you should never conclude that you must give God a reason to love you, because you never gave Him a reason to love you in the first place. When we realize the depth of our hopeless condition apart from Christ, it ultimately will magnify the love of God. When we realize He did not first love us because we did something good, but rather loved us because He is love. We never gave Him a reason to love us in the first place. You can also stop looking for good in yourself because there isn't any. This sets us free to revel in the grace of God because His grace was shown to us while we were sinners.

What does this have to do with you? You and I are the people of Romans 1:18- 3:20. We are the helpless sinners. We had a twofold problem, firstly being under sin's condemnation and authority, and secondly being powerless to do anything about it. Wait till you see what God did about it. I'll go into that in the next tutorial.

> **? DISCUSSION POINTS**
>
> **1.** What does it mean to be "under sin"?
>
> **2.** Why was the Law given?
>
> **3.** In vs. 19, we are told that "whatever the Law says it says to those who are under the law". Who was "under the law"?
>
> **4.** Since those "under the Law" could not keep it, how does that prove that the whole world is guilty before God?
>
> **5.** Why does God seek to silence men?
>
> **6.** How does all of this relate to you (Looking at Romans 3:9-20)?

3.7 The Basis for our Justification

 OBJECTIVES OF THIS TUTORIAL

Paul explains the implications of Christ's death for us as believers, one of which is being made righteous, allowing us to stand before a holy God. This module was developed from lessons presented by Bible Teacher Scot Keen.

Introduction

Last time Paul showed us that all humanity is guilty before God. No one is righteous and so mankind's only hope is grace. Now that Paul has our attention and we feel our need before a holy God, he moves on to give us the good news. He will begin to address the theological basis for our justification. He will answer questions like, "How can God declare us righteous and still remain righteous himself?" He will then provide us with some Old Testament examples of justification by faith.

Righteousness Revealed

Let's begin with the theological basis for our justification. In Romans 3:21 Paul says, "Now, apart from the law," which means apart from man's performance, "the righteousness of God has been manifested." The way to receive then righteousness of God is revealed in the Gospel Message, as seen in Romans 1:17, "For in it the righteousness of God is revealed from faith to faith; as it is written, 'but the righteous man shall live by faith'". There are a few things I want us to catch here. First of all, Paul says that the righteousness of God is revealed. Now this is not referring to God's attribute of righteousness, rather it is referring to His saving activity. The righteousness here is God's gift to believing sinners which allows them to stand before Him in all his holiness.

Philippians chapter three talks about this righteousness as well. It is righteousness that is credited to sinners who believe the Gospel Message. To clarify, it does not mean to be made righteous, meaning once we believe the Gospel everything we do is now righteous. We know that is not the case. This righteousness is also bigger than God seeing us as if we have never sinned. Granted when we believe the Gospel, when we are justified, our sins are completely removed. But that is only half the story. It is not just that our sins are forgiven, but we are also credited with righteousness before a holy God. It is a legal declaration because of God's credited righteousness. We're not just forgiven, we are also given the status of being righteous before a holy God.

Let's follow Paul as he explains this idea. Look at Romans 3:21-22, "But now apart from the law the righteousness of God has been manifested...even the righteousness of God through faith in Jesus Christ for all those who believe." This righteousness is God's righteousness. Think about the implications of this. Mankind's 'righteousness' is filthy rags, as Isaiah would say. But Paul is talking about God's righteousness. If we are credited with God's righteousness, then how could we ever be more legally right than the moment we believe the Gospel? To put it another way, if you receive God's righteousness by faith in Christ, that righteousness is perfect. It is God's righteousness and therefore cannot be improved upon.

That means you will never be more legally righteous than the moment you believe the Gospel, not in all of eternity. You cannot add to God's righteousness. You will never be more righteous than the moment you believe the Gospel. That is profound. A Christian author once said, "There are two questions that every believer must settle. Number one, does God completely accept me? Number two, if so, upon what grounds?" Does God completely accept us? If so, why? He completely accepts us because He completely accepted what Christ did on our behalf. After all, it is the righteousness of God we are talking about here which is perfect and so cannot be improved upon. Paul says the righteousness of God through faith in Jesus Christ is for all those who believe, and there is no distinction.

Righteousness Received

When Paul says, "For all those who believe, and there is no distinction," he is alluding to the Jew-Gentile division we talked about previously. Paul insists that God's righteousness is for both Jews and Gentiles. There is universal need to be right before God. Look at Romans 3:23, "All have sinned and fall short of the glory of God." There is also universal provision. Christ died for all men. The righteousness of God is for all who believe. How can God do this? What are the grounds by which He can credit sinners as righteous? Notice verse twenty four, "Being justified as a gift by his grace through the redemption which is in Christ Jesus." These terms are loaded; justified as a gift, or as some translations say justified freely by his grace. We know that if something is given by God's grace, then it is underserved.

When Paul says "freely, and by his grace" he is roughly saying the same thing. But he says it, I believe, for the sake of emphasis. God's righteousness is both free and undeserved. It is gracious on God's part to make us right through faith, "Being justified or declared righteous as a gift by God's grace, and that is through the redemption which is in Christ Jesus." Think about redemption, a term that has history in the Old Testament.

Property could be redeemed, slaves could be redeemed and prisoners of war could be redeemed. Those acts were called redemption, and the prices paid were called ransoms. Christ was a ransom for sinners. He died, and his blood paid the price for us to be set free from our sins. While Paul is speaking about redemption here, these analogies go further.

Righteousness Upheld

Look at Romans 3:25, speaking of Christ, "Whom God displayed publicly as a propitiation in his blood through faith." Propitiation is a big word. It is not one that we often use in conversation, if ever. But it is a word that also has history in the Old Testament. It refers to God's wrath turning away by means of a substitute. In the Old Testament the Israelites had a tabernacle. Inside it was the mercy seat, underneath which were the tablets of the law. The mercy seat was exactly like it sounds, a place of mercy. Blood would be sprinkled on it which communicated that what should bring judgment, God's Law, was covered over because of a provision of a sacrifice, and so sinners could find mercy there. Propitiation speaks about the turning away or the aversion of God's wrath.

I like to think of it this way. Picture a lightning rod. They are placed in a certain spot to channel the fury of a storm away from people and into the ground. They are set up for that very reason. In the same way God publicly put Christ in open view of all the world on the cross at Calvary. He did that as a propitiation, averting God's wrath away from sinners and towards Jesus as He became sin for us. Also mentioned in the Old Testament is the day of atonement. The day of atonement meant death for the lamb, but mercy for the sinner. When the lamb's blood was sprinkled on the mercy seat, it was death for the lamb, mercy for the sinner and satisfaction for God's righteous standard.

Jesus is the Lamb of God. He made propitiation for our sins. It meant death for the Lamb of God, mercy for the sinners, and satisfaction for God. This is something I hope that we pause to think about. If God is completely satisfied, the real question is, "Are you satisfied?" Don't take me wrong, I'm not saying that God exists to satisfy either you or me, but I mean that if God is accepting what Christ did, what more can be done? God is resting in what Christ did on our behalf. He is satisfied. When we believe the Gospel we are saying, "God, I place my faith where you placed my sin," and that is on the Son of God who died in our place. Remember it was death for the Lamb of God, mercy for the sinner and satisfaction for God's wrath.

I'll give an illustration that might turn your stomach. In the States we celebrate Thanksgiving every year. It's a major holiday. One of the things we do is gorge ourselves on food. We always have turkey, mashed potatoes, sweet potatoes, salad, broccoli, squash, all kinds of vegetables and cranberry sauce. We can only fit one little spoonful from each dish on our plates and still our plates are heaping over. We eat all the food we can possibly hold and then sit down on the couch and watch a football game. Then it's time for cake or pie and ice cream. It feels like we cannot eat another bite. We're satisfied.

Now, imagine being in that situation where you have eaten to your heart's content, you can't take another bite, and someone gives you some rancid meat to eat. I told you it would turn your stomach! You are so full you can't take another bite and yet they spoon feed it into your mouth. It just turns my stomach to think about it. But you know what? When we try to offer something to God with our own works while He is completely satisfied in His Son, we are doing that very thing. We are telling God that something more needs to be done when He is insisting that He is satisfied with what Jesus has done.

I have said before that the righteousness of God is not referring to God's attribute of righteousness. It speaks rather about God's act of declaring righteous those who believe in Christ. But in Romans 3:25, it is now speaking about God's attribute of being righteous. Jesus was crucified publicly to show the world that He is righteous. He demonstrated His righteousness by passing over the sins previously committed. When Adam sinned against God, God forgave Adam. When David sinned with Bathsheba, God forgave David. You could go on and on with Old Testament examples. That raises a question. How can God be a righteous God and forgive those sinners? We know from the book of Hebrews that the blood of bulls and goats cannot remove sin. How could God forgive them if their sins had been paid for?

I like to think of it like using a credit card. I pay for something with a credit card by swiping it at the store and so could argue, "I just paid for that." They let me leave the store because, after all, I did give them my credit card. I paid for it in a sense, but I don't really pay for it until I pay the bill that the credit card company sends. Likewise, it is like people were saved on credit, so to speak, prior to Christ paying for our sins. God forgave them in light Christ's future payment. And God was righteous in forgiving them because the price would be paid by Christ.

God was righteous in forgiving Old Testament believers, and He is righteous when He forgives those of us today who believe the Gospel Message, because Christ died for our sins. Notice this statement, "So that he would be just, and the justifier of the one who has faith in Jesus." A quote attributed to John Calvin comes to mind, "Just and the justifier is the marrow of theology." In other words, this is the heart of the Gospel. God can somehow be both just and the Justifier. God is not going to lower His standards to save man, He is going to maintain His justice. But He also wants to be the Justifier, the One who forgives sinners. How can God maintain a perfect standard, and yet forgive sinners who cannot live up to that standard?

In a sense, God faced a 'dilemma'. How could He maintain justice and also be the Justifier? The beauty of the Gospel is that God can be both just and the Justifier of the one who has faith in Jesus. I like to say something that raises red flags. God does not forgive sin. Let me say it again: God does not forgive sin! Here is what I mean: God forgives sinners, but He does not leave sin unpunished. He is just. When Christ died, the full weight of God's wrath fell on Him so that He could be the Justifier of the one who has faith in Jesus. God was jealous to maintain that. He wanted to be just and the Justifier.

Implications

Christ dying for our sins made it possible for God to show full justice towards sin so that He could in turn show mercy and be the Justifier of those who have faith in Jesus. In conclusion Paul says, "Where then is boasting?" It's excluded. There is no room for boasting. On what grounds? He says, "By what kind of law? Of works? No, but by law of faith. For we maintain that a man is justified by faith, apart from the works of the law." We cannot be justified by works. And if we are justified by faith we have nothing to brag about.

We cannot boast because we did not satisfy God's wrath, we simply trusted in the One who did. There is no boasting. Look at Romans 3:29, "Or is God the God of Jews only? Is he not the God of Gentiles also? Yes, of Gentiles also, since indeed God who will justify the circumcised by faith and the uncircumcised through faith is one." Paul says, "Do we then nullify the law through faith? May it never be! On the contrary, we establish the law." In this chapter Paul has laid the theological basis for our justification. God can justify us when we believe the Gospel because of the redemption that is found in Christ.

THE BASIS FOR OUR JUSTIFICATION

> **? DISCUSSION POINTS**
>
> **1.** In your own words, what do you think it means when God's Word says that Jesus was "filled with the Holy Spirit's power"? Do you think there was any time when Jesus was more or less filled with the Holy Spirit than another? Please explain.
>
> **2.** If a friend who claims to be a Christian said to you that they don't really feel free - that they've always had a sense of being restricted and weighed down in their faith - what would you say to them? How would you express how you feel about freedom and liberty as God's child?

3.8 The Results of Justification

> **OBJECTIVES OF THIS TUTORIAL**
>
> Bible presenter Scot Keen wraps up Romans chapter 4 with Old Testament examples of being justified by faith. He then introduces Romans chapter 5 with the results of justification, one of them being the security of the believer.

Introduction

In the last tutorial, we looked at the theological basis for our justification. We used two key theological terms that speak about Christ's payment which frees us from our sins and satisfies God's wrath, namely, the redemption that is in Christ and the propitiation through faith in His blood. Now Paul launches into another section with Old Testament examples of people who were justified by faith. Let's delve into those examples.

Old Testament Examples

One thing that is significant to note about Romans chapter four is that Paul elaborates on the things that he says in chapter three. At the end of chapter three, he says, "Boasting is excluded." In chapter four, he shows that Abraham has no right to boast. In chapter three, he says that boasting is excluded because we're justified by faith not by works. In chapter four, he shows that Abraham was justified by faith not by works. In chapter three, he shows that both Jews and Gentiles were justified by faith. In chapter four, he shows that both Jews and Gentiles are children of Abraham through faith. So chapter four is all about Paul elaborating on the things that he said in chapter three.

This is significant because it shows that it is Paul's desire for us to truly grasp what he said in chapter three. He wants us to know that justification is a gift and is received by faith and by faith alone. It was so important for Paul that he gave us an extra chapter just to elaborate on those things. As we look at these Old Testament examples of justification by faith, the first major point Paul makes is that men who were justified in the Old Testament were justified by faith apart from works, which is the same for us today. He begins with Abraham, and then he gives an example from David.

Justified Apart from Works

Let's look at Romans 4:1, "What then shall we say that Abraham, our forefather according to the flesh, has found?" Paul uses Abraham and David as his Old Testament examples. They were the two most respected men of God in the Old Testament by the Jews, and so to use them as examples would be a convincing case. Paul says in Romans 4:2, "For if Abraham was justified by works, he has something to boast about, but not before God. For what does the Scripture say? 'Abraham believed God, and it was credited to him as righteousness'". Paul makes it clear that Abraham was credited with righteousness apart from works. He was credited with righteousness by faith.

The term credited alludes to legal accounting. Picture our record before we had faith in God and it would look blank, as far as righteousness is concerned. We are bankrupt of righteousness. There is no one righteous. Not even one. We recognize that apart from Christ, we have no righteousness. As far as sin on our record, Paul says in Romans chapter three that both Jews and Greeks are under sin. We have all turned aside. We were condemned already and without an excuse to give. That was our record before God.

Go back to the Abraham example. He believed God, and it was credited to him as righteousness. This righteousness, we have already learned, is the righteousness of God through faith in Jesus Christ. It is God's righteousness. It is perfect and so cannot be improved upon. Abraham's faith was counted as righteousness. It was not that Abraham's belief was a righteous thing. All he did was simply believe God's promise, and God credited righteousness to him on that basis.

Notice in Romans 4:4, "Now to the one who works, his wage is not credited as a favor, but as what is due. But to the one who does not work, but believes in him who justifies the ungodly, his faith is credited as righteousness." Paul is making a contrast here between the one who works and the one who does not work. To the one who works, whatever that person receives, it is not a gift. It is just wages. It is payment for services rendered, but for the one who does not work but believes, his faith is credited as righteousness.

Really, I think this is a very important aspect in ministry to keep in mind. When we share Christ with others we need to remember that they cannot receive the righteousness of God as long as they are trying to work for it. Paul says God's righteousness is for the one who does not work but believes. As long as someone is trying to work for righteousness, they cannot have it, because God only gives it through faith in Christ. Paul is contrasting works and faith. As far as salvation goes, it is only for people who do not work for it.

Sometimes people argue that it is good to believe the Gospel, and mankind cannot do anything good. Therefore, mankind cannot believe the Gospel. This is what is called a fallacy of equivocation. It is an illogical argument. It is using a term in two different ways. It is good to believe the Gospel, and mankind cannot do anything good as far as meriting God's salvation, but we cannot extend that to say that mankind cannot believe the Gospel. Paul says God's righteousness is for the one who does not work but believes. That means that faith is not a work. It is simply receiving God's testimony as truth.

Paul says, "Now to the one who works, his wage is not credited as a favor, but as what is due. But to the one who does not work, but believes in him who justifies the ungodly, his faith is credited as righteousness." I'll give an illustration hopefully drives this point home. Years ago, I took a ministry trip to Papua New Guinea. Upon arrival, I discovered that even though I had been invited to come I was still expected to pay for my own travel. I thought it was going to be paid for by the people who invited me. When I was onsite in this ministry location, I was presented with this large bill. I thought, "Man, what am I going to do? How am I going to pay for this?"

I was studying Romans chapter four at the same time, and thought, "Wouldn't it be so cool if I received an email from someone saying, 'Scot, we paid your bill, you don't have to worry about it any longer'". Of course that never happened, and so I had to pay the bill myself. However if I had received a note saying that the bill was paid for, I would not have tried to pay it. In other words, if I really believed that someone had paid my price, I would not worry about paying that price any longer. When we trust Christ the Savior, we are not trying to pay Him back for what He has done. We are not trying to atone for our sin. We are resting because we believe God's promise that our penalty has been paid in full.

Paul gives another example, this time King David. In Romans 4:6, Paul says, "Just as David also speaks of the blessing on the man to whom God credits righteousness apart from works." Then he quotes from Psalm thirty-two, "Blessed is he whose transgression is forgiven, whose sin is covered! How blessed is the man to whom the Lord does not impute iniquity, and in whose spirit there is no deceit!" This is really significant. Please catch this. Justification is more than "just as if we had never sinned."

Justification is more than our sins being forgiven. It is also being credited with righteousness. Abraham believed God and it was credited to him as righteousness. That speaks about something positive being placed on his account. Then Paul uses David as an example in Romans 4:6, "The man to whom God credits righteousness," it sounds like he's talking about something positive placed on our account. Then it is all about the negative (sin) being removed when he says, "Blessed is he whose transgression is forgiven, whose sin is covered!"

Justified Apart from Circumcision
These two examples show that justification deals with our sins being removed, and God's righteousness being credited to our account. In Romans 4:9, Paul says, "Is this

blessing then on the circumcised, or on the uncircumcised also?" He says, "We say, 'Faith was credited to Abraham as righteousness'. How then was it credited? While he was circumcised, or uncircumcised? Not while circumcised, but while uncircumcised." This brings us to the next major point. Paul is showing that not only are we justified by faith apart from works, but we are also justified by faith apart from circumcision.

Now, that may seem irrelevant to you. However, it was very relevant to the Jews in the first century. Paul is explaining that people who came from a Jewish background had no advanced standing over the Gentile believers. They were all one in Christ. He insists that works could not save, nor could divinely prescribed rights (such as circumcision). In Romans 4:10, Paul says again that Abraham was not credited with righteousness when he was circumcised, but rather when he was uncircumcised. When Abraham believed God in Genesis fifteen, he had not yet been circumcised.

In that sense, Abraham was a justified man who was uncircumcised. Later he received the sign of circumcision, "He received the sign of circumcision, a seal of the righteousness of the faith which he had while uncircumcised, so that he might be the father of all who believe without being circumcised, that righteousness might be credited to them" (Romans 4:11). It is interesting that Abraham was justified when he was uncircumcised. That makes him the father of all who believe who are uncircumcised, such as the Gentile believers. He was also a justified man who was later circumcised. In that sense, he is also the father of circumcised believes or Jewish believers.

Paul goes on to say that Abraham is the father of all who believe both the circumcised and uncircumcised. Paul is doing is the same thing he did in chapter three. He is showing that both Jew and Gentile believers are united as children of Abraham through faith. Abraham is the father of all who believe. He goes on to speak about some of the blessings that come by faith. Paul reminds us that Abraham and the promises were given apart from law, and on that grounds, the promises extend to Gentile believers as well.

Abraham's Faith
Let's move onto Romans 4:17-25. Look at Abraham's faith and how it was an example for all. Notice verse seventeen, "As it is written, 'A father of many nations have I made you in the presence of him whom he believed, even God, who gives life to the dead and calls into being that which does not exist." We find these obstacles to Abraham's faith as Paul is showing his faith as a model. He wants us to see the obstacles that Abraham faced. There are more obstacles in verse eighteen, "In hope against hope he believed, so that he might become a father of many nations according to that which had been spoken, 'so shall your descendants be.'" Then verse nineteen, "Without becoming weak in faith he contemplated his own body, now as good as dead since he was about

a hundred years old, and the deadness of Sarah's womb." This is a beautiful picture of faith. Abraham didn't ignore his circumstances, although they were against him. He was almost a hundred years old, and he considered that. He knew he was an old man. Not only that, he knew that Sarah was in no place to be a mother because her womb was barren.

The beautiful thing is that Abraham recognized that he was too old to father a child. He knew too that Sarah was past the age of child-bearing, and yet he hoped against hope. Circumstances offered him no hope, but God's Word did. He believed that God could do the impossible. Specifically, he believed (verse seventeen) in a God who gives life to the dead. Sarah had a dead womb, but God gives life to the dead. Not only that, but he believed in a God who calls into existence things that do not exist. Just like God said, "Let there be light," and there was light. God called light into existence. God was going to call into existence a nation from Abraham, and similarly he was going to call into existence a nation from Sarah's dead womb. After all, He is a God who can call into existence things that do not exist and give life to the dead.

Look at Romans 4:20-22, "With respect to the promise of God, he did not waver in unbelief but grew strong in faith, giving glory to God, and being fully assured that what God had promised, he was able also to perform. Therefore it was also credited to him as righteousness." Paul is saying that Abraham gave glory to God, believing God could do what God said he would do. When you and I believe God's Word, we simply trust that God can do or has done what He said He will do or did do. We are trusting God's word. When Abraham did that, it was credited to him as righteousness.

That is a quick overview of chapter four Paul used Abraham and David as examples of people who were justified by faith apart from works. He showed us that circumcision had nothing to do with that, a very important statement for the Jews. He showed that God's promises are realized by faith and not by law, another important point for the Jews to hear. Then he gave Abraham's faith as an example for all who would later believe, and therefore be justified. Next Paul talks about the results of justification, what comes as a result of having trusted Christ as our Savior. We will find the benefits of being justified by faith in Romans 5:1-11. We will also see an emphasis on our security as believers.

Results of Justification

Let's look at Romans 5:1, "Therefore, having been justified by faith, we have peace with God through our Lord Jesus Christ." What I want you to catch in this section is Paul's excitement. I have to make a confession here. When I first studied Romans 5:1, I was keen to bypass it to get to Romans 5:12 for some meaty theology. But I discovered a lot of good stuff in Romans 5:1 -11. Notice Paul's excitement here. Paul uses phrases like we have, also we have, and not only this, but we also, much more than, much more, and not only this. Paul was obviously excited with all the things that we have because of our faith in Christ.

Present Benefits

Paul says, "Having been justified by faith," which shows that justification is not a process. It is an event. We are not in the process of being justified. We have been justified. Since we have been justified in the past, the promises are things that are true of us now. They are present possessions as believers. The promises include, first of all, peace with God. It refers to the fact, not of a subjective feeling, but of a legal standing. We were enemies of God and under God's wrath, and now we are at peace with God. There is no hostility towards us. This peace is not a subjective feeling, but rather a state of being at peace with God. The war is over, so to speak.

Paul says, "We have this peace with God through our Lord Jesus Christ," and then, "Through whom (through Christ) we have obtained our introduction by faith into this grace in which we stand." Consider Paul's language here. He says we are standing in grace. How can we stand in grace? What does that mean? Well, standing speaks of being positioned somewhere. My standing is in grace, and grace speaks of God's unearned favor. Since we have been justified by faith, we are positioned in God's unearned favor. God's posture towards us is one of grace, one of favor. And that is always true. We are always standing in the God's favor.

When I was a child I would make new friends and it felt like we were best friends for a whole day, and then I would do something wrong, or they would do something wrong, and then I moved on to my next best friend, only for the pattern to be repeated. In contrast, God says in Romans chapter five that we are standing in His favor. His posture towards us is one of kindness and that will not change. We are standing in God's grace. Not only that, but Paul says, "We rejoice in hope of the glory of God."

I have a few comments on that statement. Hope in Scripture speaks of anticipation that is based on certainty. It speaks of something I know is going to happen, and because of that, I have excitement now even though it has not taken place yet. When Paul says, "We rejoice in hope of the glory of God," he is speaking about glorification. He is saying that we rejoice now because we are going to share in glory, we are going to be glorified together with Christ. In other words, we are celebrating the ultimate aspect of our salvation, which is glorification. And Paul is excited about that even now.

Of course it is something to rejoice about. But we may be surprised at what Paul says next, "Not only this, but we also exult in our tribulations." This is a worldview paradigm shift. To rejoice in tribulations is to rejoice in difficulties. Why would Paul say that we rejoice in tribulations? He goes on to say that we rejoice knowing that tribulation brings about perseverance. Perseverance brings about proven character. Proven character brings about hope. We rejoice in the difficult circumstances of life because God uses them to mature us in the faith.

That is not something we know by experience, so much as something we know by faith in God's word. "We know," Paul says, "We know that tribulation brings about perseverance; and perseverance, proven character; and proven character, hope; and hope does not disappoint." The idea is that as God takes us through the difficulties of life, we come to trust His character even more and more and more. Think about David and Goliath. Remember when David wanted to go out and fight Goliath? His brothers tried to discourage him. David replied that his God had delivered him from the paw of a bear and from a lion. David trusted God. God delivered him from a bear and a lion, and because of that, David was willing to trust God in his fight against a new enemy, which was Goliath.

My point is that when we go through stretching circumstances and find that God is faithful, we are ready to trust Him in even bigger areas. That is what Paul is alluding to here, "And our hope in God is not disappointed." Our hope in God will not be disappointed because of God's love. Note that Paul is speaking about our ultimate hope of being glorified together with Christ. We rejoice in hope of the glory of God. Our glorification will not be disappointed, and we know that based on the love of God.

Security in Christ

Look at Romans 5:6-8, "For while we were still helpless, at the right time Christ died for the ungodly. For one will hardly die for a righteous man; though perhaps for the good man someone would dare even to die. But God demonstrates his own love toward us, in that while we were yet sinners, Christ died for us." I will walk you through Paul's arguments here. Sometimes people get tripped up on the terminology in the verse above because Paul says, "A righteous man," and then "A good man." A righteous man here would be someone who lived according to the standard of the Law, but a good man would be someone who went above and beyond the call of duty.

Paul says that one would hardly die for a righteous person, but maybe for a good person someone would possibly die. Let me just put that another way. There are certain people of whom you would say, "I might possibly die for that person." For example, you may say you would be willing to die for one of your children or for your wife or husband. There are certain people you are so fond of that you may be willing to die for them. In essence, Paul is saying, "Human love at its best would die for some people, but not for all."

In contrast look at verse eight, "God demonstrates his love, in that while we were yet sinners, Christ died for us." Paul says human love might die for some people. God's love is so powerful that He would die for even the most undeserving of us while we were still sinners. God's love exceeds even the most extreme form of human love. I love verse eight. Paul says, "God demonstrates his love." God is (present tense) showing His love, and the way He is (present tense) showing His love is that in the past, Christ died for our sins. He uses past tense at the end.

Sometimes people say, "If God really loves me, why doesn't He show me that He loves me?" Paul says, "He did show you, and He is showing you now by what He already did in history when Christ died for our sins." He gives another example in verses nine and ten, "Much more then, having now been justified by his blood, we shall be saved from the wrath of God through him. For if while we were enemies we were reconciled to God through the death of his son, much more, having been reconciled, we shall be saved by his life." And we also see in verse eleven, "And not only this, but we also exult in God through our Lord Jesus Christ, through whom we have now received the reconciliation."

Paul is emphasizing the security that the believer has in Christ. He says that hope does not disappoint because of the love of God. As a believer is expecting glorification, Paul says, "They have confidence in that because, first of all, God's love is greater than human love." That is his first statement of defense. Then he says in verse nine, "Having been justified...we will be saved from the wrath of God through him."

In essence, Paul is saying, "If He has already justified us, surely He is going to continue His work in us. If God did the more difficult thing (Christ dying for our sins while we were sinners) then surely now that we are reconciled, He will complete His work in us." Both verses nine and ten have basically the same argument. God did something while we were sinners, verse nine, "Having been justified by His blood," and verse ten, "We were reconciled." If God justified us, if He reconciled us while we were sinners, surely, He will continue His work and save us from His wrath. Paul is giving an argument for the security that a believer has in Christ.

? DISCUSSION POINTS

1. Why does Abraham have nothing to boast about?

2. What verse indicates that faith is not a work?

3. Why would Paul use Abraham and David as examples of those who were justified by faith? How would that help him connect with his audience?

4. What is the "blessing" that Paul refers to in verse 9?

5. What is the meaning of the phrase; "in hope against hope he believed"?

6. What are the results of justification that we find in 5:1-11?

7. What does it mean to be "standing in grace"?

3.9 From Justification to Life

 OBJECTIVES OF THIS TUTORIAL

Bible presenter Scot Keen analyses the transition from justification to life for the believer in Romans chapter five. He contrasts Adam with Christ and helps us to identify with them.

Introduction

So far we have discussed Paul's thesis for the book of Romans. He is not ashamed of the Gospel because it is the power of God for salvation for everyone who believes, to the Jews first and also to the Gentiles. Paul then launched into a discussion on the righteousness of God that we find in the Gospel. He elaborated on justification by faith. He also explained the theological basis for our justification, for our redemption and for the satisfaction of God's wrath. In Romans chapter four, Paul went on to deal with Old Testament examples of justification by faith. Then in chapter five we looked at the results of justification. We now stand in God's favor, we have hope that is guaranteed and our future rejoicing is in the glory of God.

Justification to Sanctification

Now we will explore Romans 5:12-21 and look at the transition from justification to life. This section focuses on the journey from justification to sanctification, a journey of Christian growth and maturity. It is foundational as Paul will talk about our identification with Adam and his sin and also identification with Christ. This will be the basis for all the Christian life principles that come in chapter six through to chapter eight. So it is foundational in that sense. Also, we are going to find that Paul will elaborate on the abundance (or riches) of God's grace and the impact that they have on the believer's life. The keyword of Romans 5:12-21 is 'one'. As we transition from justification to life, Paul will emphasize the oneness of those identified either with Adam or with Christ. We find death through Adam and life through Christ.

Listen to all the words that describe oneness, or the identification principle. We find that through one man sin entered into the world. It was the transgression of one that caused many to die. God's gift of grace came through one man. There is one who sinned.

Judgment arose from one transgression. Death reigned through the one and we reign in life through the one, Jesus Christ. One transgression brought condemnation to all people. One act of righteousness results in justification. One Man obeyed and one man disobeyed. We find a contrast between Adam and Christ in the picture. We have moved on from contrasting the Jews and Gentiles. We are now contrasting Adam and Christ. Adam's one sin is what set us all up as sinners. Christ's one act of righteousness is what sets us up as belonging to God. We have been declared righteous through faith in Him. Through Adam came sin and death, and through Christ comes righteousness and life. Those are the contrasts in this section.

Let's think about how we can identify with Adam in his sin. In Romans 5:12 Paul says, "Therefore, just as through one man sin entered into the world, and death through sin, and so death spread to all men, because all sinned." And so the question is, "How did we sin along with Adam? Why are we brought into his judgment?" There are several different views on this. One is the Seminal View. In this approach, we sinned in and with Adam because we were in him biologically, meaning we can be traced back to him by our DNA. So when Adam sinned, we were inherently in Adam and therefore we sinned along with him. The other major view is called Federal Headship and it argues that just as a team captain makes decisions for the entire team, so Adam, when he sinned, was representative of the human race and therefore brought us all into death and condemnation. At the end of the day, it does not really matter how we get there. The result is still the same: through one man's sin, death entered into the world and it spread to all people because all sinned.

Before I delve into the details, I want you to understand what I believe is Paul's goal here. His aim is not to explain why people go to Hell when they die. Paul already accomplished that thoroughly in Romans 1:18-3:20. He has already established the fact that all the world is guilty before God. So Paul is not trying to make the same point all over again. Rather he wants to show that just as there were ramifications from being united with Adam, so there are ramifications of being united with Christ, just further reaching ramification this time.

The Damage of Sin

Let's look at the damage caused by the first man, Adam. Paul says, "As through one man sin entered into the world and death through sin and so death spread to all men because all sinned." Death (the divinely appointed penalty for sin) came into the world through Adam's sin. Now death is the penalty that God appointed for sin. Remember God said of the fruit in the garden, "The day that you eat of it you will surely die." Cranfield, author of a commentary on Romans, says, "Death is not sin's soldier or servant or instrument. It is the sign of God's authority. Death is appointed by God as the inseparable and inescapable accompaniment of sin." Wherever there is sin there is death, and God was the One who set it up that way. So whenever we see death we are reminded that all of humanity is under the God's authority, as death is the divinely appointed penalty for sin.

In some cultures we almost numb ourselves to the realities and pain of death. Maybe we do this to take some of the sting out of it. Death is supposed to be a reminder to all of humanity that something is wrong in God's perfect world, a reminder that there is a problem now and that we are not in the garden any longer. So death reminds us that there is something wrong and also that we are under God's authority. It is experienced by all because all sinned in and with Adam and so death spread to all people because all sinned. This reminds us of our mortality.

Look at Romans 5:12 again, "Therefore, just as through one man sin entered into the world, and death through sin, and so death spread to all men, because all sinned." Then Paul says in Romans 5:13, "For until the law sin was in the world, but sin is not imputed when there is no law. Nevertheless death reigned from Adam until Moses, even over those who had not sinned in the likeness of the offense of Adam." I'll slow down and explain this technical section as best as I can.

Some look at the verse, "Sin is not credited or imputed where there is no law", and think that God did not judge sin until the law came along. But remember, God judged sin in the days of Noah. There was no Mosaic Law then. God also judged sin in the days of Sodom and Gomorrah, so he is not saying that God did not judge sin. Paul is saying Adam had a clearly stated consequence. He was told that when he ate the forbidden fruit, his punishment would be death. Moses' Law prescribed what people must and must not do. If the Israelites disobeyed God, in some cases, death was the clearly prescribed penalty. Both Adam and Moses had a clear prohibition and a clear warning that death would be the consequence if people disobeyed God. Paul is saying that death reigned from Adam until Moses, even for those who did not sin in the same way as Adam. These people did not transgress a clearly stated prohibition. The reason that death reigned for them is not because they were disobeying a clear-cut command, but because they were sinners because of Adam's sin and we know death is always the accompaniment of sin. So Paul is making the point that through Adam's sin death established its reign over mankind. The reign of sin and death is universal and inescapable. No one gets out of here alive. God has appointed death as the penalty for sin.

I remember years ago being at a Civil War graveyard when I was doing missionary training. We were on an excursion and were learning to use GPS and navigational tools. I had been studying Romans chapter five at the time, and so as I looked at the tombstones I was reminded that death is inescapable and universal. The reign of sin and death through Adam is something that all people face.

Paul says, "Death reigned from Adam until Moses, even over those who had not sinned in the likeness of the offense of Adam" (Romans 5:14). And then he says that Adam was a type of Him who was to come. Adam is a representative, and although death came through him, he is also a type of Christ. There two Adams- the first Adam and the last Adam. Now there are similarities between them: both are representatives of a race of people and both performed significant acts that had consequences for those associated with them. So there are similarities but there are also major dissimilarities. Notice the first difference: in verse fifteen, Paul says, "But the free gift is not like the transgression. For if by the transgression of the one the many died, much more did the grace of God and the gift by the grace of the one man, Jesus Christ, abound to the many."

Adam did much for bad and Christ did much more for good. We know that what Adam did is true and it had ramifications that are known and recognized by all. But even more true than the reign of death through Adam's sin is the abundance of grace through Christ and what He did. Now how can one thing be truer than another? Well of course both are equally true. Paul is just being emphatic to make the point that if we believe that what Adam did had consequences on those associated with him, then we need to be even faster to believe that being associated with Christ has ramifications on our lives.

There is also a difference in number, "The gift is not like that which came through the one who sinned; for on the one hand the judgment arose from one transgression resulting in condemnation" (Romans 5:16). God responded to Adam's one sin, not all of Adam's sins in his entire lifetime, not the accumulated sins of the human race. God responded to the one sin of Adam by bringing condemnation on all of humanity. If God judged one sin that severely, how would we expect God to respond to the accumulated sin of all of humanity? Look at Romans 5:16, "On the one hand the judgment arose from one transgression resulting in condemnation." God responded to Adam's one sin by bringing condemnation on all of humanity. God responded to the collective sin of all humanity by showing His amazing and unexpected grace through the Lord Jesus Christ. Paul is shocking us with this difference here. In grace, God responded to humanity's sin by dying in our place.

There is also a difference in consequence, "For if by the transgression of the one, death reigned through the one, much more those who receive the abundance of grace and of the gift of righteousness will reign in life through the one, Jesus Christ" (Romans 5:17). And so we know that through Adam's one transgression death reigned. Paul says, "much more," meaning even more sure than death's reign through Adam is the reign of life in Christ.

I remember listening to a song years ago that talked about Jesus' return, "We will leave this land where death reigns to ever be alive." I remember contemplating the words of that song, "Man, how great it will be when Christ comes back and we're ever alive with him." And then it hit me from the Scripture that the moment we believe in Christ is when life begins, not when Jesus comes back but the moment we trust in Christ.

Paul says, "Those who receive the abundance of grace and the gift of righteousness," that is referring to justification by faith. "Those who receive that will reign in life through the one through Jesus Christ." So the gift of righteousness, or justification, is the gift to stand before God. We begin to reign through life through the One, which is Jesus. Paul is talking about the ability through the indwelling spirit, Christ through us, to live the Christian life. The reign in life begins when we receive by faith the righteousness that comes through Christ. Paul is encouraging believers to accept that Truth. He says, "much more". We picture this reign of God's grace and righteousness resulting in life.

Life through Faith in Christ

Paul summarizes this section in verses eighteen and nineteen. He says, "So then as through one transgression there resulted condemnation to all men, even so through one act of righteousness there resulted justification of life to all men." I'll pause there for a while. If all we had was verse eighteen, it would sound like Paul was saying Adam's sin condemned everybody and Christ's death justified everybody. Christ's death did make the payment for all sin, but notice again in verse seventeen that it is for those who receive the abundance of God's grace. Adam's sin automatically impacted all of humanity, whereas Christ's payment of sin potentially impacts all of humanity. We receive his gift by faith and then we find its impact. So it is not automatic and therefore has to be received by faith.

Look at Romans 5:19, "For as through the one man's disobedience the many were made sinners." We were placed in the camp of sinners because of Adam's one sin, "Even so through the obedience of the one the many will be made righteous." When he talks about the obedience of the one, he's talking about Jesus being obedient by dying as the book of Philippians would say, "even the death of the cross." It's that one act of righteousness when He died for us, "through that the many will be made righteous."

What about the Law? Paul says that the Law was created so that transgression would increase. The Law increases sin in certain ways. It increases it in clarity because we have clear standards that we violate when we sin. It increases in clarity. It also increases in character because it shows that what people are doing is not just an act of sin but actually an act of rebellion, a violation of a clearly stated standard. The Law also increased in terms of quantity, as we will discover in Romans chapter seven. But when people feel that their autonomy is threatened by the Law, they actually want to fight against it. So the Law actually increases sin, "The law came in so that the transgression would increase; but where sin increased, grace abounded all the more." See this as a big picture of the Old Testament. Watch God's interaction with humanity, specifically with Israel. Israel went from bad to worse throughout her history. God, in His grace, sent Christ to die for our sins. So sin abounded but grace abounded all the more. He says, then, that just as sin reigned in death, grace would reign through righteousness through eternal life through Jesus Christ our Lord. The result of what Christ did is eternal life. We have eternal life (life knowing God) and can live in fellowship with Christ because we are alive in Him.

? DISCUSSION POINTS

1. What is the gift of righteousness?
2. Who are the ones that "reign in life"?
3. What is the key word of this passage?
4. What came through Adam?
5. What came through Christ?
6. What is the difference between the "Seminal View" and "Federal Headship"?
7. What is Paul's goal in this section?
8. In what ways are Adam and Christ similar?
9. Those who believe the gospel receive what?
10. What does Paul mean by "much more" in verse 17?
11. How does "transgression" increase under the Law?

ACTIVITIES

1. A friend comes to you and says: "I sometimes doubt my salvation. I am constantly wondering if I did enough, if I did it right, etc. I don't have peace in my heart, and I don't see how God could accept me. I find myself still struggling with sin, so if I sin after God has forgiven me, then what does that mean?" He was told by a friend that if he was really saved he would have peace (Rom.5:1), and that if he still struggled with sin maybe he wasn't saved. The man told him maybe he didn't do enough, that he didn't really commit. How can you help them only using Romans 3:21 – 5:21?

3.10 Living a New Life

 OBJECTIVES OF THIS TUTORIAL

Bible presenter Scot Keen discusses sanctification in the believer's life in Romans chapter 6. He explains that we are no longer slaves to sin and but slaves to righteousness. Believing this will help us live out our new lives in Christ.

Introduction

So far Paul has dealt with the fact that we are all guilty sinners before God. He touched on God's salvation, justification by faith and will now talk about sanctification, or Christian growth and maturity. We will first look at Romans chapter six, which deals with the believer's relationship to sin and the idea that we are alive from the dead. Then in chapter seven we will touch on the believer's relation to the law and the struggle with the flesh. Finally in chapter eight, we will discuss our deliverance through Christ.

Our relation to sin

Let's begin in Romans chapter six with the believer's relation to sin. I want you to see that we are no longer dealing with sins plural, meaning the fruit, we are dealing rather with the thing sin itself, so singular. We are dealing with the root of the problem. Sin is pictured as a reining power. We remember this from all the way back in Romans 3:9, where Paul says that he has proved that all men are under sin. Being under sin speaks of being under the condemnation of sin and the authority of sin. Paul dealt with the condemnation of sin when he described justification. Now as he talks about sanctification, he deals with our being set free from the authority of sin. We are looking at sin being personified.

Doug Moo, in his commentary on Romans, says, "Sin reigns, it can be obeyed, it pays wages, it seizes opportunity, it deceives, and it kills. In a word, Paul personifies sin. He pictures it as a power that holds sway in the world outside of Christ bringing disaster and death on all humanity." So again, we are dealing with the root of the problem, not just the fruits of that problem.

Here is an analogy I took from Watchman Nee and his work The Normal Christian Life. He compared sin in the life of a believer to the prohibition that took place in the United States. A lot of Christians were trying to do away with alcohol completely and so they would pour out alcoholic beverages and in doing so try to rid the world of alcohol. Watchman Nee made the argument that, until the distilleries were shut down, it would never effectively work. It had to happen at the root level. That is what Paul does with sin in Romans chapter six through eight. He does not try to clean up people's behavior. He deals with the behavior later on. In this section, Paul talks about our relationship to sin (that we are no longer salves of sin) and in doing so, he deals with sin at a root level. Paul insists that believers need to know that they have been set free from the authority of sin. He asks the question in Romans 6:1, "Shall we sin, or shall we continue in sin, so that grace may abound?"

Know you are free

In chapter five Paul said, "Where sin abounded, grace abounded all the more." The natural, logical question would be, "What shall we say then? Are we to continue in sin so that grace may increase?" Paul's answer is very strong. He says, "May it never be. How shall we who died to sin still live in it?" Paul will make the argument that we should not continue in sin because it is entirely inconsistent with who we are in Christ. How can we who died to sin still live in sin?

I'll give you an analogy that is kind of crazy, but maybe it will help you to remember it. Imagine being a scuba diver. It is entirely appropriate and necessary to wear scuba gear when you are under water, but if someone was to wear scuba gear just walking down the street, you would wonder what that person was doing. It is entirely inconsistent when being out of the water. Paul is saying that, now that we are in Christ, it is entirely inconsistent to live as slaves of King Sin because we died to sin.

Look at Romans 6:2, "How shall we who died to sin, still live in it?" Paul is saying that believers should not continue in sin, and yet, it obviously possible for a believer to continue in sin. We know that because Romans 6:12 says, "Don't let sin reign in your mortal bodies." So sin is present and desires to reign in us, and yet we have been set free and are responsible to not let sin reign. Chapter six will tell us how we are to go about that. We do not need to sin because we died to sin with Christ.

Look at Romans 6:3, "Or do you not know that all of us who have been baptized into Christ Jesus have been baptized into his death? Therefore we have been buried with him through baptism into death, so that as Christ was raised from the dead through the glory of the Father, so we too might walk in newness of life." When Paul says, do you not know, it is implied that his audience does not know, and he wants them to. Do they not know that, having been baptized with Christ, they were baptized into His death?

Chapter five spoke about being identified with Adam and with Christ, which begs the question, how are we identified with Christ? Paul explains that here in chapter six. He says, "We were baptized with Christ into his death." We were connected to Him. In Corinthians Paul says, "By one spirit, we were baptized into one body." When we believed the Gospel, the Spirit of God placed us into the Body of Christ. We were connected with Him through Spirit baptism. Because of that, Paul can say that we have died and our lives are hidden with Christ in God. Not only that, but he says in Galatians, "All who were baptized into Christ have clothed yourself with Christ." So we are connected. We are clothed with Christ. We identify with Him through baptism. When we believed the Gospel, the Spirit placed us into Christ, and therefore we are connected to Him. Since He died to sin, we died to sin with Him.

Believe you are free

Listen to this again. In verse Romans 6:4, "Therefore we have been buried with him through baptism into death, so that as Christ was raised from the dead through the glory of the Father, so we too might walk in newness of life." Look too at Romans 6:10-11, "For the death that he died, he died to sin once for all; but the life that he lives, he lives to God. Even so consider yourselves to be dead to sin." We are connected to Jesus so we also died to sin, and therefore we have been set free from its authority. It is logical. Christ died to sin, we were in Christ and so we died under sin.

Let me give you a story from back in the Civil War days in the United States. There was a man named George Wyatt who was drafted to be in the military. George Wyatt had a wife and three kids and didn't want to leave his family because he was afraid he would never return. There was young man by the name of Richard Pratt who had no family, and Richard Pratt agreed, for a certain sum of money, to go instead of George Wyatt. George Wyatt was drafted, but Richard Pratt went in his place and fought in the civil war. In the course of battle, Richard Pratt was killed. Years later, they tried to draft George Wyatt again, and he legally avoided that draft by saying that he died in the person of Richard Pratt. That is the concept that Paul is bringing out. You and I died to sin through another. We died in the person of Christ. He died under sin, and we died in and with Him.

When Paul talks about dying under sin, he is talking about being separated from the authority of sin. Remember in Romans 3:9 that when we were in Adam we were slaves of sin, under its condemnation and also under its authority. We were slaves of King Sin. We were slaves of King Sin until we died. When we died with Christ we were raised to walk in newness of life in freedom from the dominion of sin. That is what Christ has done for us.

Look at Romans 6:5-6, "For if we have become united with him in the likeness of his death, certainly we shall also be in the likeness of his resurrection, knowing this, that our old self was crucified with him, in order that our body of sin might be done away with, so that we would no longer be slaves to sin." Paul says our old self, our old man, was crucified with Christ. The old man is who I was in Adam and from Adam. I died with Christ, and so I was raised as a new creation in him. I still have a propensity to sin, or else Paul would not say in verse twelve not to let sin reign in my body. Sin is still present, but it is no longer my legal master. I died to the authority of King Sin. Paul says do you not know, which implies that his audience obviously did not.

Hiroo Onoda was a Japanese soldier in World War Two who fought in the Philippines. He was twenty-two years old when he went into battle, and his commanding officers told him, "Do not leave. Do not retreat. Only carry out your mission to the point of death." As soldiers came in and fought this battle, Hiroo Onoda and those with him retreated into the mountains, and they hid there from 1944 until 1974, thirty years in hiding, and he would not come out until he was discharged from a superior officer. In essence, he was living as if the war was taking place, when in fact the war was over. He did not know that he was free to return home. That is how it is with many believers. We have been set free from sin as a reigning power, but if we are ignorant of that fact, we cannot enjoy the new life that we have in Christ. We cannot glorify God with the new life that He has given us. So Paul says, "Do you not know we have been set free from the authority of sin?"

In verse seven Paul goes on to say, "He who has died is freed from sin." We died with Christ under King Sin. I would be confident to say that as you hear these truths from Romans, you are probably struggling to understand how you died with Christ. How are you alive with Him? How does it all work? It is a process to grow in our understanding of these things. Even if you cannot understand how it worked, please trust God's word in verse seven that says, "He who has died is freed from sin." When you recognize the impulse to sin (the sin that Paul personifies as a reigning power), would you please believe God's Word which says that you don't have to yield to that any longer because you have been set free? You are no longer a slave of sin.

Paul says do you not know. He wants all believers to know that they have been set free from sin. Not only does he want us to know this, he wants us to believe it. He says, "Believe that you have been set free." Look at Romans 6:8, "Now if we have died with Christ, we believe that we shall also live with him, knowing that Christ, having been raised from the dead, is never to die again; death no longer is master over him." "Even so," verse eleven, "Consider yourselves to be dead to sin, but alive to God in Christ Jesus." One author said in a book, "If you feel like you've died to sin, you've died to sin, and if you don't feel like you've died to sin, you've still died to sin." This is an issue of faith, not feelings. The desire to sin is not weakened in the believer, but the separation from its authority is there. We have the freedom to say no to King Sin. God has set us free from its authority. We need to know that, but we also need to believe that.

Live your new life in Christ

In Romans 6:12 Paul says, "Therefore do not let sin reign in your mortal body so that you obey its lusts." Did you catch that? Sin is in us and it has desires and we are responsible not to obey those desires. Sometimes people say, "I can't help but do," fill in the blank, whatever it is that they are struggling with as a sin. Paul says we can help it. We have been set free, and we are under obligation to not let sin reign in our mortal bodies. Paul wants us to believe this and he wants us to act on it as well. We need to know and believe what is true of us, that we died to sin's authority and have been raised to walk in newness of life.

In verse thirteen Paul says, "Do not go on presenting the members of your body to sin as instruments of unrighteousness; but present yourselves to God as those alive from the dead, and your members as instruments of righteousness to God." Some people call this the Gospel to the saved. This is the Good News, not of how Christ has set me free from the penalty of sin, but of how He set us free from the power of sin. This is the Good News to believers, and Paul exhorts us to live out our new life in Christ. Do not let sin reign in your mortal body. Sin is present and desires to reign, and we are responsible to say no to it. Instead we are to present ourselves as instruments of righteousness to God. As believers we can use our hands, feet and minds as instruments of sin, or we can use them as instruments of righteousness. Paul is telling us not to yield to sin, but to yield instead as instruments of righteousness under God. We do that by faith.

Look at Romans 6:13 again, "Present yourselves to God as those alive from the dead." That is a strong statement. Let me give you another example of how this works. If we were at an event and they asked for all the men aged thirty to forty-five to come forward, then I would go forward. I wouldn't tell my age, but I would be presenting myself as a male who is between thirty to forty-five years old. If we were at an event and there was an announcement for all Christians to come forward and receive a free gift, then it would be as a Christian that you would present yourself.

Paul says, "Present yourselves to God as those alive from the dead." That means yield to God as one alive from the dead. Yield to Him by believing that you are alive from the dead. This is meaty here. If you yield to God as alive from the dead, it means that you must believe that you died to sin and that you are not a slave to sin. You believe that you are alive under God in Christ, and so you yield to the Spirit of God at work in you believing those things are true. So it is a believing submission. You are conscious of the fact that this is true of you in Christ, that you are not a slave of sin, and you yield to God on that basis.

It took me several years of chewing on Romans to understand these truths. It didn't come overnight. As a new believer, I'd be faced with temptation, and my immediate prayer would be, "Oh God, please help me not to give in to this. Please enable me not to do this." I literally remember the day when faced with a temptation and, instead of saying, "Oh God, set me free from this," I said, "God, thank you that you did set me free." I had a believing attitude in God's word. When we feel a strong desire to sin, it is our privilege to be able to claim the Word of God that even though the desire to sin is present, it is not our authority. We died to sin and are alive under God in Christ Jesus.

Watchman Nee, as I mentioned earlier, uses an analogy that will help us remember this. He uses the illustration of a ship captain. The evil ship captain is running the ship, and he tells people to mop the deck, hoist the mainsails, or scrape the barnacles underneath the boat. The people run and carry out all the orders that this evil dictator gives. Along comes someone else, a new captain, and so the evil ship captain is tied to the mast of the ship. He is still there barking out orders, but he is no longer the one in charge. Christ is in charge now. You and I both have a desire to sin, and we also have a desire to do the things of God. Although both desires are present, God says we are supposed to yield ourselves, not to sin, but to righteousness as those alive from the dead. We need to believe God's Word and yield to Him on that basis.

The truth about sin

Being dead to sin means that we are not under the authority of sin, and being alive under God means we have the life of Christ and so can live the Christian life. Look at the conclusion in Romans 6:14, "For sin shall not be master over you, for you are not under law but under grace." How does being under grace set us free from sin? We will talk about that in chapter seven. Paul just alludes to it now before moving on. He says that sin is present, but it is no longer our master, and therefore, we should treat it as an evil power that has been deposed of its authority.

Look at Romans 6:15, "What then? Shall we sin because we are not under law but under grace? May it never be! Do you not know," Paul says, "that when you present yourselves to someone as slaves for obedience, you are slaves of the one whom you obey, either of sin resulting in death, or of obedience resulting in righteousness?" Understand that Paul is talking to believers here. He is not doubting their salvation. He says that we died to sin with Christ. We are no longer slaves of sin legally and yet, for all practical purposes, we are slaves to the one we obey. Even though we are not slaves of sin, if we yield to sin, we are being a slave of sin in that moment. We can yield to sin resulting in death (which I think speaks of separation of fellowship with God) or we can yield ourselves to God resulting in righteousness. This is practical sanctification.

Look at verse seventeen, "Thanks be to God that, though you were slaves of sin," that is when we were unsaved and slaves of King Sin, "you became obedient from the heart to that form of teaching to which you were committed." They responded in faith and were freed from sin. They were set free from sin's authority and became slaves of righteousness.

So Paul says, "I'm speaking in human terms because of the weakness of your flesh. Just as you presented your members as slaves to impurity and to lawlessness, resulting in further lawlessness, so now present your members as slaves to righteousness resulting in sanctification." We are progressively being sanctified. Paul says, "Yes, you used to be slaves of sin, and you yielded to sin and it just took you down a downward path of shame and lawlessness and ungodliness." He says, "Now, present yourselves as instruments to righteousness, and the end of that road is sanctification."

Look at Romans 6:20, "For when you were slaves of sin, you were free in regard to righteousness. Therefore what benefit were you then deriving from the things of which you are now ashamed?" Paul is asking, "What good came out of that, when we yielded to sin? Those are the things that we are ashamed of now." So, in contrast now, "Having been freed from sin and enslaved to God, you derive your benefit, resulting in sanctification, and the outcome, eternal life." Paul is saying that we are not to yield to sin because the end of that road is death. Instead, we are to yield ourselves to righteousness and that results in sanctification and eternal life. I believe this eternal life is an experience of fellowship with God. Life in the knowledge of God, as John chapter seventeen would define it, is eternal life; knowing God and knowing Jesus Christ. So Paul is urging believers to not continue in sin. He raised a question in verse one, "Shall we continue in sin that grace may abound?" He now says, "No, you died to sin. No, you're not under law, you're under grace. No, when you yield to sin, you practically make yourself a slave of sin. No, because sin brings death." The answer is an emphatic no. This concept raises many questions in our minds because, as I said earlier, we don't feel dead to sin or that we are free from sin, but this is when God calls us to walk by faith and not by sight.

Clarifications

To conclude, here are some helpful clarifications. It was not sin that died in Romans chapter six, but rather we who died to sin. This means that the desire to sin is still present. Paul says in Romans 6:12, "Don't let it reign," which means it could reign, but we are not supposed to let it. Being dead to sin then, does not mean that sin died, and it does not mean that we are unable to respond to sin. After all, why would he say, "Don't let it reign," if it is not possible to respond to sin? It does not mean that the propensity to sin has weakened. It is still present. It does mean that our relationship to sin has radically changed. We are no longer slaves to sin. We need to know this. We need to believe it is true, and we need to yield ourselves to God on that basis.

At the end of the civil war in the United States, Abraham Lincoln signed the Emancipation Proclamation which gave freedom to all slaves. Interestingly, when you look at history, there were some people who still served as slaves because they did not know that Lincoln had signed that bill. The first thing we need to know is that we died to sin and have been emancipated, that we are no longer slaves of sin. Other slaves knew they were free but had a hard time believing it. They did not feel like they had been set free. It was really an act of faith for people to step out and enjoy their freedom. We need to know that we have been set free. We need to choose to step out in faith in God's Word and trust that we are no longer slaves of sin. Instead, we yield ourselves as instruments of righteousness under God. When we do that, we find that we are practically being set apart and sanctified day after day. That is what Paul teaches about sanctification in Romans chapter six.

❓ DISCUSSION POINTS

1. From this passage of Scripture (Romans 6:1-23), give at least three reasons why we should not continue in sin. Who are the ones that "reign in life"?

2. How does Spirit baptism relate to our death unto sin?

3. What does "death" speak of?

4. What were we "separated" from?

5. Who is "our old man"?

6. If our "old man" was crucified, why do we still sin?

7. Who or what died in Romans 6? Us, or sin? Why does it matter?

8. According to Romans 6:7 who is it that is freed from sin?

9. What does it mean to "reckon yourselves to be dead indeed unto sin"?

10. What are the two main points of application we are exhorted to make?

11. What does it mean to "present yourself to God as alive from the dead"?

12. In Romans 6, Paul gives at least four reasons why believers should not continue in sin. What are they?

13. Give at least two descriptions of what being dead to sin does NOT mean.

14. Give at least two descriptions of what being dead to sin DOES mean.

ACTIVITIES

1. In our last scenario, we encouraged a new believer regarding the fact that, through faith in Christ, they are accepted before God. You hopefully were able to encourage your friend and now he is confident of his justification. The struggles he sometimes has do not shake his confidence in the finished work of Christ. He knows that it is not a question as to whether he did enough; he is resting in the fact that Christ did more than enough. However, the struggle with sin is very tiring and he knows that where sin abounds, grace abounds all the more. He knows he's secure in Christ. Now he finds himself giving in to sin more often. He wonders why it even matters. Why should he even resist? What do you tell him from Romans 6?

3.11 Brought to Despair

✓ OBJECTIVES OF THIS TUTORIAL

Bible presenter Scot Keen continues to discuss sanctification in the believer's life in Romans chapter seven. We must come to the end of ourselves and depend fully on the in-dwelling Spirit in order to live our new lives in Christ.

Introduction

In this tutorial Paul continues to discuss sanctification in chapters six through eight. Last time we dealt with the believers' relationship to sin. As believers we have been set free from the authority of sin because we are dead to sin and are alive to God. Now in Romans chapter seven Paul will deal with the believer's relation to the law and also with the believer's struggle with the flesh.

An illustration from marriage

We firstly need to realize that we have been joined to another. In Romans chapter seven Paul gives an illustration from marriage to show the believer's relation to the Law. He says, "Or do you not know, brethren (for I am speaking to those who know the law), that the law has jurisdiction over a person as long as he lives? For the married woman is bound by law to her husband while he is living; but if her husband dies, she is released from the law concerning the husband. So then, if while her husband is living she is joined to another man, she shall be called an adulteress; but if her husband dies, she is free from the law, so that she is not an adulteress though she is joined to another man."

Paul is making the point that death ends a legally binding relationship. A wife is legally bound to her husband in marriage until he dies. But once he dies, she is free to enter a new relationship. You may ask why Paul brings this up here in Romans. The Jew had made a covenant with God at Mount Sinai in Exodus chapter nineteen. They said, "Whatever God is commanding we will do." They entered into a legally binding relationship and were bound in successive generations to that Mosaic covenant.

Now Paul is saying that believers have been set free from the Law. The Jew are probably wondering how this is possible. Paul shows them that they can be set free through death with Christ. In the same way that believers die to sin, they also die to the Law. In chapter six Paul says sin will not be our master because we are not under Law but under grace. Now in chapter seven he shows us how that is possible.

A new relationship

Look at Romans 7:4, "Therefore, my brethren, you also were made to die to the law through the body of Christ, so that you might be joined to another, to Him who was raised from the dead." Obviously the only people who were bound by covenant at Sinai were the Jews; but Paul is speaking to all believers here. As a matter of principle no believer is under the Mosaic Law. All believers have died to the Law and are joined to Another (to Him who was raised from the dead). They are joined to the person of Christ. Why are we joined to Christ? So we can bear fruit for God. Some theologians call the statements dead to sin, alive unto God, dead to the law positional truths. They are things that are true of us regardless of whether we know that they are true or not. They are simply true because we are connected with Christ.

It is fascinating that these positional truths are always intended to have practical results. Go back to chapter six. We died to sin so that we could walk in newness of life. In chapter seven we found that we died to the Law and we were joined to Another so we could bear fruit for God. So God desires practical results in our life and these positional truths are the foundation for that.

We died to the law to be joined to Another so that we could bear fruit for God. The implication is that fruitfulness could not come under the law of paradigm. It comes by being joined to Another. Colossians touches on this. Look at Colossians 2:20, "You died with Christ to the elementary principles of the world. Do not handle, do not taste, do not touch." Paul says, "These are the commandments and teaching of men and they have the appearance of wisdom and religion and abasement; but they are of no value against the flesh." Paul is saying that simply having a set of rules does not make a believer fruitful. Fruitfulness comes by being joined to Another.

We'll talk more on this in Romans chapter eight; but for now I will mention that the idea of being fruitful is not subjugated to the book of Romans. Galatians chapter five, for example, describes the fruit of the Spirit. Philippians chapter one refers to the fruit of righteousness which comes through Jesus Christ. And here in Romans seven we are told that we are to bear fruit for God. All this requires us to be connected with Jesus. As believers we can be fruitful only because we are connected to the Lord Jesus as He is the source of our fruitfulness. It will be the Spirit of God who produces fruit in us as we walk by faith.

Paul says, "You were joined to another in order that you might bear fruit for God." Paul gives an illustration from marriage to make the point that death ends a legally binding relationship, which in turn enables us to enter a new relationship. Paul says, "But now we have been released from the law, having died to that by which we were bound, so that we serve in newness of the spirit and not in oldness of the letter" (Romans 7:6).

Paul contrasts the law and grace here. Paul says, "We serve not in the oldness of the letter; but, in the newness of the spirit." Sometimes when we talk about law and grace, people think we are talking about God's disposition. They think God used to be stern and legalistic and now He is gracious. Law and grace deal with systems by which God governed people at various times in history. God governed Israel under the paradigm of the Mosaic Law. God governs believers in this age under this paradigm called grace. Under grace, man has a responsibility to not let sin reign. He has a responsibility to walk in newness of life. One of the major differences now is that under grace believers have the indwelling spirit, and that makes all the difference in the world.

Death under the law
Let me contrast Law and grace to help Romans become clearer. "Under law man is told to do this and live," (Leviticus 18). Under grace, we are alive, now walk in newness of life. Under Law, the Law demands duty and then offers blessing. Look at Deuteronomy chapter twenty-eight, "If you do this I will bless you." Under grace, we have been blessed with all spiritual blessings in Christ. The Law speaks of human performance. It tells us what to do but it does not enable us to get there.

John Bunyan used to say, "Run John run, the law demands; but, gives me neither feet nor hands." The Law told people what to do, but there was no indwelling Spirit to enable them to get there. Grace speaks of God's enablement because God tells us what to do. There are lots of commands and exhortations in the New Testament; but they are carried out with the knowledge of and independence upon the in-dwelling Spirit to enable us to get there.

Let's go back to John Bunyan's quote, "Run John run, the law demands; but, gives me neither feet nor hands. A grander noose God's grace does bring, he bids me fly and he gives me wings." God's grace enables the believer to do that which God commands the believer to do.

C.A. Coates on the law
Author C.A. Coates says, "I cannot imagine anything more calculated to fill an honest soul with despair than the New Testament if you leave Christ out." He goes on to say that many believers treat the New Testament as the superior Law of Moses. If we are honest, God raises the expectations in the New Testament to a whole new level. Jesus says we are not just to love, but to love as He has loved us. Husbands are to love their wives as Christ loved the Church! The expectations are infinitely higher. In fact, what

God commands us in the New Testament is so unobtainable that it can only be obtained by means of the in-dwelling Spirit.

So C.A. Coates makes the point that if we try to live the Christian life apart from the Holy Spirit, we are essentially placing ourselves under the Law with no divine enablement. Under grace God tells the believer what to do and also makes provision for that accomplishment.

Legal system versus grace system

Lewis Perry Chaufer has been known to say, "Any aspect of life or conduct undertaken in dependence of the flesh, is to that extent purely legal in character." He is just making the point that the Christian life cannot be lived by the power of the flesh. It has to be lived through the enablement of the Spirit of God. The question is not whether or not God wants us to live a godly life, that is clear enough. The question is, "How does God want us to get there?" The answer? "Not in the oldness of the letter, but in the newness of the spirit." It is God's enablement.

A friend told me once that God's moral absolutes never change; but the way He governs those absolutes have changed. That is why we find so many things from the Law repeated in the New Testament. God's moral absolutes have not changed; but the way He governs those have changed and now He governs with the provision of the Spirit of God who is at work in our lives. This is critical for us to understand as we live the Christian life.

A struggle with the flesh

Let's tackle the believer's struggle with the flesh now. This is another important theme in Romans. Now some people look at Romans 7: 14-25 and conclude that Paul is not a believer here. They say that Paul is alluding to a time in his life when he was not a believer and the struggles he experienced then. I don't agree. I think Paul was describing an experience he had as a believer in this passage. He is just referring to a time before he came to understand God's provision of the in-dwelling Spirit to live the Christian life. After all, we are talking about sanctification here and Paul wants to encourage believers in their growth in the Lord. It would not be encouraging to say that yes, I struggled too, but I wasn't a believer. That would not encourage anybody. Paul shows us his struggle that lasted until he came to understand the Spirit's enablement to live the Christian life. He uses that to encourage his audience to also trust God as they struggle in the Christian life.

Brought to despair

In Roman 7:14 Paul says, "For we know that the law is spiritual, but I am of flesh, sold into bondage to sin." Paul is talking about being brought to a place of despair. He says,

"I am sold into bondage to sin." Some people argue that Paul must not have been a believer here because otherwise how could Paul say he say that he is sold into bondage to sin? I think Paul is simply saying that there is a part of him, the flesh, that is irrevocably committed to sin. It is called the flesh. It is not getting better and it is not going away. Paul recognizes that the problem is not the Law. There is something in us that bristles against the Law of God. Paul speaks about the confusing experience he had as a believer struggling with sin and how he came to clarity. We can also be encouraged as we have probably faced that same confusion and now God's word gives us clarity as well.

So we have Paul's experience. Now, here's a quote by William R., "If you claim that the wretched man of Romans seven is an unregenerate man, under conviction of sin, the complete reply is this that the man of Romans seven is crying for deliverance not from sins, guilt or punishment but from its power. Not from forgiveness of sins, but help against in-dwelling sin. This man is exercised not about the day of judgment, but about a condition of bondage of which he hates."

In Romans 7:14-25, Paul is not asking who will set him free from the penalty of sin, he is asking who will set him free from the power of sin. This is a believer struggling to live the Christian life. You and I can learn from his experience that first of all, there is a conflict of desires. Look in Romans 7:15, "For what I am doing, I do not understand; for I am not practicing what I would like to do, but I am doing the very thing I hate". And then again in verse nineteen, "For the good that I want, I do not do, but I practice the very evil that I do not want." And further along in verse twenty-one, "I find then the principle that evil is present in me, the one who wants to do good."

There is a conflict of desires here. You have felt the same thing, no doubt. On one hand we have these new desires because God has given us the divine nature and the in-dwelling Spirit; but on the flip side, we still have the flesh. Sin is still in believers and it desires to reign. So we have a frustrating conflict of desires. Look at verse fifteen again, "What I'm doing I do not understand."

I will never forget, after becoming a believer, the day that I was plagued with an awareness that even though my sins were forgiven, I was still wretched on the inside. I remember struggling so much. Was there something wrong with me? Why did I still want to sin? When would it go away? That is exactly what Paul is talking about, "I do not understand. I am not practicing what I would like to do; but I am doing the very thing that I hate."

Many of us of experience trying to do good, failing and then getting discouraged. Yet we get this renewed vigor and we try harder. We fail again and get frustrated again. We come to a point of despair and we have a choice to either throw ourselves on God and trust Him for deliverance or to become discouraged and throw in the towel.

As a fairly new believer, I remember praying that God would take away my desire to sin. I won't go into details because it is too personal, but I would pray about this every day, day after day after day. I remember one morning I was praying that same prayer and I literally I just stood up and said, "Forget it, it's never going to go away. The desire to sin is never going to go away." I was so discouraged. Why bother even trying? That is how believers sometimes feel. Even as painful as that is, it is actually an important part of our growth. Paul came to realize that sin was present in him, someone one who wanted to do good and it was not going to go away. The desire to sin was going to go away.

Paul identifies the problem, and the source of the problem is sin. He says in verse seventeen, "So now no longer am I the one doing it; but, sin that dwells in me." Paul is not avoiding responsibility, he is simply recognizing that the problem is in-dwelling sin and it is not getting any get better. The source of the problem is sin.

It is interesting that Paul recognizes that sin is in him, but at the same that it does not define him. He is a new creature in Christ. Yes, sin is in him, the one who wants to do good. See the distinction there, God does not define him by his sin, although it is still resident in him.

There is nothing good about our flesh. Look at verse eighteen, "For I know that nothing good dwells in me, that is, in my flesh." Our flesh cannot be fixed. Coming to accept that the desire to sin is not going away is a part of our growth. Sanctification is not the desire to sin going away. The flesh is not getting any better.

Look with me at verse twenty-one, "I find then the principle that evil is present in me, the one who wants to do good." Paul accepted the fact that sin is was in him and it was not getting any get better or going away, not until he gets a new body. Peace comes not because our flesh is going away; but because we realize that, although it is not going away, it does not define or rule us.

Paul has the desire to do good but that in and of itself is not enough. Look at verse eighteen again, "Willing is present in me, but the doing of the good is not." When we are created new in Christ, we have a new set of desires and we have the in-dwelling Spirit. If you are like me as a new believer, you may have also determined that you have a desire to serve God and do the right thing so therefore you will do it. But you come to find that the desire is not enough. "Willing is present, but how to perform that which is good, I do not find" (Romans 7:18).

What does this mean then? We have to live by faith. God has left us dependent upon Him to do the good that we want to do. The desire is present, but that desire is not enough to carry the good out. We have to depend on the indwelling Spirit to live this out.

A cry for deliverance

So believers are brought to an end of themselves in Romans seven. Look at Romans 7:24, "Wretched man that I am! Who will set me free from the body of this death?" There is nothing more painful than this experience. Many of you believers can identify with this. You have been there. Maybe you are there now. It is a painful, but it is also necessary because throughout this process God teaches us that we are entirely dependent upon Him. "Wretched man that I am, who will set me free from the body of this death?"

Dennis McCallum in his book Walking in Victory says, "Although we now realize we cannot save ourselves by good works, we may secretly believe that we are able to follow God in our own strength. Even if we say yes, I know I'm unable to change myself, God may detect a lingering confidence in self and he will smoke out this confidence by allowing us to tangle with his law, just as Paul does in Roman seven."

In other words, God allows us to try to do what He says to do. At times we try to do that apart from trusting in the Spirit to enable us. And God uses that to teach us that regardless of desire, we still need the in-dwelling Spirit's enablement to carry it out. Of course He is already resident in us but still we need to trust in Him day by day to carry out the things He wants us to do. When Paul says, "Who will deliver me?" he recognizes that the Law cannot deliver him. The Law furthered his bondage. Paul recognized that self-determination could not deliver him because in the flesh dwells no good thing. He recognized that even a new nature could not deliver him, because although willing was present, how to perform that which was good he could not find.

As William R. says in his commentary on Romans, "Only the deliverer can deliver." In fact, he says it this way, "Sinners don't get saved until they trust the Saviour and saints don't get delivered until they trust the deliverer." We have to trust God through His in-dwelling Spirit to enable us to walk in this newness of life.

A resolution

The resolution comes after the believer has gone through the agonising process of being brought to the end of himself and finally realizes his need. That is how we escape this wheel of disappointment and frustration. We realize that it has to be God working through us.

Paul says in Romans 7:25, "Thanks be to God through Jesus Christ our Lord." Through our death with him (Romans six) and through His life in us (Romans seven) is newness of life. The Spirit of God (Romans eight) living in the believer enables us to walk in this newness of life. That is what Paul teaches in Romans chapter seven.

? DISCUSSION POINTS

1. Does the description of baptism here line up with what you have been taught previously?

2. Do you feel this view of baptism is consistent with the flow of God's Narrative, as it has described His character and purposes so far?

3. If you have been baptized, what was your understanding at the time? Was it done in such a way as to reflect the rich illustration of a believer dying, being buried and then being resurrected with Jesus?

4. Do you feel that it is important to be baptized as a believer through immersion, or do you see this as one of the "negotiables" of our faith?

5. Do you have any thoughts on *who* should baptize someone else? Is there anything in the Narrative so far that might guide us in this?

3.12 Deliverance Now and in the Future

 OBJECTIVES OF THIS TUTORIAL

Bible presenter Scot Keen concludes the discussion on sanctification here in Romans chapter eight. He explains the two types of deliverance for the believer, both present and future.

Introduction

Last time we discussed the believer's relationship to sin and that we are alive from the dead. We also looked at the believer's relationship to the Law, that we died to the Law in order to be joined to Another so we might bear fruit for God. And then we looked at the believer's struggle with the flesh in Romans 7:14-25. Paul realized that his flesh was still present; it was not getting any better and it was not going away. All these truths have built up to the climax of Romans chapter eight, which is Paul's conclusion on sanctification.

Let's briefly review the Christian life principles that we have observed so far. We are identified with Christ, just as like we were identified with Adam (Romans chapter five). Now, we have died to sin and its authority. Sin is still present. It desires to reign but we are not under obligation to let it do so. We have been raised to walk in newness of life. We also learned that neither the Mosaic Law or any other law are God's means of deliverance because deliverance does not come from the Law.

We also found that although we are positionally free from sin's authority, we still need God's enablement to do the good things that we desire and to refrain from the evil that we do not want to do. Remember that Paul said that willing is present, "How to perform which is good, I do not find." Paul cried out in desperation in Romans 7:24, "Wretched man that I am. Who will set me free from the body of this death?" The answer is found in Christ, "Thanks be to God through Jesus Christ our Lord" (Romans 7:25). He develops his answer later in chapter seven, "Deliverance is found as we walk in the spirit."

Now let's move onto Romans chapter eight. It can be divided into two major sections. Believers are delivered now as they walk according to the Spirit, however they find deliverance ultimately when they are glorified.

Escaping the law of sin and death

Let's begin first of all with the deliverance now as we walk with the Spirit's enablement. Paul says, "Therefore there is now no condemnation for those who are in Christ Jesus. For the law of the spirit of life in Christ Jesus has set you free from the law of sin and of death" (Romans 8:1-2). You may already be aware that whenever the word therefore is used it means that what has been said so far is being summed up, transition into a new section.

Keep in mind that the chapter divisions you see are were not in the original text. Paul has cried out for deliverance, "Who is going to set me free from the body of this death? Thanks be to God through Jesus Christ our Lord." He then says, "Thanks be to God through Jesus Christ our Lord! So then, on the one hand I myself with my mind am serving the law of God, but on the other, with my flesh the law of sin" (Romans 7:25). He recognizes that his inner-man is always going to desire the things of God, and the flesh is going to always desire the things of sin. "Therefore, there is no condemnation for those who are in Christ Jesus for," he explains, "for the law of the spirit of life... has set you free from the law of sin and death."

It is doubtful that that Paul is referring to eternal condemnation here because his explanation in verse two is has to do with how we live our lives now. Most likely when he says there is no condemnation, he is talking about the experience of struggle and defeat that we saw at the end of chapter seven. Believers are set free from that experience when they walk according to the Spirit.

Notice Romans 8:2, "For the law of the spirit of life in Christ Jesus has set you free from the law of sin and of death." Paul uses the word law here to speak about a principle that acts uniformly. Think about the law of gravity. What goes up must come down. That is a principle that acts uniformly. That is the concept here. And the law that Paul speaks about is the law of the Spirit of life in Christ Jesus, and it delivers believers from the law of sin and death.

Now I understand the law of sin to be the principle that sin always brings death. We have actually seen this in Romans previously. Paul was trying to live by the law when he said, "This commandment, which was to result in life, proved to result in death for me" (Romans 7:10). I take it that Paul is talking about his experience of separation of fellowship with God when he tried to walk in the power of the flesh.

Paul talks about how this law, the law of sin, brings about death, "Who will set me free from the body of this death?" (Romans 7:24). When he talks about sin and death, I think he is alluding to an experience of separation of fellowship. We know that is always going to be the case unless there is a superior law to set us free from that.

Think again about the law of gravity; what goes up must come down. There is another law that supersedes this law and it is the law of aerodynamics. And in the same way, the law of sin producing death can be superseded by the law of the Spirit of life in Christ Jesus.

We are talking about the Spirit of God producing life in the believer, as the believer walks according to the Spirit. We are talking about this walk of freedom that comes through the Spirit's enablement, mentioned in the previous tutorial. We should not serve in the oldness of the letter, but in the newness of the Spirit. That is how we find life, by walking according to the Spirit.

Now Paul says, "For what the law could not do, weak as it was through the flesh, God did" (Romans 8:3). Which begs a question. What was it that the Law could not do? Well, in the context of Romans, we are looking at a believer trying to live by the Law and trying to be fruitful. But the believer has to be set free from that and instead joined to Another, in order to bear fruit for God.

The Law cannot cause a believer to be fruitful, because the it is about performance. Remember our quote from John Bunyan, "Run, John, run, the law demands, but gives me neither feet nor hands." Now the Law can tell us what is right and it can reprimand our sin, but it cannot enable us to do the right thing. So God did what the Law could not do, weak as it was through the flesh. The problem with the Law is not the Law in and of itself. It is what the Law had to work with that lets it down. God did what the Law could not do, and he did it by sending His own Son in the likeness of sinful flesh, and as an offering for sin He condemned sin in the flesh.

Please understand that we are not talking about justification any longer. We are talking about sanctification. We are talking about Christian growth and maturity, fruitfulness and things of that nature. The Jews would have been terrified to try to live a righteous life apart from the Law. And while Paul is arguing here that it is possible to live a righteous life, he is clarifying that it is only possible apart from the Law.

God did what the Law could not do. He firstly condemned sin in the flesh (Romans chapter six). Our old self was crucified with Him in order that the body of sin might be annulled, or rendered inoperative. Paul is saying, again, that God made it possible for the believer to live a Christian life, a righteous life, and He did that first of all by setting us free from the authority of sin (Romans 8:3). He condemned sin in the flesh. And secondly, He made it possible for us to live a righteous life through the indwelling Spirit. Look at verse four, "So that the requirement of the law might be fulfilled in us, who do not walk according to the flesh but according to the spirit." Paul beautifully brings together the things that he has been saying so far.

Notice that he says so that. God had a goal in mind in what He did for us through Christ. He did it so we could live a godly life. Paul says, "So that the requirement of the law might be fulfilled in us." What is the requirement of the Law? It is quite simple, as you may remember from the gospels. Jesus summed up all the Law and the Prophets in two commands. Love the Lord your God with all your heart and your neighbor as yourself.

Paul is going to take that and condense it down to one word. He says, "He who loves his neighbor has fulfilled the law" (Romans 13:8). So love was ultimately what the Law was aiming for, as was lived out in the life of the Old Testament believer. But there was a problem; the Law would command love, but it did not enable love. There was no indwelling Spirit. But now God has condemned sin in the flesh, set us free from the authority of King Sin, and not only that, but has made it possible for the requirement of the Law, love, to be fulfilled in us.

I think Paul's choice of words here, under the inspiration of the Spirit, is very precise. He does not say the Law would be fulfilled by us. He says it would be fulfilled in us. I take that we are talking here about the Spirit's ministry of producing the fruit of the Spirit, first and foremost of which is love. The Spirit produces love in us which in turn makes it possible for us to live a godly life, something that the Law required but never enabled because there was no indwelling Spirit.

Paul says that this godly life is possible because of what Christ has done, and yet notice that it is contingent on our walk. He says again that, "The requirement of the law would be fulfilled in us, specifically those of us who do not walk according to the flesh, but according to the spirit." This lets us know that as believers we have a choice. God desires for us to walk according to the Spirit. If we walk according to the flesh the requirement of the Law will not be fulfilled in us. But if we walk according to the Spirit, the Spirit produces love, and I will be doing what God wants me to do.

That is the essence of what Paul is describing here. God has made it possible for us to live the Christian life when we walk according to the Spirit. Let's define what it means to walk according to the Spirit. First of all, this concept of walking comes from the Old Testament when Enoch walked with God, as did Noah and Abraham. And Paul says that those who live their life walking according to the Spirit will find the requirement of the Law being fulfilled in them.

The idea is that we live our life in dependence upon the Holy Spirit, and at the same time live our life believing that we died to sin and that we are alive to God. We live our lives believing and yielding to the truths in Romans chapters six to eight. That is the major idea that Paul is bringing out here. This walk is idiomatic for one's life, and it is to be lived according to the Spirit of God with God's enablement to live the Christian life.

We escape the law of sin and death by walking according to the Spirit. Who will set us free from this body of death? Christ will as we walk according to the Spirit.

Motivation to walk with God

Now Paul gives us a motivation to live this way, to walk with God in this pattern. Look at Romans 8:5-6. He says, "For those who are according to the flesh set their minds on the things of the flesh, but those who are according to the spirit, the things of the spirit. For the mind set on the flesh is death, but the mind set on the spirit is life and peace."

He seems to be referring to worldview here. Their worldview is shaped by God's Word, and as they walk according to the Spirit they find life and peace. Those who walk according to the flesh, they find an experience of death. Why is it that a walk according to the flesh brings death? Take a look at verse seven, "The mind set on the flesh is hostile toward God; for it does not subject itself to the law of God, for it is not even able to do so." When believers walk in the flesh, they are yielding to something that is hostile to the things of God.

Remember Paul said, "Willing is present, but how to perform that which is good I do not find." Paul realized that evil was present and it was not going to go away. That desire to sin is present and it is not going to get better. If you yield to it, then you are yielding something that is hostile towards God. So obviously the result is death or separation of fellowship. Paul encourages believers here to make the right choice and to choose to walk according to the Spirit instead of the flesh.

Now notice Paul says, "Those who are in the flesh cannot please God." They cannot please God. And you could study this further if you like, but for now notice there are two different prepositions that Paul uses. He talks about according to the Spirit and he talks about in the Spirit. Two different prepositions. All believers are in the Spirit, but not all believers consistently walk according to the Spirit.

Paul says in verse nine, "You are not in the flesh but in the spirit, if indeed the spirit of God dwells in you." And I think he is saying why in the world would we walk according to the flesh, when God says we are not in the flesh? Why not rather walk according to the Spirit, because we are in the Spirit? In other words, why not live consistently with who God has made us in Christ? Paul is arguing that we should be motivated to choose to walk according to the Spirit.

Notice that the believer is under no obligation to the flesh. "If Christ is in you, though the body is dead because of sin, yet the spirit is alive because of righteousness. But if the spirit of him who raised Jesus from the dead dwells in you, he who raised Christ Jesus from the dead will also give life to your mortal bodies through his spirit who dwells in you" (Romans 8:10-11).

As an encouragement, think about Christ when He lay in the tomb. He was dead and the Spirit of God gave life to His mortal body, and the Spirit of God gives life to our mortal bodies also. Whenever you doubt whether or not the Spirit of God can enable you to live the Christian life, just remember the resurrection. The one who raised Christ from the dead gives life to your mortal body now when you walk according to the Spirit. You are I are under no obligation to the flesh. "So then, brethren, we are under obligation, not to the flesh, to live according to the flesh- for if you are living according to the flesh, you must die" (Romans 8:12-13). Look again at the phrase under obligation not to the flesh.

When I was twelve years old, I remember going to a basketball game with my dad at Rupp Arena, which is where the Kentucky Wildcats play in Lexington Kentucky. We were watching a high school tournament ball game. Clay County Kentucky got to the final game which was totally unexpected. They were a Cinderella team that just happened to make it to the final game. Everybody in this arena stood on their feet waiting to see how the game would turn out. And I stood up on my tip toes beside my dad with excitement, trying to see the game. Then I heard a voice behind me thundering, saying, "Sit down!" I felt a chill of fear flow through my body, and I slowly started to sit down. I looked over at my dad and he looked at that guy, then looked at me and said, "You don't have to sit down." I realized, "That's right, I'm not obligated to this guy. I obey my dad."

I see the same thing here in Romans eight. Pauls says, "You are under obligation not to the flesh." We have sinful desires. And Paul says we are not under obligation to them. Here's why. Look at Romans 8:14, "For all who are being led by the spirit of God, these are sons of God." Because of our identity as Christians, sons and daughters of God, we are set free from sin's dominion and we are not obligated whatsoever.

In fact, Paul says, "If you live according to the flesh, you must die." He is talking to believers. Note that he is not talking about eternal death but, as I've been saying, an experience of separation of fellowship. And when the believer yields to the flesh, Paul says, "I refuse to call that life. It is not life as God intends." "We are under obligation, not to the flesh, to live according to the flesh- for if you are living according to the flesh, you must die; but if by the spirit you are putting to death the deeds of the body, you will live." As the believer chooses to yield to the Spirit of God, the desires of the flesh are nullified (not carried out to execution), so we put to death the deeds of the body, but remember we do this by the Spirit.

I love the terminology if you, by the Spirit. It is my responsibility, but it is His enablement, "If by the spirit you are putting to death the deeds of the body, you will live." So there is our motivation to walk according to the Spirit.

A glimpse of glory

We finally get a glimpse of glory in Romans 8: 15-17. Paul brings up the idea of sonship in verse fourteen and elaborates, "For you have not received a spirit of slavery leading to fear again, but you have received a spirit of adoption as sons by which we cry out, 'Abba! Father!'" This walk that the Spirit is leading us as believers is our birth right. It is ours as believers. So, "We cry out, 'Abba! Father!' The Spirit himself testifies with our spirit that we are children of God, and if children, heirs also, heirs of God and fellow heirs with Christ." In fact, Paul says, "If...we suffer with him so that we may also be glorified with him."

Deliverance through glorification

Paul is making a transition here. He is moving from deliverance now to our ultimate deliverance, when Christ comes back and we are glorified. Paul has talked about being delivered now by the indwelling Spirit. Now he is going to talk about being delivered ultimately through glorification. We are now in the second half of Romans chapter eight, specifically in Romans 8: 18-39. Paul touches on the hope of redemption. Notice where this is going. I realize I just said this, but I will say it again. Paul wants us to realize we have deliverance now, but we not going to have deliverance ultimately until we are glorified. We need to be realistic. Although we have the first fruits of the Spirit and the enablement to live the Christian life, there will always be a struggle at some level until we are glorified.

The hope of redemption

More on the hope of redemption. Paul says, "I consider that the sufferings of this present time are not worthy to be compared with the glory that is to be revealed to us." Paul proceeds to lift our eyes away from the here and now and the present sufferings towards eternal glory. And by doing that, he motivates us to be encouraged to keep living for Christ, knowing that we are not going to be here forever.

Paul mentions, "The sufferings of this present time." Those are things that naturally happen to us living, first of all in a broken world, and secondly, as believers living in a world that is hostile to our faith. If you look at Paul's catalogue of suffering in first and second Corinthians, you will know that Paul is not making a thoughtless comment. He suffered as much or more than anyone may ever suffer. And yet as Paul considers that, he says, "It's not worthy to be compared with the glory that's going to be revealed."

Let's move onto verse nineteen, "For the anxious longing of the creation waits eagerly for the revealing of the sons of God." Sons of God is a phrase that refers to all believers. Paul pictures creation standing on its tiptoes, nervously biting its fingernails, waiting for the canvas to be lifted in order to see the beautiful work of art, which is the revealing of the sons of God. In other words, creation longs to see our glorification.

That begs the question, why would Paul picture creation as wanting to see our glorification? "The creation was subjected to futility, not willingly, but because of him who subjected it, in hope that the creation itself also will be set free from its slavery to corruption into the freedom of the glory of the children of God" (Romans 8:20-21). Paul is alluding to Genesis chapter three. God included creation in the curse, so that it could also be included in redemption. He subjected creation to futility. And the idea is frustration of purpose, that creation, as beautiful as it is, does not live up to its full potential. It's futility now.

C. S. Lewis in the Chronicles of Narnia described it this way. It's always winter, but it's never Christmas. What a more melancholic, depressing picture. Always winter, but never Christmas. Others have said that creation sings in a minor key. It is a beautiful world, but it is not what it was and it is not what it will be. It was subjected to futility in hope that it would be set free from its corruption into the glory. Look at verse twenty-one, "That the creation itself also will be set free from its slavery to corruption into the freedom of the glory of the children of God." So God included creation in the curse so it could also be included in redemption. Creation waits for the believer to be delivered.

Paul says, "For we know that the whole creation groans and suffers the pains of childbirth together until now. And not only this, but also we ourselves, having the first fruits of the spirit, even we ourselves groan within ourselves, waiting eagerly for our adoption as sons, the redemption of our body" (Romans 8:22). These are amazing statements. Paul says that creation groans. It is waiting to be delivered. And then he says, almost in disbelief, that even we ourselves, "We... having the first fruits of the spirit, even we ourselves groan within ourselves."

It is almost unthinkable that the very sons of God would experience the same thing. But he says yes even us, the ones who had the first fruits of the Spirit, experience this groaning. And this concept of the first fruits of the Spirit reminds us that we have a taste of the future now, but the final picture has not come.

We are delivered day by day, as we walk according to the Spirit, but we will ultimately be delivered at glorification. So creation is longing for our deliverance, and we too, the ones who have the first fruits of the Spirit, wait eagerly for our adoption as children.

Now we have already seen in both Romans and Galatians that we are adopted, we are sons and daughters of God. So when Paul says we are waiting eagerly for our adoption, he means we are waiting for the "redemption of our body" (Romans 8:23). He's talking about the completion of our salvation. We have been justified, we are being sanctified and we wait eagerly to be glorified. We are waiting for the redemption of our body.

Paul says, "In hope we have been saved." We are saved in hope. There is more to come and so we anticipate the completion of our salvation. "Hope that is seen is not hope, for who hopes for what he already sees? But if we hope for what we do not see, with perseverance we wait eagerly for it." Paul says hang tight, it is coming, just keep trusting God and one day your salvation will be complete.

So far we have discussed creation groaning, the believer groaning waiting to be delivered, and not only that, but also the Spirit groaning on our behalf. Paul speaks about the ministry of intercession when the Spirit of God is praying for us, even when we are unaware of it, and at a loss as to how we should be praying ourselves. God is active on the part of the believer.

The certainty of our hope

We finally arrive at the certainty of our hope here in Romans 8:28-39. Paul says, "And we know that God causes all things to work together for good to those who love God, to those who are called according to his purpose." And these two phrases those who love God and those called according to his purpose are used interchangeably. We are simply talking about believers. Paul says we know that God causes all things to work together for believers. This is something we know by divine revelation, not through experience, and Paul is so confident of it that he says we know.

When Paul says all things it means that it is all inclusive. Whatever believers face in their life, God uses it ultimately for their good. It is not saying here that everything is good, or that God causes everything, but it rather that God causes everything to work together for good.

For those of you who like to bake, think of it this way. When my wife makes a cake, she puts two or three sticks of butter, flour and raw eggs into a bowl. None of those things would probably be tasty alone. The raw eggs, flour and stick of butter are not good in and of themselves, but they can be made into something that accomplishes good.

Paul says that God causes all things to work together for good for those who love God. God is at work in history to use the trials of life, the persecutions we face, the discouragement, whatever it might be, to accomplish good. But what is meant by good? I think we frequently try to fill that in with our own expectations of what is good, when in reality the good that God has in mind is conforming us to the image of His Son.

Look at Romans 8:29, "For those whom he foreknew, he also predestined to become conformed to the image of his Son, so that he would be the firstborn among many brethren." You firstly notice the phrase those whom he foreknew, which is another conversation in itself, but whatever the case, we know we are talking about believers. And what did God predestine these believers for? To be conformed to the image of God's Son. Because God predestined believers to be conformed to the image of His Son he is going to use all things towards that end.

There are two aspects of conformity here. There is gradual conformity, sanctification, as we have concluded from Romans chapters six to eight. For example, Paul says in Galatians that he is laboring until Christ is formed in them. That is what sanctification is about, becoming more like Christ. There is gradual conformity, and there is also final and ultimate conformity. Paul goes on to say, "Those whom he predestined, he also called, he also justified, and he also glorified." All things ultimately work together towards God's good end of making us like His Son. In fact, it is so certain that we will become like Christ that he says, "Those whom he has justified, he also glorified."

There is an argument here for eternal security which I think is very strong. My counter-argument to losing your salvation would be, if you could lose your salvation, wouldn't you agree that you would have to have salvation to begin with? Of course people would say yes. You have to have something before you can lose it. In other words, you would have to be justified, and then fail to be glorified. But what does Paul say? Those whom He justified, He also glorified. Every believer will be glorified, every believer is secure in Christ, so those whom He justified he also glorified. Our salvation is a certainty, and God will accomplish that in our lives.

Not only that, but nothing can separate us from the love of God. Paul says, "What then shall we say to these things? If God is for us, who is against us?" (Romans 8:31). And it is not that Paul is actually looking for someone who is against us, but the idea that if God is the one who is for us, then it doesn't matter who is against us, because God is God. "He who did not spare his own Son, but delivered him over for us all, how will he not also with him freely give us all things?" If God has given Christ for us, He is surely not going to stop short of completion. He has already given His Son on our behalf, so He is going to freely give us all things with Him.

In fact, talking to believers he says, "Who will bring a charge against God's elect? God is the one who justifies" (Romans 8:33). If the supreme court has declared us righteous before God, who can bring counter-charge that? Of course the answer is no one. "Who is the one who condemns?" There is no one who can condemn believers because we have been justified. "Christ Jesus is he who died, yes, rather who was raised, who is at the right hand of God, who also intercedes for us." So, Christ is interceding for believers. The highest Judge in the universe has declared us righteous, so we stand secure.

Moreover, Paul says, "Who will separate us from the love of Christ?" And then he asks several questions, "Will tribulation, or distress, or persecution, or famine, or nakedness, or peril, or sword?" Paul thinks through every possibility that someone could give, every counterargument that might emerge. And Paul says, "In all these things we overwhelmingly conquer through him who loved us." His synopsis is, "For I am convinced that neither death, nor life, nor angels, nor principalities, nor things present, nor things to come, nor powers, nor height, nor depth, nor any other created thing, will be able to separate us from the love of God, which is in Christ Jesus our Lord."

Catch what Paul is saying. Sometimes we can be skeptical. Sometimes it can take a lot of convincing for us to become assured of our eternal security in Christ. Paul thinks of every possibility that someone might offer, and then, just to make sure he covers all the bases, he says, "Nor any other created thing." No created thing can separate us from the love of God that is in Christ.

If no created thing can separate us from the love of God, what else is left? Only the uncreated eternal God. And what has he said? He says He is for us. God the Father is for us, and He gave His Son for us. God the Son intercedes for us. God the Spirit is making groanings too deep for words; the Triune God is for us. We cannot and we will not be separated from the love of God.

And this is the exclamation point on Paul's description of sanctification. If believers are going to grow, they need to know that they are not growing towards acceptance and security. They are growing as accepted and secure people. And as they struggle and fail, they are struggling and failing as people who are secure in Christ. And that sets us free to grow in Him.

DELIVERANCE NOW AND IN THE FUTURE

? DISCUSSION POINTS

1. What is meant by "the law of sin and death"?

2. What is meant by "the Spirit of life in Christ Jesus"?

3. What are the "two factors of freedom"?

4. Who finds the deliverance spoken of in Romans 8:1-4?

5. What benefit comes to the believer because God has "condemned sin in the flesh"? Why did God condemn sin in the flesh?

6. What is the significance of the wording in 8:4 "in us"?

7. Walking in the Spirit results in…?

8. Walking in the flesh results in…?

9. What does Paul mean when he says "If you live according to the flesh, you will die?"

10. What is meant by his statement, "If you, through the Spirit, put to death the deeds of the body, you will live"?

11. What does the term "adoption" speak of?

12. When will this futility be lifted?

13. When Paul speaks of our "hope" he is referring to…?

14. Why was creation subjected to vanity/futility?

15. God is working all things together towards what goal?

➡ ACTIVITIES

1. Scenario for Romans 8: A friend asks you how they can find deliverance from a sin that they have struggled with for some time. How do you help them from Romans 8? Make sure you explain what it means to walk according to the Spirit. Also, explain how future hope impacts present choices.

3.13 God's Faithfulness to Israel

 OBJECTIVES OF THIS TUTORIAL

Bible presenter Scot Keen discusses Israel's rejection here in Romans chapter nine. He clarifies that God is still faithful to His promises to Israel, and so we can be sure that He will be faithful to us as well.

Introduction

In this tutorial we will talk about God's dealings with Israel as a nation, which was an important topic in the first century. First let's look at Romans chapter nine. To give you an idea of how much this chapter refers to Israel, notice how many times Paul mentions them. Paul talks about his brethren, his kinsmen, Israel, Abraham's descendants, Jews, the sons of Israel, the posterity, disobedient obstinate people, remnant, my fellow countrymen, natural branches and also uses some pronouns referring to them: they, their, themselves, you and them. As you read Romans chapter nine, keep in mind that this is a literary section, as that is important when interpreting this passage. So we can conclude that this chapter is about Israel.

In Romans chapter nine Paul will say he has great sorrow for his kinsmen, who are Israelites. In chapter ten his prayer is for their salvation. Paul has great concern for them because they have been temporarily set aside in God's program. God has turned His focus from the Jews to the Gentiles. We will look at this is more detail in chapter eleven, but for now we can know that at a future time God will resume His program with Israel. Getting back to Romans chapter nine through eleven, this section is about a vindication of God's dealings with Israel. Someone could rightfully ask the question: How could God not keep His promises to Israel? Is God just? Is He righteous? Paul says it is not as though God's Word has failed. He wants to lay to rest our fears that God has broken His promises to Israel.

God's faithfulness to Israel

Let's address God's faithfulness to Israel. The question about Israel surfaced in Romans three, with minimal explanation on Paul's part. It was in that passage that Paul said that there is no distinction between Jews and Gentiles. The question was raised, "What advantage do Jews have?" Paul gave it a brief response. He said, "Much in every way, to them were committed the oracles or the promises of God." There were advantages of being a Jew, but Paul didn't go into the details then. But now Paul will flesh out the topic. Why would Paul do this? Paul had just stated that nothing can separate the elect from the love of God. If I was a believer in the first century, the first question that would come to mind would be, "What about Israel?" Israel was God's elect people, and they had been separated, it appears, from the love of God. So this was a very natural question that could be asked and answered, and that is what Romans nine through eleven sets out to do.

Examples from the Old Testament

Here are some Old Testament references of God's promises that Israel would never be separated from him. Zion said, "The Lord has forsaken me, and the Lord has forgotten me" (Isaiah 49). God responded, "Can a woman forget her nursing child? These may forget, but I will never forget you." It would be a rare occurrence for a nursing mother to forget her child. And yet, even if she was to forget her child, God says He would not forget Israel. God says, "The mountains may be removed, and the hills may shake, but my loving kindness will not be removed from you, and my covenant of peace will not be shaken" (Isaiah 54). God uses His covenant love for Israel as a guarantee that they would never be separated from His love.

Another Old Testament reference is a wonderful promise in Jeremiah thirty one. "Thus says the Lord who gives the sun for light by day, and the fixed order of the moon, and the stars for light by night. If this fixed order departs from before Me, then the offspring of Israel shall cease from being a nation before Me forever." My point with this small smattering of examples is that God has made several promises to Israel, that they would always be His people, that He would not forget them, etc. With that being said, Paul tells believers in Romans eight that they will never be separated from the love of God. He has to address the issue of God's faithfulness to Israel, and here is why. If God doesn't keep His promises to Israel, how do we know that God will keep His promises to us? So Romans nine through eleven becomes a very relevant passage of Scripture for all believers, because it is only because God is faithful to Israel that we can have certainty that God will be faithful to us.

Paul's answer is found in Romans 9:6, "It is not as though the word of God has failed." Before he explains himself further, Paul says that regardless of how things appear, God's promises to Israel have not failed. This will set the stage for the rest of what He says in this very important section of Scripture. The first thing that Paul mentions is that God is just in setting Israel aside. He shows that God is just in Romans 9:6-29. God was just when He chose Isaac instead of Ishmael. God was just when He chose Jacob instead of Esau. God was just when He hardened Pharaoh and when He showed mercy to Israel. Now too, God is just when He shows mercy to Gentiles and when He hardens the Israelites. God is just in setting Israel aside.

And then Paul explains that God in fact had a reason to set Israel aside. Setting Israel aside was not the result of an arbitrary choice of sovereignty, but because of Israel's unbelief. God did have a reason to set Israel aside. Then Paul will proceed to show us that there is still a remnant of believing Jews. They have not been rejected as a whole, and God is using this time of Israel's fall to mean salvation for the Gentiles. Paul concludes that Israel has not been set aside forever. God will yet resume His program with Israel. All Israel will be saved. It is important for us to keep these pieces of the puzzle in mind as we look at the Romans chapters nine to eleven when Paul tells us that God's promises to Israel have not failed.

The tragedy of Israel's rejection

Paul begins his explanation with the tragedy of Israel's rejection in Romans 9:1-3, "I am telling the truth in Christ, I am not lying, my conscience testifies with me in the Holy Spirit, that I have great sorrow and unceasing grief in my heart. For I could wish that I myself were accursed, separated from Christ for the sake of my brethren, my kinsmen according to the flesh." Paul grieves the tragedy of Israel's rejection. Paul's heart is broken for his kinsmen. He says, "I… wish that I myself were accursed, separated from Christ for the sake of my brethren, my kinsmen according to the flesh." Paul is talking here about Jewish people who do not believe in Christ. His heart is sorrowful for them, to the point that he says he wishes, if possible, he could be accursed for them. We see the tragedy of Israel's rejection and Paul's heart for his kinsmen.

This tragedy is amplified in light of the privileges that they possessed. Paul says, first of all, they received the adoption as sons. This takes us back to Exodus chapter four where God says, "Israel is my firstborn son." They were the Lord's chosen possession. They had the adoption as sons, and also the glory. The glory here talks about God's Shekinah Glory, the presence of God that was manifest first at the tabernacle, and then later in the temple. It was indicative of God's favor, His presence and His protection. To them belonged the glory. Not only that he says, but to them also belonged the covenants. The covenants here refer to the Abrahamic covenant: God's gift of the land forever. It also refers to the Mosaic covenant: God's promise of a regathering and a regeneration of the nation. The Davidic covenant: God's promise that a descendant of David would reign forever. And finally it refers to the new covenant: God's promise to give them a new heart. These are all covenants that God made with Israel.

Notice that Paul looks at unbelieving Israelites and he says, "These covenants belong to them." It is something that they can anticipate in the future. He also mentions the giving of the Law. And of course, references the fact that out of all the nations, Israel alone possessed God's special revelation. As Psalm 147 says, "He shows his word to Jacob. His precepts and his judgments to Israel." Again, Paul says, "To them belong the fathers." This alludes to the patriarchs from which Israel was descended. "The lord your God, to him belong heaven and the heavens of heavens. The earth and all that is in it. Yet the Lord set his heart and his love on your fathers, and chose their offspring after them" (Deutoronomy 10). There are all Israel's privileges. The glory, the covenants, the fathers. Then Paul adds the Law, the temple services, and the promises to the list above. All these things belong to them, and ultimately from them is the Christ, the promised One.

The privileges Israel had put them in a great position to know God and glorify Him, but instead they, "turned their table into a snare," as Paul will say later on in chapter eleven. They stumbled over the stumbling stone. The tragedy of Israel's rejection is amplified by the privileges they possessed.

The justice of Israel's rejection

Now we will look at the justice of Israel's rejection. How is it that God can set them aside and still maintain faithfulness to his promises? Paul deals with this firstly by showing that physical descent does not guarantee that one will inherit God's promises. Look at Romans 9:6, "It is not as though the word of God has failed." In light of all these promises and privileges God's Word did not fail. The explanation is simply this. They are not Israel who are descended from Israel. They are not all Israelites who are descended from the man Israel. In other words, Paul is beginning to talk about an Israel within Israel; a remnant.

Paul says, "They are not all Israel who are descendant from Israel, nor are they all children because they are Abraham's descendants, but through Isaac your descendant will be named." One can be a biological child of Abraham and not be a recipient of the promise, and yet God is still faithful to His Word. To develop that promise, Paul talks about Isaac and Ishmael. "It is not the children of the flesh who are children of God, but the children of the promise are regarded as descendants" (Romans 9:8). Speaking of Isaac, verse nine, "This is the word of promise, 'At this time I will come and Sara shall have a son'. And not only this, but there was Rebecca also." Paul will go on to talk about Jacob and Esau shortly, but first he explains that one can be a physical descendant of Abraham, as Ishmael was, and still not inherit the promise of God. Ishmael was not a child of promise. He was a biological child, and no one would accuse God of failing to keep His promise to Abraham when God chose to keep it with Isaac instead of Ishmael.

One can be a physical descendant and not inherit the promise of God. Some might argue, "Yeah, but that example involved two different mothers." And so Paul goes a step further and uses Jacob and Esau as examples. "And not only this, but there was Rebekah also, when she had conceived twins by one man, our father Isaac; for though the twins were not yet born and had not done anything good or bad, so that God's purpose according to his choice would stand, not because of works but because of him who calls, it was said to her, 'The older will serve the younger'. Just as it is written, 'Jacob I loved, but Esau I hated.'" (Romans 9:10-13). I want to pause and unravel that for a moment. Remember that according to custom Esau was the one in the rightful place for blessing, and Jacob had no claim on that. It was the firstborn who was supposed to be blessed. The one who was in the rightful place did not receive it, and the one who had no claim on it did receive it, and that was God's freedom of choice in that matter.

Think about the larger context of what was happening in the first century. Paul is addressing the ones who are in the rightful place for blessing but did not receive it, the Jews. He is addressing too the ones who had no claim on it but did receive it, the Gentiles. And God is free to do that because He is God. He says again, "The older will serve the younger, just as it is written; Jacob I loved, but Esau I've hated." God has right to choose who will be the recipients of His promises, whom He desires to bless. And Paul is using individuals to throw light on God's dealings with Israel and Gentiles. The larger context shows that God is free to do this. Not only do we have Ishmael and Esau, but we also have another example here with Pharaoh.

God chose who was going to be the recipients of the promises. By the way, I do want to add that if you read Genesis you will perceive that Ishmael was not reprobated to hell, and neither was Esau. This was a matter of who was going to carry the covenant promises. With that being said, the question still would naturally arise: What do we say then? Is there injustice with God? May it never be. You get this emphasis of God's freedom, and question remains: Is God being unjust? Is God simply doing what He wants to do, and is that okay? Paul says yes, God can do this, "For he says to Moses, 'I will have mercy on whom I have mercy, and I will have compassion on whom I have compassion.'" (Romans 9:15).

Now, the context of this is Exodus thirty-three. This is where Israel has worshiped the golden calf, and Moses comes off the mountain and he is angry with them. God says He is not going to personally continue with them on their journey, but He will send his angel with them. And Moses not only begs God to accompany them, but also begs God for assurance that He will do this. company them. And God shows Moses His glory as a sign that He is going to continue with the nation on their journey. In this context God says, "I will show mercy to whom I show mercy." The idea is that God is showing mercy to Israel, not because they deserve it but because God is a gracious God.

So the question that Israel would have to grapple with in the first century is this: Is it okay for God to show mercy to those who are undeserving of mercy? Of course they have to answer yes. That is exactly what God did with Israel at the nation's beginnings, when God constituted them a nation and led them out of slavery in Egypt. Paul says in Romans 9:16, "So then it does not depend on the man who wills or the man who runs, but on God who has mercy. For the Scripture says to Pharaoh, 'For this very purpose I raised you up, to demonstrate My power in you, and that My name might be proclaimed throughout the whole earth'. So then he has mercy on whom he desires, and he hardens whom he desires."

Let's briefly go to the book of Exodus to decipher this. God demonstrates to all the world that he alone is God. God says that He will take them for Him as a people. "I will be your God, and you shall know that I am the Lord when I bring you out from the burden of the Egyptians" (Exodus 6:17). You have this theme of you will know that I am the Lord that is developed throughout the exodus. "By this you shall know that I am the Lord" (Exodus 7:17). "The Egyptians shall know that I am the Lord" (Exodus 7:5). "That you may know that there is no one like the Lord your God" (Exodus 8:10). And it goes on and on throughout the Exodus account. When the spies when into Jericho, you remember what Rajab said? She said, "We heard about what your God did, how He dried up the Red Sea, and when we heard this our hearts melted with fear, because your God is God in heaven above, and on the earth beneath."

God's name was declared throughout the earth. The reason God's name was declared throughout the earth was because God hardened Pharaoh. He solidified Pharaoh in his decision to rebel. He locked him into his choice. When that took place, we have not one plague, not two plagues, but ten plagues. And because we have ten plagues, God made a mockery of the gods of Egypt over and over again, and His name was proclaimed throughout the whole earth. Back in Romans 9:17 God says, "For the Scripture says to Pharaoh, 'For this very purpose I raised you up, to demonstrate My power in you, and that My name might be proclaimed throughout the whole earth.'" Paul's conclusion is in verse eighteen, "He has mercy on whom he desires, and he hardens whom he desires."

Let's just picture ourselves as Jews in the first century. We know that God has turned His attention away from the Jews, and towards the Gentiles, and we are struggling with this. How is it okay for God to harden the Jews, and to show mercy to the Gentiles?

Paul, in essence, is telling them that by their own theology they must agree to this. He asks, "Is it okay for God to show mercy to whom He desires?" He showed mercy to Israel so he can show mercy to Gentiles. Is it okay for God to harden whom He desires? God hardened Pharaoh. No Jew would have difficulty with that, but when the tables are reversed and God is hardening Israel, it is harder to contemplate. Paul says, "He has mercy on whom He desires, and He hardens whom He desires." Keep in mind that this is in the larger context of God setting Israel aside and turning His attention towards the Gentiles. We see that God is free in the exercise of His mercy and His judgment. In fact, we see this here in Romans 9: 17-18. Pharaoh again is an example of God hardening whom He desires. Israel is an example of God showing mercy to whom He desires. Now the tables are turned. God is showing mercy Gentiles, and He has hardened the nation of Israel. So Paul moves into the next aspect of this argument, a defense of God's freedom.

A defense of God's freedom

God is God, and He can do what He wants to do. He will always be consistent with His nature and His character. Look at verses nineteen and following. Paul anticipates the question. He says, "You will say to me then, 'Why does he still find fault? For who resists his will?'" It appears like someone visualizes themselves as a helpless pawn as God is moving the chess pieces to accomplish his purposes. Paul's first answer is this, "On the contrary, who are you, O man, who answers back to God?" Paul addresses this by first putting man in his place, "Who are you oh man." He reminds them: you are just a human being and He is God, so be careful with the questions that you ask. "Who are you oh man, who answers back to God?" Then he uses an analogy, "The thing molded will not say to the molder, 'Why did you make me like this,' will it?" He illustrates his point with an example of a potter making pottery.

Of course it would be ludicrous for a piece of pottery to say, "Why did you make me like this?" God is the Potter and so has freedom, and Paul wants the objector to know that. God is free in the exercise of His mercy and His judgment. God is God, and we are not, and so He is free. God is free. Paul defends God's freedom. Let's go progress with this further. "Or does not the potter have a right over the clay, to make from the same lump one vessel for honorable use and another for common use?" (Romans 9:21). You know what? That is exactly what God did with Israel. Out of the clay of humanity God made one lump for honorable use, Israel, and everything else was common. If God wants to do that now in a different way, He is able to do that. He has freedom. He is the potter, and we are the clay. Paul now begins to answer this objection in another way. The question remains: why does God find fault who resist His will?

His first answer is we are human and He is God. He is the Potter, we are the clay. Let's get that straight first. But now he goes on to explain, "What if God, although willing to demonstrate his wrath and to make his power known, endured with much patience vessels of wrath prepared for destruction?" This brings to mind a couple of images. First of all we think of Egypt and Pharaoh, through which God demonstrated His wrath and power. If God wished, He could have demonstrated His wrath to Israel, but in fact He is forbearing His wrath in order to show mercy. In essence Paul is saying yes God is free, God is God, but at the same time God is not dealing too severely with Israel, in the sense that there is no opportunity for mercy. God is showing mercy to Israelites. He is withholding wrath in order to show mercy.

So Paul says, "What if God although willing to demonstrate his wrath and to make his power known, endured with much patience vessels of wrath prepared for destruction? And he did so to make known the riches of his glory upon vessels of mercy, which he prepared beforehand for glory, even us, whom he also called, not from among Jews only, but also from among Gentiles." I'd like to make a comment here. First of all, I believe that the concept of vessels of wrath prepared for destruction does not involve a fixed quantity, at least not the way I understand it. I think this because, in Ephesians chapter two, Paul talks about vessels of wrath, and mentions that at one time he saw himself as being a child of wrath, who is now a child of God. You have vessels of wrath prepared for destruction (unbelieving Israelites) and God is holding back wrath in order to show mercy. He did so to make known the riches of his glory upon vessels of mercy which he prepared beforehand for glory, "Even us, whom he also called, not from among Jews only, but also from among Gentiles."

I believe Paul is eluding to believing Jews whom God has shown mercy, and now they are prepared beforehand for glory. But it is not just believing Jews, it is also believing Gentiles, "Even us, whom he also called, not from among Jews only, but also from among Gentiles." He backs this theologically in Romans 9:25, "As he says also in Hosea, 'I will call those who were not My people, 'My people,' and her who was not beloved, 'beloved.' And it shall be that in the place where it was said to them, 'you are not My people,' there they shall be called sons of the living God." This is a beautiful quote in Hosea, and it recalls that Israel had gone from being God's people to being rejected. And God said He would call them once again His people. The amazing thing is that Paul applies this here to Gentiles because of a point of similarity. "Isaiah cries out concerning Israel, 'Though the number of the sons of Israel be like the sand of the sea, it is the remnant that will be saved; for the Lord will execute his word on the earth, thoroughly and quickly.'" (Romans 9:27).

And just as Isaiah foretold, "Unless the Lord of heaven's armies had not left to us a remnant, we would have been like Sodom and Gomorrah." Paul states here that Israel's rejection is just. He shows that physical decent does not guarantee one will inherit the promises of God. He also shows that God is free in the exercise of His mercy and judgment. No one would accuse God of breaking His promises to Abraham when God showed Isaac mercy instead of Ishmael, to Jacob instead of Esau, nor should they say that in Paul's day either. God's freedom is defended. He can show mercy to whom He desires, and He can harden whom He desires, because He is God. He is the Potter and we are the clay. Yet there is a flavor of God's mercy in this, that even though God is willing to show his wrath, He is actually holding it back in order to show mercy. And not just to Jews, but also to the Gentiles who come to faith in Jesus.

? DISCUSSION POINTS

1. Why is the issue of Israel's rejection relevant for the church?

2. What is the main issue that Paul is addressing in Romans 9-11?

3. Paul uses God's choice of Isaac and Jacob as well as His hardening of Pharaoh to illustrate...?

4. Who are presently the recipients of God's mercy?

5. Who is presently under a judicial hardening?

3.14 An Unfathomable Plan

 OBJECTIVES OF THIS TUTORIAL

Bible presenter Scot Keen concludes the discussion of God's faithfulness to Israel and to the Gentiles in this tutorial. He marvels along with the Apostle Paul about God's unfathomable wisdom and mercy in the face of our failure and sin.

Introduction

In this tutorial we move into the remainder of Paul's argument concerning God's faithfulness and his promises to Israel. This brings us to Romans 9:30- 10:21 and then to chapter eleven for a look at the reason for Israel's rejection. Let's jump in. Paul has already shown us the justice of Israel's rejection. He said that physical descent does not guarantee one will inherent the promises of God. He explained that God is free in the exercise of His mercy and judgment. In essence Paul said first of all God is God and He can do what He wants, of course always consistent with His nature and character.

The reason for Israel's rejection

Now Paul will explain that God in fact had a reason to set Israel aside. Israel sought righteousness the wrong way. Look at Romans 9:30, "What shall we say then? That Gentiles, who did not pursue righteousness, attained righteousness, even the righteousness which is by faith." The Gentiles were not looking for God's salvation. They were living their lives apart from God and were not even thinking about salvation and yet they found God's righteousness by faith when the Gospel Message went to them.

"But Israel pursuing a law of righteousness did not arrive at that law." Why? "Because they did not pursue it by faith but as though it were by works" (Romans 9:31). Israel did not get righteousness, Paul says, because they were trying to earn it by works. They stumbled over the stumbling stone just as it is written, "Behold I lay in Zion a stone of stumbling and a rock of offence and he who believes in him will not be disappointed."

Paul is using Isaiah chapters eight and twenty-eight to show that the Messiah would be a stumbling stone for some. He would also be salvation for others and those who trust in Him would not be disappointed. Their hopes and expectations would be fulfilled when they trusted in Him. Israel had sought righteousness the wrong way. The sought it by works instead of by faith. They stumbled over the stumbling stone. When Jesus came and told the Jews that their self-righteousness was not good enough, they stumbled over that. Some were offended by His Message but there were others who believed in Him as Messiah, and as Paul says, they were not disappointed.

Paul says his heart's desire and his prayer to God for Israel is for their salvation (Romans 10:1). Paul says, "I testify about them that they have a zeal for God, but not in accordance with knowledge. For not knowing about God's righteousness and seeking to establish their own, they did not subject themselves to the righteousness of God. For Christ is the end of the law for righteousness to everyone who believes."

Paul's prayer is for Israel's salvation but they are missing out because they are trying to gain righteousness by works when Christ is the final answer. Christ is the end of the law of righteousness to everyone who believes. They are zealous but are ignorant of God's righteousness that is provided through faith in Jesus. Notice that Paul's desire and his prayer is for Israel's salvation. This is bigger than personal, individual salvation. Paul's desire is that Israel would have everything that God promised them.

If you have been following along in previous modules you will know that God has been pointing towards the Messiah who would come and reign and bring in Israel's golden age. The Messiah would bring about their salvation. As Isaiah and other prophets foretold, Israel would have a period of great blessing where they would beat their swords into ploughshares and their spears into pruning hooks. Paul longed for Israel to have their salvation. The salvation would begin first of all with individual Israelites trusting in Jesus as Messiah and would ultimately arrive when God conquered the nations and brought the Messiah to reign over all the earth.

In verses five onwards, Paul shows that Israel was seeking to do something when the work had already been done. They were zealous but ignorant and now they are trying to work when the work has been done. Notice that the righteousness of the law deals with what must be done. Moses writes that the man who practices the righteousness based on law shall live by their righteousness but the righteousness based on faith speaks as follows. "Do not say in your heart, 'Who will ascend into heaven?' (that is, to bring Christ down), or 'Who will descend into the abyss?' (that is, to bring Christ up from the dead).' But what does it say? 'The word is near you, in your mouth and in your heart'- that is, the word of faith which we are preaching, that if you confess with your mouth Jesus as Lord, and believe in your heart that God raised him from the dead, you will be saved; for with the heart a person believes, resulting in righteousness, and with the mouth he confesses, resulting in salvation."

The righteousness of the law tells you to do something but the righteousness based on faith tells you that you don't have to do anything because the work has already been done. Faith does not say ascend into heaven and bring the Saviour down. Faith believes he has already come. Faith does not say descend into the abyss and raise him up from the dead. Faith believes he has already resurrected. Paul says that the righteousness based on faith speaks of what has been done is within reach of all.

Paul goes on to say, "The word is near you, in your mouth and in your heart that is, the word of faith which we are preaching." The message that Israel needed was right in front of them but they ignored it. All they had to do was to confess with their mouth that Jesus is Lord and believe that God raised Him from the dead and they would be saved. In fact, God is rich in mercy on Jews and Gentiles and so saves any who call on His name. Paul argues that Israel sought righteousness the wrong way and that is why God set them aside. They did not believe.

Israel tried to do work when the work had been done. As Paul said, "Being ignorant of the righteousness of God, they sought to establish their own righteousness." Then Paul goes on to say that Israel rejected her opportunity to be saved. Now verses fourteen to twenty-one is a large section that needs to be given more time, but for now I will simply say that Paul's basic argument is that Israel heard the Message but they refused to believe it. As He says, "All day long I have stretched out my hand to a disobedient and obstinate people" (Romans 10:21).

This is important because back in chapter nine the question was raised: Why does He still find fault who resists God's will? Paul was so emphasizing God's sovereignty in chapter nine that someone could conclude that they are helpless under God's sovereign hand. Paul was emphasizing God's sovereignty, that God has freedom to set Israel aside, but now he is showing in fact that God had a reason and should not be blamed. If anyone is to be blamed, it is Israel because God stretched out his hand to the disobedient people. We find that in the gospels as well as the book of Acts, and so Israel was set aside because of her unbelief.

The extent of Israel's rejection

Let's move on and talk about the extent of Israel's rejection. So far we have discussed the justice of Israel's rejection, that God is God and we are not. We know the reason for Israel's rejection, unbelief and rebellion, and now we'll see the extent of Israel's rejection in chapter eleven. Paul is going to show us first of all that the rejection of Israel is partial in number. Look with me Romans 11:1, "I say then, God has not rejected his people, has he? May it never be! For I too am an Israelite, a descendant of Abraham, of the tribe of Benjamin."

No one can conclude that God has rejected the Jews completely because Paul was a Jew and he had received God's mercy and so we have Paul as proof. Then Paul goes on to speak about a believing remnant as additional proof. "God has not rejected his people whom he foreknew. Or do you not know what the Scripture says in the passage about Elijah, how he pleads with God against Israel? 'Lord, they have killed your prophets, they have torn down your altars, and I alone am left, and they are seeking my life'" (Romans 11:2). Elijah felt like he was the only one. And what is the divine response to him? God says, "I have kept for myself seven thousand men who have not bowed the knee to Baal." It appeared that Elijah was the only one but in reality God had preserved a remnant. Paul draws a similarity with the believing remnant even in his day. "In the same way then, there has also come to be at the present time a remnant according to God's gracious choice. But if it is by grace, it is no longer on the basis of works, otherwise grace is no longer grace" (Romans 11:5-6). There was a remnant of believing Jews because of God's gracious choice.

"What then? What Israel is seeking, it has not obtained, but those who were chosen obtained it, and the rest were hardened" (Romans 11:7). God showed mercy on some and yet He hardened the rest. He quotes the Psalms and other passages as well, such as Deuteronomy. He says here, "Just as it is written, 'God gave them a spirit of stupor, eyes to see not and ears to hear not, down to this very day.' And David says, 'Let their table become a snare and a trap, and a stumbling block and a retribution to them. Let their eyes be darkened to see not, and bend their backs forever.'"

Partial rejection

It looks like God has completely rejected Israel but the rejection was partial in number. It was not complete. There was a remnant, a group of believing Jews because of God's grace, but the rest of them were hardened. He quotes these passages to show that they have the spirit of stupor. They are blind and, as David says, their table became a snare. The things that were intended to be for their blessing became a snare to them.

This goes back to chapter nine where we saw their blessings, their promises, their covenants, their glory and their fathers. These were their blessings, their table, but they came to be a snare when they trusted in them as their salvation. They trusted in their Jewishness as that which made them right with God instead of seeing it as a privilege, as a portal which gave them access to the knowledge of God through the Hebrew Scripture. So Paul has shown us that that the rejection of Israel is partial in number. It is partial because Paul is proof and the believing remnant is also a proof.

Temporary rejection

Now Paul will show that the extent of Israel's rejection is only temporary. It is not forever. He is will show that through Israel's fall the Gospel is released to the Gentiles. Paul says, "I say then, they did not stumble so as to fall, did they?" (Romans 11:11). There are two different Greek words used here and one means to be tripped up and one means to fall beyond recovery. Paul in essence is saying Israel did not mess up so bad that there is no future and he adds, "May it never be!" But rather by their transgression, salvation has gone to the Gentiles to make them jealous.

Gospel for the Gentiles

When Israel rejected the Gospel it resulted in God turning to the Gentiles. Now something amazing emerges in the book of Acts. You see it in Acts chapters thirteen, eighteen and twenty-eight. In all three passages Paul is speaking to Jews who have rejected his message. Paul says, "Let it be known to you from now on we go to the Gentiles." Paul is revealing that the result of Israel's rejection of the Gospel is the platform and the transition by which the Gospel goes to the Gentiles. The Jews rejected it and so it goes to the Gentiles.

Paul says in verse twelve, "Now if their transgression is riches for the world and their failure is riches for the Gentiles, how much more will their fulfillment be!?" He says their fall resulted in the Gospel going to Gentiles. Let's pause and have a brief grammatical conversation here. When Paul says their in verses twelve to fourteen, who is he referring to? He is talking about unbelieving Israelites and says their fall has resulted in the Gospel coming to the Gentiles. Then he talks about their fulfillment.

This language speaks of Paul's anticipation of a future restoration of Israel. He sees a future for them. Paul says Israel's rejection of the Gospel means riches for the world and the Gospel's arrival to the Gentiles. Nevertheless, he sees a future for national Israel. "For if their rejection is the reconciliation of the world, what will their acceptance be but life from the dead?" (Romans 11:15). Paul speaks about their rejection as synonymous with reconciliation for the world. It means that the message of reconciliation, the Gospel, came to the world because the Jews rejected the Gospel Message which in turn became the occasion of the Gospel coming to us Gentiles.

A plea for humility

Paul continues his argument in verse seventeen and onwards. He suggests the Gentiles ought to be humble. Israel's fall equals the Gospel to the Gentiles but the Gentiles need to be humble and realize that they are coming into this by grace. He says, "But if some of the branches were broken off, and you, being a wild olive, were grafted in among them and became partaker with them of the rich root of the olive tree," (Romans 11:17). Paul says, "Do not be arrogant toward the branches."

As Gentiles we did accept the Gospel and so our tendency might be to look down our noses in pride at the Jews and somehow believe that we are better than them. Paul says that we are like wild olive branches grafted in. We came into something that God was already doing in history. He says, "Do not be arrogant toward the branches." "Remember", he says, "that it is not you who supports the root, but the root supports you."

I take these verses that we as Gentiles were grafted as probably speaking about the Abrahamic Covenant and the promises of God that came there. As Gentiles we came into what God was already doing in salvation history. We were wild olive branches grafted in and we became partakers with Israel of these promises that God gave to Abraham. We are blessed with Abraham as we've already seen in Romans chapter four. We shouldn't be proud towards Jewish people because we came into something that God was already doing in history.

"You will say then, 'Branches were broken off so that I might be grafted in'" (Romans 11:19). In other words, the Gentiles might say Israel was set aside so that we Gentiles could be brought in. Paul says, that they are partly right. They were broken off because of their unbelief. Can you see that again? That gets back to the reason why God set Israel aside. They were broken off because of their unbelief. And because they rejected the Gospel, God turned towards us. But as that is something that God in his grace did, we should not look down our nose on Jewish people.

In fact Paul says that we should be humbled by God's grace coming to us. He goes on to say they were broken off because of their unbelief but you- the Gentiles- stand by faith. Here is why we should fear. If God did not spare the natural branches, He will not spare us either. Paul, I believe, is talking at a bigger level than individual. If God set aside Jewish people because of their unbelief and he turned towards the Gentiles, Paul is saying that if Gentiles do not keep responding in faith, God will turn away from them as well. I don't think he is talking to individuals here. I think he is talking to the Gentiles as whole.

Then Paul says in verse twenty-two, "Behold then the kindness and the severity of God to those who fell." God was in fact severe. God's treatment towards the Jews was so severe that he set them aside and they have been that way now for almost two thousand years and counting. However, He was kind towards us Gentiles. If the Jews do not continue in their unbelief will be grafted in, for God is able to graft them in.

Paul is presenting a plea for humility. If God set aside the natural branches then we need to be humble and realize God could bring the natural branches back in. He simply set them aside because of their unbelief. Now Paul turns to Israel's future salvation. He says, "I do not want you, brethren, to be uninformed of this mystery" (Romans 11:25).

When Paul uses this language, it means he is about to pull back the curtains and let us see into God's plan. He is saying, "I don't want you to be ignorant of this mystery so that you will not be wise in your own estimation that a partial hardening has happened to Israel until the fullness of the Gentiles has come in."

When he says partial hardening, he means partial in number, as obviously not all Jews have been hardened. Paul is proof, as is the believing remnant. It is also partial in duration. Notice that it is limited by time. He says wait until the fullness of the Gentiles has come in and then all Israel will be saved. Paul sees a future for Israel. They have been hardened temporarily but not indefinitely. It will only last until the fullness of the Gentiles has come in. Even today the Gospel is going out to the Gentiles, but when God is ready He will turn His attention back to the Jews and all Israel will be saved.

We know all Israel will be saved because it is written, because of the fathers and because of God's desire to show mercy to all. Let's look at these as individual aspects, but first of all because it is written. "And so all Israel will be saved; just as it is written, 'The deliverer will come from Zion, he will remove ungodliness from Jacob'" (Romans 11:26). Then he quotes from Jeremiah thirty one, "This is my covenant with them when I take away their sins." Paul sees a future fulfillment of Israel in the new covenant. At least, it is in the future from his vantage point.

Paul believed that Israel would find her salvation in the future when the Deliverer comes (alluding to Christ's return). He says, "From the standpoint of the gospel, they are enemies for your sake" (Romans 11:28). In other words, the Jews were enemies of the Gospel, but from the standpoint of election they are beloved for the sake of the fathers. Paul goes back to the fact that God made promises to the patriarchs, and because of that, Israel can have confidence that their salvation will come in the future. All Israel will be saved because it is written and because of the fathers.

"The gifts and the callings of God are irrevocable" (Romans 11:29). God had called Israel to be His people and they will indeed once again be His people. Paul says, "For just as you once were disobedient to God, but now have been shown mercy because of their disobedience, so these also now have been disobedient, that because of the mercy shown to you they also may now be shown mercy. For God has shut up all in disobedience so that he may show mercy to all" (Romans 30-32). This is a complex statement, so I will take the time to elaborate on this.

Paul establishes a precedent and the precedent is that the Gentiles were disobedient but they were shown mercy because of Israel's rejection of the Gospel. Speaking about the Gentiles, he says, "Just as you once were disobedient to God, but now have been shown mercy because of their disobedience, so these also now have been disobedient, that because of the mercy shown to you they also may now be shown mercy. For God has shut up all in disobedience so that he may show mercy to all." This is a fairly confusing wording here but basically Paul is saying is that God has set a precedent that He shows mercy to disobedient ones. He showed mercy to the Gentiles because of Israel's disobedience, but Gentiles were also disobedient. Since God showed mercy to disobedient Gentiles, that gives Him grounds for showing mercy to disobedient Jews. He has put all people under disobedience so that He might show mercy to all. This is what I call God's benevolent sovereignty.

God in His amazing kindness and grace used Israel's rejection of the Gospel as an occasion to take the Gospel to the Gentiles. God used the Gentiles receiving the Gospel as a precedent to show mercy to disobedient people, therefore He will show mercy to disobedient Israel. God has done all of this because of His desire to show mercy to all.

An appropriate doxology

That brings us then to verses thirty-three and following where Paul says, "Oh, the depth of the riches both of the wisdom and knowledge of God! How unsearchable are his judgments and unfathomable his ways! For who has known the mind of the Lord, or who became his counselor? Or who has first given to him that it might be paid back to him again? For from him and through him and to him are all things. To him be the glory forever."

I like to call this an appropriate doxology. Who would have ever thought to use Jewish rejection as Gentile inclusion? Who would have ever thought to use Gentiles being saved to make Jews jealous and then on occasion to show mercy to them? No one thought of this. No one gave this idea to God. No one was His counselor. Rather this demonstrates the depths of the riches of the wisdom and knowledge of God, and because of that from Him, through Him, and to Him are all things. To Him be the glory for ever and ever. Amen.

This concludes Romans chapter eleven but I want to bring us back to where we started. The question was raised back in chapter three: what advantage is there in being a Jew? Paul gave a brief answer and he moved on. In chapter eight Paul said that nothing can separate us from the love of God in Christ. The natural question for a Jew to ask is, "If God broke his promises to the Jews, how do I know that he won't break his promise with me? If something can separate Israel from the love of God, how do I know that I won't be separated from the love of God?"

Remember Zion said, "The Lord has forsaken me, God has forgotten me" and Isaiah said, "A nursing mother might forget her children but God would never forget Israel." In Isaiah fifty-four we learned that the mountains may shake and the hills may be removed but God's loving kindness would not be taken from them. Then in Jeremiah thirty-one we found that God made a covenant to Israel, promising that they would not cease from being a nation before Him.

The climactic answer of Romans nine through eleven is God's Word has not failed. God will not let go of Israel and therefore God will not let go of you. God has not broken His promises to Israel. They have not been separated from the love of God and so neither will you ever be separated from the love of God. That is why Paul needed to deal with this topic on the heels of making the promise that nothing can separate us from the love of God.

❓ DISCUSSION POINTS

1. What was the cause of Israel's rejection?

2. What does the righteousness of the law speak of?

3. What does the righteousness of faith speak of?

4. Who are presently the recipients of God's mercy?

5. According to 10:21, was Israel's rejection due to a lack of concern on God's part?

6. How do we know that the rejection of Israel is only partial?

7. What is meant by becoming a partaker of the rich root of the olive tree?

8. Using phrases from the text of Romans 11, list as many possible evidences that the rejection of Israel is only temporary.

3.15 Righteousness Practiced

 OBJECTIVES OF THIS TUTORIAL

Bible presenter Scot Keen describes a transformed life in this tutorial. He shows how the first eleven chapters of theology in Romans helps prepare believers for the application discussed here in chapter twelve.

Introduction

In this tutorial, we will delve into the final section of Romans which is deals with application. So far we've looked at Paul's introduction and his thesis statement: he is not ashamed of the Gospel of Christ because it is the power of God to salvation to everyone who believes, to the Jew first and also to the Gentile. Then we discussed condemnation and Paul unified his audience by showing that both Jews and Gentile are under God's wrath, that there is no distinction He then gave us an answer to our condemnation problem: righteousness is provided through justification. Just as both Jews and Gentiles were united in their condemnation under God, both can be justified by faith through the Lord Jesus Christ.

Paul then explored sanctification and he dealt with Christian life principles such as being dead to sin and being alive to God. He concluded that we died to the Law and that the Spirit of God indwells believers. Lastly we tackled God's vindication. We analyzed God's promises to Israel and discovered that they have not failed. Israel has simply been temporarily set aside in God's program. God used Israel's rejection of the Gospel as an occasion to turn to the Gentiles and reach out to them.

Application

And so we will now look at application, how righteousness is practiced. As we move into chapter twelve, note that the basis for all application is found in Romans 12:1-2, and so I like to call these verses hinge verses. They appeal to the previous content in Romans one through eleven and they lay the foundation for the application in the rest of the book.

Walking in love

Let's look at the text. Romans 12:1-2, "Therefore I urge you, brethren, by the mercies of God, to present your bodies a living and holy sacrifice, acceptable to God, which is your spiritual service of worship. And do not be conformed to this world, but be transformed by the renewing of your mind, so that you may prove what the will of God is, that which is good and acceptable and perfect." Notice that Paul has written eleven chapters without giving us anything to do. It is only now that we arrive at the application section. I like to contrast this with a lot of discipleship models that we see.

Sometimes it appears that the believer, a new believer, is instantly given a list of things to do and not to do. And what I love about Romans is that before Paul tells us what to do, he gives us the theological basis for it. He does not tell us what to do until he tells us first why and how and I think that is extremely significant. The why behind this is not to gain or maintain a standing with God. In fact, the why is a response of worship to God because of His mercy that shown.

Let's look at this again. He says, "I urge you, brethren, by the mercies of God." Some translations say, "I beseech you brothers by the mercies of God." Doug Mo and his commentary on Romans calls this an exhortation of grace. It is stronger than a suggestion but it is weaker than a command, and that is because Paul wants our response to be that of genuine worship, not something that is an obligation so much as it is a response to the mercy shown.

Paul's appeal based on the mercies of God has in view all the mercies of God seen in the book of Romans up to this point. This would include God in His grace providing redemption when we were all guilty before God. There are none righteous, not even one, none that does good, none that seeks after God, but now we find that "Apart from the law the righteousness of God has been manifested, being witnessed by the law and the prophets, even the righteousness of God through faith in Jesus Christ" (Romans 3:21-22).

And so when Paul speaks of the mercies of God, we have in view redemption through Christ. We have propitiation (satisfaction with the payment for our sins) and not only that, but we also have reconciliation (mentioned in chapter five). In chapter four, we found that our sins are not counted against us and instead we have been credited with righteousness. We enjoy reigning in righteousness and grace through Jesus Christ (chapter five). We are dead to sin and alive to God, dead to the law, joined to another, indwelt by the Spirit of God. There is no condemnation, no separation and God is working all things together for good.

We anticipate future glory...we could go on and on and on, but I think it is very important that we meditate on the mercy shown to us and use it as a foundation and basis for our endeavor to live a godly life. Listen to this quote by William R. Newell. He says, "We may venture to say that it's only those who learn to regard themselves as the object of divine mercy, that the deepest foundations for godliness of life will be or can be laid." And what Newell is saying is that the better we understand the mercy shown us, the greater the foundation and appeal to live a godly life.

Think about the woman in Luke chapter seven who poured perfume on the Jesus' feet and wiped his feet with her hair. Jesus said that she loved much because she was forgiven much. In reality, it took the same sacrifice of Christ for all of us to be saved, and as we meditate on how much we have been forgiven it moves us to worship. And so that is what you see in Romans chapter twelve: this urge, this appeal, this exhortation based upon the mercies of God to present our bodies as a living sacrifice.

The imagery Paul uses here comes from the Old Testament sacrificial system, but in Paul's analogy it is not an animal sacrifice but a human one, bringing ourselves before the Lord. It is a beautiful picture. Now if you look at the book of Exodus (and also Leviticus and Numbers) you will find that some sacrifices were mandatory and others were termed freewill offering. The latter were not obligatory, the worshiper was not required to bring them, but here's the catch. If they choose to bring a freewill offering, then it belonged to the Lord the moment it was presented to Him.

Exodus chapter twenty-nine puts it like this, "Whatever touches the altar is holy to the Lord." It was a freewill offering but, once given, was completely dedicated to God. And that is the imagery that Paul uses here. He is urging us to present our bodies, our entire selves, completely over to God, to remember that we no longer belong to ourselves but to Him instead. And so I want to challenge us. If this is what Paul says we should do, why is it that we are so afraid to do it? Do we not trust God character? He has already shown His character and His attitude towards us in this book of Romans.

I think we are often scared because we know what it might cost us and yet, in reality, this is the greatest thing that a believer can do, our highest worship. Notice that Paul calls this a living sacrifice. In the Old Testament of course we picture a slain sacrifice given to a priest, and by virtue of that, given to God. Paul says present your bodies as a living sacrifice and the idea is that we are to go on living as if we have died. We go on living as if we have been slain. It is all about Him and not about us at all. A complete and utter sacrifice to Him is our spiritual service of worship. And the beautiful thing about our submission and surrender is that it is actually an act of worship.

Now God could tell us to do this completely apart from a context of worship. Think of it this way, we belong to Him by virtue of creation. He made us and so He can tell us what to do. We are His by virtue of creation and by virtue of redemption. First Corinthians says, "You were bought with a price.

redemption. First Corinthians says, "You were bought with a price. Therefore, glorify God with your bodies." Paul could make this argument based on creation, or even based on redemption, but he makes his appeal that we would do this not because we have to, but as an act of worship in response to the mercies of God.

And I challenge you to come to grips with this. Paul says I beseech you brothers. So he is speaking to believers and not assuming that they have already come to the point of complete surrender to God. Of course you would know, if you've ever surrendered to God in this manner, you have to surrender again and again because we easily drift away from this frame of mind. As one person has said, the problem with living sacrifices is that they keep removing themselves from the altar. God wants us to be completely given over to Him as our spiritual service of worship.

Be transformed

Note verse two. Paul says, "Do not be conformed to this world, but be transformed by the renewing of your mind." And when Paul speaks about conformity and transformation, we need to understand what he is touching on here. He says don't be conformed to this world and the tense of the verb is passive, literally meaning stop allowing the world to conform you. It is something that passively happens as we interact with the cultures around us. We begin to accept the worldview and values and norms of those around us. And Paul says stop. Stop being conformed to this world but instead be transformed by the renewing of your mind.

When Paul speaks about the world he is talking about this world system, this present evil age, as he puts it in Galatians chapter one. Again we are talking about the world's systems and values which are under the dominion of Satan the god of this world. And so Paul is challenging us as believers to learn to recognise and reject the thinking of this world. It's worldview transformation: we learn to evaluate our thoughts based on God's Word. Again he says, don't be conformed to this world but be transformed by the renewing of your mind.

Think about these examples from Scripture. Remember when the disciples came to Jesus and said, "Should we forgive seven times?" The world would say that someone who is truly forgiving would forgive seven times. But Jesus said, "I say not seven times but seventy times seven." And so Jesus contrasted what the world would say with His thoughts. Here is another example. The disciples were discussing the issue of greatness and Jesus said, "Those who are great in the world system have authority over those who are under them." Jesus turned that upside down when he added, "The one who's greatest among you will be servant of all."

One more example of a life transformed is in Matthew chapter sixteen. Jesus talked about life saying, "The one who seeks to save his life will lose it but the one who loses his life for my sake, that person will find it." As usual, Jesus found the worldview that was present and challenged them with His Word. That is exactly what Paul is pointing out here. We learn to reject the thinking of this world and to embrace what God's Word says about certain things.

Now, I have some examples that I will share very quickly and then move on. Think about ethics. The world speaks frequently about moral relativism; that all truth is relative and that what is true or good for you may not be true or good for me. But God's Word gives moral absolutes.

The world declares that the purpose and meaning of life is to have fun, enjoy yourself and have other people like you. God says that the purpose of life is comes from being made in His image and likeness and therefore we should live in fellowship with Him and honor Him with our lives. And so I want to encourage you to learn to evaluate the belief systems you come across, especially your own, and let them be challenged by the God's Word. That is the worldview transformation and growth that God wants to bring about in our lives.

And so Paul says, "Do not be conformed to this world but be transformed." This too is passive. He says, "Be transformed by the renewing of your mind." The beautiful thing about this is that it is an imperative or a command. Paul is commanding us to be transformed and yet using passive tense. We cannot transform ourselves but are supposed to expose ourselves to that which does transform us, being transformed by the renewing of our minds. The idea is that as we expose ourselves to the Truth of God's Word, His Word renews our mind and changes our thinking, our values and our worldview so that we are thinking God's thoughts after Him. We learn to believe what God says instead of what the world says.

This is phenomenal. When you minister to others, remember that the way God wants to bring about change in lives is not on the outside but the inside; transformation starts on the inside, by the renewing of our minds. Worldliness is not about externals, it is the way we think, and we change that by changing what we think. Christian growth and maturity starts with the renewing of our minds. It is God's Word that changes the way we think. God's methodology for change is from the inside out. You may have noticed that we have only just arrived at the application section of Romans. The first thing God says about it is to be separate from the world for the purpose of being separated for Him. This will be crucial as we move into the rest of the application section.

Finding God's will

Paul says that as our minds are renewed we can know the will of God. Often when we think about the will of God, we think about where we should live, where we should serve, whom we should marry, where we should go to college or what kind of career we should have. Those are some decisions people typically think of when they consider the will of God. I want you to understand that when Paul speaks about God's will in this context, he is talking about a correlation between knowing the Word of God and knowing the will of God. Knowing the Word of God directly impacts our knowledge of the will of God. We know what God wants us to do when we understand His Word.

Here's a quote from D.A. Carson in his book on prayer A Call to Spiritual Reformation. His comments are in reference to Colossians chapter one on the topic of the will of God, but the same principle applies. He says, "We must think through what Paul means by the knowledge of God's will, with which he wants believers to be filled. Very frequently, we're inclined to use the expression, the will of God, to refer to God's will for my vocation or some aspect of my future that is determined by choice." He says that we seek the Lord's will about whom we should marry, major purchases, what church to attend and when we want to move to a new city.

None of this is intrinsically bad as there are many ways in which the Lord does lead us and we should not despise them. Nevertheless, this focus is often quite misleading, perhaps even dangerous, because it encourages us to think about the Lord's will primarily in terms of my future, my vocation and my needs and can become a form of self-centeredness. Instead of thinking about what God means by His will, we approach this in a self-centered way.

Foundation for application

We need to let God's Word show us what His will is. The foundation for application then is Romans 12:1-2, that we would yield ourselves to God as a living sacrifice as an act of worship. Here is what is awesome about this concept. Whatever we do after surrendering ourselves to God is an act of worship, because it begins with giving ourselves completely to God. Therefore when we are serving the body (mentioned in verses three to eight) and interacting with other people (verses fourteen to twenty-one), whatever we are doing can automatically become an act of worship to God because we are doing it as a living sacrifice.

Serving the body

When Paul gets into specifics, the first thing he mentions is serving the body through our spiritual gifts. I love the picture of Jesus washing the feet of the disciples. That is what we do as we serve the body of Christ, we meet the needs of others and reach out to them in compassion. Before we get into the specifics of serving the body and the other details of application, I want you to see that the basis for this, the theological foundation, is a living sacrifice. When Paul moves into application, people frequently end their study of Romans at this point. They conclude that they have got the theology and that is all that they need. But understand that the theology came for the very purpose of having healthy application, and so there is a practical purpose for doctrine. It is intended to lead us to a place of worshiping God with our lives and serving the saints, meeting the needs of others.

And so, let's talk about this in verses three and following. We serve the body through our spiritual gifts, first of all in humility. Paul says, "Through the grace given to me I say to everyone among you not to think more highly of himself than he ought to think; but to think so as to have sound judgment, as God has allotted to each a measure of faith" (Romans 12:3). Now it is interesting what Paul says here. He says that God has given to each a measure of faith, but then as we move through the text, he will also talk about the grace and the gifts that are given to us. He uses faith and grace and gifts interchangeably here in Romans chapter twelve to talk about the gifts that God has given to the body and the capacity to use those gifts in serving one another.

When Paul wrote Romans, he was in Corinth, and the believers there had a lot of pride in their gifts. Knowing this, Paul gives a caution here. He says not to think more highly of ourselves than we ought to think, but to have sound judgment. And the concept is that God has given gifts to every believer and so we should not become proud of them, but realize that they are gifts given not for our sake, but for the sake of the body.

And so Paul says in verse four, "For just as we have many members in one body and all the members do not have the same function, so we, who are many, are one body in Christ, and individually members one of another. Since we have gifts that differ according to the grace given to us, each of us is to exercise them accordingly." In other words, Paul is saying, "Whatever your gift is, it's not for your sake, it's for the sake of the body." He is reminding us that we are servants of one another, and we should serve first of all in humility, recognizing that God is the giver of the gift and that He gave it for the sake of others.

Paul says in verse six, "If prophecy, according to the proportion of his faith; if service, in his serving; or he who teaches, in his teaching; or he who exhorts, in his exhortation." In other words, whatever your gift is, then serve in that capacity and be faithful in it because that is how you contribute to the overall growth and function of the body.

Love in action
Paul goes on to speak about love and action. We are moving through this section fairly quickly. This section of Romans is unique because Paul gives short exhortations without much explanation or background, and yet the overarching theme here is love in action.

First of all love as it relates to righteousness. In verse nine Paul says, "Let love be without hypocrisy." And so Paul is making an appeal for a genuine love that would abhor or hate what is evil and cling to what is good. That is what genuine love looks like. Also he says, "Be devoted to one another in brotherly love, give preference to one another in honor." And so Paul says we should put other believers before ourselves. That runs completely in confrontation with our flesh. The way our flesh works is we want everything to be about us, but that should not be a problem remember, because we are supposed to be living sacrifices, and a living sacrifice has already died to itself.

So Paul says, "Be devoted to one another… give preference to one another." How does love relate to laziness? Paul says, "Not lagging behind in diligence, but fervent in spirit serving the Lord." Part of our service to Christ and to others is to choosing not to be lazy, but to be fervent and to serve the Lord in that way. Look at verse twelve, "Rejoicing in hope, persevering in tribulation, devoted to prayer." I'll briefly comment on the latter.

Often when people pray, they fall into one extreme or another. Some fall into the ditch of legalism and they feel extreme guilt if they do not pray for an excessive amount of time every day. Others fall into the opposite ditch. They conclude that if they are devoted to anything, then maybe it becomes a form of legalism. Well, Paul strikes a perfect balance and says, "We should be devoted to prayer." He is saying prayer is something to which we need to commit and prioritize. Paul goes on to admonish the believers to also contribute to the needs of the saints and practice hospitality. In the first century world, there were many opportunities to reach out to saints, to other believers who were in need. God would challenge us to do the same thing even in our day and time.

Overcoming evil with good

Let's look now at overcoming evil with good, the final section of Romans chapter twelve. We firstly see love pushed to the limits. Look at verse fourteen. Paul says, "Bless those who persecute you, bless and do not curse". When we are persecuted, our tendency us to desire for the person who is persecuting us to face God's judgment. Paul says, "Don't desire their condemnation, but instead, desire their spiritual well-being. Bless those who persecute you, bless and do not curse."

Remember in the Book of Acts, when Saul of Tarsus was watching Stephen being martyred? Saul was guarding the coats of those who were executing Stephen. And when Stephen was being executed, do you remember what he said? He said, "Lord Jesus, do not lay this sin to their charge." Stephen was blessing those who persecuted him. He desired their salvation instead of their condemnation. When Paul says, "Bless those who persecute you, bless and do not curse," I have to believe that he remembers watching that scene and sees Stephen's desire for their salvation instead of their condemnation. No doubt that marked Paul forever.

Well Paul says, "Rejoice with those who rejoice, and weep with those who weep." This involves entering into the joys and sorrows of others. He then talks about humility and persecution. He says, "Be of the same mind toward one another; do not be haughty in mind, but associate with the lowly." And then finally, he discusses how we should respond to those who inflict harm on us. Verse seventeen, "Never pay back evil for evil to anyone. Respect what is right in the sight of all men." The tendency is to pay back bad for bad. Paul says, "Do not do that, it's not our right to revenge ourselves. It's not our place."

When I consider this, I think of David being chased by King Saul. David had opportunities to over and over again to take King Saul's life, but over and over again he would not touch the Lord's anointed. In essence, David was leaving room for God's wrath. He was not paying back evil for evil, he was trusting God with the difficulties that he faced. And so Paul says in verse eighteen, "If possible, so far as it depends on you, be at peace with all men." Paul adds a helpful disclaimer because he recognizes that sometimes it is not possible, as sometimes the other person does not want to be at peace. And so Paul simply says, "As far as it depends on you."

"Never take your own revenge, beloved, but leave room for the wrath of God." If we take our own revenge, we are not leaving room for the wrath of God. So Paul says, "Never take your own revenge, beloved, but leave room for the wrath of God, for it is written, 'Vengeance is Mine, I will repay,' says the Lord'". Now, I don't think that God intends us to find comfort in the fact that He is going to punish the wicked. We see throughout the Psalms that God will ultimately bring judgment on the wicked. And we don't find pleasure in it, as we seek their blessing not their condemnation. Nevertheless, we do know that we do not have to take justice into our hands, because the God of Justice will one day right all the wrongs.

Our posture should be what Paul says in verse twenty, "But if your enemy is hungry, feed him, and if he is thirsty, give him a drink; for in so doing you will heap burning coals on his head." Now, sometimes people take the phrase heaping burning coals on his head to mean that if we are kind to other people, it will bring greater judgment upon them later on. I don't think that is what Paul has in mind here. I think he is saying that when you feed your enemy, you are going well beyond what would be expected of you. You are showing God's kindness and grace.

I'll give you some background to the phrase heaping burning coals. In the first century world, people heated their homes with fires, they cooked with a fires and so they was an essential part of their daily lives. But they didn't have matches or a lighter to start their fire, so they would use existing coals to start a new fire. And from what I understand, it was a cultural expectation that if someone came to you to borrow fire, you were obligated to at least give them a burning coal. But it would be going above and beyond what was expected culturally if you gave them burning coals in the heaps.

RIGHTEOUSNESS PRACTICED

What Paul says is that when we feed our enemy, it is as if we are going above and beyond what would be expected. We are heaping burning coals upon their head, we are being extremely generous, and in that way, we win. And here is what I mean by winning, Paul says, "Do not be overcome by evil, but overcome evil with good" (Romans 12:21). When we pay back bad for bad, evil for evil, we are losing. We are being overcome by evil. When we show grace and kindness even to those who are evil to us, we are overcoming evil with good. And in that way, we are showing the grace of God to those who are undeserving, just like you and I are undeserving of God's grace as well.

? DISCUSSION POINTS

1. What's the significance of the fact that Paul beseeched the Romans on the basis of God's mercies?

2. What does it mean to present your bodies as a living sacrifice to God?

3. Not all Christians have presented themselves to God as living sacrifices. What are some possible reasons for their failure to do so?

4. What is indicated by the imperative mood of 12:2 "be transformed"?

5. What is indicated by the passive voice (be transformed) of 12:2?

6. How does Biblical transformation take place?

7. Now that we have arrived at the application section of the book, what does God say to us?

8. Are you allowing this reality to effect the way you view yourself and the way you live?

9. Have you presented yourself to God as a living sacrifice? If not, on a separate sheet of paper, write down the reasons for not doing so, and think about the validity of your reasoning.

10. In what ways have you been conformed to the world?

3.16 Relating to Authority

 OBJECTIVES OF THIS TUTORIAL

Bible presenter Scot Keen delves into Romans chapter thirteen in this tutorial. After a rich discussion on truth so far in Romans, the author of Romans now practically shows us how these beliefs transform our lives.

Introduction

In this tutorial, we move on to Romans chapter thirteen, the next chapter that deals with application. This chapter deals with relating to authority, specifically governing authority. Paul's major premise is will be that believers should submit to God-given authority as if they are submitting to God. This raises the question, "Why would Paul say this to the believers in Rome?" Let me first give you some background. I have previously mentioned that Paul is writing to the church in Rome made up of believers from both Jewish and Gentile backgrounds.

In 49 AD Emperor Claudius expelled all the Jews from Rome because of Messianic movements and because of general distrust for Jewish people. Later these Jewish people were able to move back to Rome, and it is approximately ten to fifteen years after this that Paul wrote the book of Romans. So evidently there were still some sentiments against the government that were held among the believers there in Rome, most likely by the Jewish believers. This corresponds with the Jewish worldview at the time. For example, the Jews believed if they recognized Caesar, then that meant they were denying God as the rightful king over Israel. Remember the people asking Jesus if it was lawful to give taxes to Caesar or not? Some people saw it as treason to recognise Caesar in this way.

Many people think a clue as to why the Jews held this worldview is found in Deuteronomy chapter seventeen, when they come into the land that God would set a king over them.

"You shall surely set a king over you whom the Lord your God chooses, one from among your own brethren. You may not set a foreigner over you who is not your brother." So based on Deuteronomy and the idea that God is the rightful King, some felt it would be treason to recognise Caesar and so refused to submit to the governing authorities in Rome.

Submission to God-given authority

Paul takes up this issue because it had become a problem. Peter also addressed this issue in the book of 1 Peter, "Submit yourselves for the Lord's sake to every human institution, whether to a king or governors, for such is the will of God that by doing right, you may silence the ignorance of foolish men." So together they challenged believers to submit to the governing authorities, and in so doing, ultimately to submit to God.

Since God is the one who established human government, to resist authority is to resist the ordinance of God. "Every person is to be in subjection to the governing authorities. For there is no authority except from God, and those which exist are established by God" (Romans 13:1). Paul's argument is that believers should submit to government because God is the One who established it.

We know God established government all the way back in the book of Genesis, when He set up a basic form of human government by saying, "Whoever sheds man's blood, by man his blood shall be shed." And so God instituted a certain form, you could say, of human government. But it goes beyond that. As Paul says here, there are no authorities that exist except from God. Those who are in power are ultimately there by the providence of God.

This is consistent with Jesus' claims in John chapter nineteen. When Pilate said, "Don't you know that I have power to release you?" Jesus responded by saying, "You could have no power at all against me unless it had been given you from above." Jesus is telling Pilate that he would not even be in power were it not for the providence of God. And so God is the One who establishes authority, and therefore believers should submit to that authority.

Consequences of resisting authority

Look at Romans 13:2, "Therefore whoever resists authority has opposed the ordinance of God; and they who have opposed will receive condemnation upon themselves." Now, the condemnation that Paul speaks of is not eternal condemnation. He is simply saying that when believers disregard governing authorities they can expect to be punished by them.

Paul goes on to talk about this punishment in verse three. He says, "For rulers are not a cause of fear for good behavior, but for evil. Do you want to have no fear of authority?

Do what is good and you will have praise from the same." Governing authorities do not typically punish people for doing good things. They punish them for doing wrong things. So there is no need to be afraid, providing one is doing what is right.

In fact, Paul says in verse four, "It is a minister of God to you for good." When he talks about it being a minister of God, he is saying that human government is God's servant, and it exists for a good reason. Human government is intended to deter evil. Now, granted, you are probably thinking about the exceptions to this that you have seen, when power is corrupted or things of that nature. We will investigate that shortly. Paul says, generally speaking, that civil authorities are a minister of God, and so a minister for good.

So Paul says that if you do what is evil, be afraid, for human government does not bear the sword in vain. When he talks about the sword, he is alluding to the ability of government to bring about the death penalty, which is common in many places. We know that James, John's brother, was put to death by the sword. That is one example. So Paul says the government is a minister of God, an avenger who brings wrath on the one who practices evil. So therefore, Paul says it is necessary to be in subjection to the government, not only because of wrath, but also for conscience sake.

I will touch on this briefly here. Notice the first reason that Paul says believers should submit to government is because it is a delegated authority given by God. We see this elsewhere in Scripture. Husbands are to love their wives, and wives are to submit to their husbands. In essence, for a wife to submit to her husband is to ultimately submit to God, who gave that delegated authority. Likewise, children are to obey their parents in the Lord. To submit to a parent as a child is ultimately to submit to God who gave that authority. And so we see this throughout Scripture. We see this again in the local body, where Paul and other authors of Scripture would tell believers to submit to church leadership. That too is a God-given authority. And by submitting to God-given authority, one ultimately submits to God.

So Paul says that we submit to government for two reasons. Firstly for wrath's sake, meaning we submit so we do not face a penalty. We keep the speed limit, for example, because we do not want to pay a speeding ticket. Secondly, we submit to government for conscience sake. We submit because of what we know to be true, and since we know that God established these delegated authorities, we know that submitting to them means ultimately submitting to God.

What does submission look like?

Look at verse six, "For because of this you also pay taxes, for rulers are servants of God, devoting themselves to this very thing." Paul makes an interesting application here. He says that we pay taxes as an act of submission to government. Now some would read this and say, "Well, Paul just doesn't know how bad it is where I live, and how much tax I have to pay." Well, according to New Testament scholars, the taxes would be approximately 33% of a person's wage. And if you were a Jew, and you paid temple tax as well, you would spending 48% of your earnings on tax. So when Paul said this, things were extremely difficult. Nevertheless, Paul says that we submit to government by paying taxes.

I also want you to notice why Paul says we pay taxes, "Because of this, you pay taxes, for rulers are servants of God." Now the Greek word for servants is diaconos. It is the same word that we use for a deacon. Obviously Paul is not saying that governing authorities are deacons in a local church. But he is using that language to emphasize that they are servants of God. Just as we support missionaries because they are devoting themselves to a certain work, or we pay pastors because they are devoted to the ministry, so also we pay taxes because civil authorities are devoting themselves to maintain order and safety within a society. They are serving God and we pay them accordingly. Of course it is not the same as supporting a missionary, in the sense that governing authorities do not normally recognise that they are serving God's purposes. But according to Paul, they are doing that nonetheless.

Look at verse seven, "Render to all what is due them: tax to whom tax is due; custom to whom custom; fear to whom fear; honor to whom honor." Paul has shown that we submit to government because it is established by God and because we want to avoid punishment. One way we submit is by paying taxes, and also by honoring those who are in public authority. In doing so we recognise them for who they are and what they do.

Exceptions to the rule

Now the question comes up, and rightfully so: Are there any exceptions to this? In fact, in his commentary on Romans, Doug Moo says, "It's only a slight exaggeration to say that the history of the interpretation of Romans thirteen is the history of trying to avoid what seems to be the obvious meaning." Are there times that it is okay to disobey human government? And I think we can sum that up in a very simple way. The only time a believer can justify disobedience to governing authority is when it requires disobedience to the Word of God. Our default is to always obey God. And God says to obey government. But if there happens to be a conflict between the two, then obviously believers must submit to God's authority. And so there are certain instances where that might be the case.

I will give you some of the exceptions I have found in Scripture. One is when it requires taking innocent life, as seen in Exodus chapter one. The Hebrew midwives did not take the lives of the Hebrew babies. Another exception is when it requires the worship of idols. In the book of Daniel, Shadrach, Meshach, and Abednego refused to bow down to the idol. And Daniel did submit to the edict that said he was not allowed to pray to God. These instances posed a conflict between obeying God and obeying government. And so these individuals chose to obey God instead of the government. And so there may be rare exceptions, but please keep in mind that the default is to obey human government, and if there is a conflict between that and obeying God, then obviously obey the Lord.

Love - the fulfillment of the law

Let's move on to the next subsection here. Paul says love is the fulfillment of the law. In verse eight he says, "Owe nothing to anyone except to love one another; for he who loves his neighbor has fulfilled the law." We saw how love takes place back in chapter eight. It comes by the Holy Spirit's indwelling. Now we are told to show this love to others. Paul says that love does no wrong to a neighbor, and therefore is the fulfillment of the Law.

So what should we do? Love. Why? Because we know the time. We have motivation. And notice what Paul says in verse eleven, "Do this, knowing the time, that it is already the hour for you to awaken from sleep; for now salvation is nearer to us than when we believed." Remember when we believed, according to the book of Romans, we were justified by faith. We believed and were saved. But Paul says our salvation is nearer than when we believed. Now he is speaking about our final salvation, glorification. He is talking about the consummation of our salvation. And it is nearer than when we first believed. Every day we get closer to our final and ultimate salvation.

Motivated - knowing the time

And because that is true, Paul says it is time to awaken from sleep. It is possible for a believer to live in slumber, not fully engaged in what God is doing in history, and not walking with Him. And Paul says it is time to wake up. Years ago my wife and I were staying with another family, and we had a newborn who was about eight months old at the time. In the middle of the night, I woke up and saw that my son's head had fallen between two bars on the bed. I remember being so sleepy that I could barely wake myself up enough to do something about it. But I also knew that his life could be in danger. And so I just forced myself through the slumber to wake up and address this issue.

Well, that is what Paul is telling believers to do, to awaken from sleep, to shake off the slumber, and to be sober-minded because our salvation is nearer than when we first believed. I would be confident to say that almost all believers have thought before at some point that they would really like to live their lives completely dedicated to the Lord. Romans 12:1-2 would say there is a question that should come before. If you really want to live for the Lord, when are you going to start?

Paul says our salvation is nearer than when we first believed, and it is time to wake up. There is no time like the present to choose to start walking with the Lord. Paul says the night is almost gone, and he is using night as a reference to this present evil age. Time is running out. Therefore, let us lay aside the deeds of darkness. Let us not live like unbelievers, Paul urges. Let us lay aside the deeds of darkness. Let us put on the armor of light. Let us behave properly, as in the day. How are we going to live when Jesus comes back? Paul says live that way now. Live like it is day.

And Paul adds, "Let us behave properly as in the day, not in carousing and drunkenness, not in sexual promiscuity and sensuality, not in strife and jealousy." We do not want to live that way, so how do we avoid those things? Look at what Paul says, "Put on the Lord Jesus Christ, and make no provision for the flesh in regard to its lusts." Paul admits that our flesh still desires the things that he just mentioned. We avoid those things by putting on the Lord Jesus Christ. In other words, we live like who God has made us in His Son, which we learned about in Romans chapters six to eight. Living like Jesus is an application of those Christian life principles.

Look at the chart below to understand this. Paul gives facts, and then he gives the application

Fact	Application
"...You have laid aside the old self..." (Colossians 3:9).	"...Lay aside the old self..." (Ephesians 4:22).
"....[You] have put on the new self..." (Colossians 3:10).	"...Put on the new self..." (Ephesians 4:24).
"You have clothed yourselves with Christ" (Galatians 3:27).	"...Put on Christ..." (Romans 13:14)

In Colossians, he says, you have laid aside the old self. In Ephesians, he says to lay aside the old self. And the idea is that we are to live as though it were true, because it is. In Colossians, Paul says we have put on the new self. In Ephesians, he says to put on the new self. Again, live as though it is true. And then in Galatians he says we have clothed ourselves with Christ. In Romans he says to put on Christ. It is true that we died to sin. It is true that we have been raised to walk in newness of life. We need to believe that this is true and yield ourselves to God on that basis. In a nut shell Romans thirteen is Paul's appeal to live according to Romans six to eight, and the principles we found there.

❓ DISCUSSION POINTS

1. What are some reasons given for submitting to governing authorities?

2. What is the only exception to this rule?

3. In 13:11, when Paul refers to "salvation" what is he talking about?

4. What is the proper attitude towards the flesh?

5. What consequences might you face for obeying God instead of 'Caesar'? Is it worth it?

6. How can you live in such a way that is a positive testimony in society?

3.17 Christian Liberty

 OBJECTIVES OF THIS TUTORIAL

Bible presenter Scot Keen delves into Romans chapter fourteen in this tutorial. The author of Romans addresses the unique issues of Christian liberty in the first century and we will find that the same principles apply today.

Introduction

In this tutorial we get into the last section on application in Romans and this time we are dealing with the issues of Christian liberty. This takes us back to the purpose of the book. If you remember the beginning of this module, Paul is writing to the church in Rome and it is made up of believers from both Jewish and Gentile backgrounds. These brought with them differing convictions because of their unique backgrounds which resulted in differing convictions on issues such as holy days, food and drink.

Attitudes towards other believers

Paul wrote this section (Romans 14:1-15:13) to provide instruction for believers to live together in unity. What I love about this section is that Paul does not say who is right or wrong, he simply gives principles that will unify believers regardless of what the issue is. That is relevant for us today because we often work and worship in multicultural communities made up of people who have differing backgrounds and differing convictions. We need to learn how to dwell together in unity. Romans fourteen and fifteen reveal not only that it is possible for us to function in unity, but it is possible because of God's provisions.

The Gospel is the answer for Jews and Gentiles, both are sinners before God and both are justified by faith. So now we get into these practical issues of why they were divided. Romans fourteen and fifteen deal with holy days, food and drink, but in order to make this more practical and relevant I want you to consider certain things that might be issues of conscience in your congregation or community. I can think of some things that I have witnessed in my sphere of interaction. At the beginning of this module I mentioned that in the south where I grew up, most believers would not think of alcoholic beverages as being permissible, whereas tobacco was no problem at all. At the same time, people in the north had no problem with alcoholic beverages but were deeply disturbed by tobacco users.

Accept and don't condemn

Other things I have heard people debate are thing like appropriate versus inappropriate clothing, tattoos and home schooling versus mainstream schooling. Whatever the issue is, it is worth knowing that Scripture gives us a certain amount of liberty and often does not command or forbid specific things. Paul teaches us that we are to accept one another and not condemn. Look at Romans 14:1, "Now accept the one who is weak in faith, but not for the purpose of passing judgment on his opinions."

Paul introduces us to this person called the weak in faith, a person who is not confidence concerning their freedom in Christ. They are not sure whether it is okay or not to do certain things. The weak in faith in Rome would most likely be the Jewish believers who were not confident that they could eat certain meats, not confident that they could neglect certain days and not convinced of the freedom that they had in Christ. Paul says to accept the weak in faith, but not for the purpose of passing judgment on their opinions. He goes on to say that some people have faith to eat all things but others who are weak eat only vegetables. So there were some believers who were confident they could eat anything they desired, and others who believed that they could only eat vegetables.

Paul says the one who eats is not look down on the one who does not eat. The temptation is for believers who are convinced of their liberty to disdain people who do not enjoy their liberty, as if that makes them inferior. On the other hand, Paul says believers who do not eat certain foods are not to judge those who do because God has accepted them, and with this Paul introduces us to the strong in faith. You have the weak in faith who are not certain of their liberty in Christ, then you have the strong in faith who are confident of their liberty. The strong are not to look with contempt on the weak, and the weak are not to judge the strong. It would be tempting for a weaker brother to conclude that the believer who has freedom is somehow excessive or over the top or worthy of God's judgment. But Paul says not to judge.

Assume the best

And so they were supposed to accept one another because God has accepted them. Now Paul will say that we need to assume the best of others. We should assume that others are likely trying to please the Lord through their convictions. Going back to the context of Romans, picture the Jewish believer judging the Gentile believer who eats meat. The temptation for each party would be to scorn the other. Paul says God has accepted them, so the implication is we should accept them as well. We would do well to realize that other believers are probably trying to please the Lord through the freedom they take or refrain from taking. Look at verse five, "One person regards one day above another, another regards every day alike." So Jewish believers would likely conclude that certain holy days must be observed, whereas Gentile believers would view every day as being alike.

Paul does not say who is right or wrong, he simply says that each person must be fully convinced in their own mind. Look at verse six, "He who observes the day, observes it for the Lord, and he who eats, does so for the Lord." Imagine interviewing Jewish believers from the first century and asking them why they observed the Sabbath day. They would most likely say that they were doing it for the Lord, as they sought to please him through their convictions. On the other hand Gentile believers would most likely say that they were eating in thankfulness for the Lord, thankful for their freedom. Both Jewish and Gentile believers were seeking to please the Lord through their use of liberty, and Paul says for that reason neither should be judged. In fact, we should assume that they were united in their desire to please the Lord just as we are.

We answer to God

Remember that every individual has to give an answer to God. Look at verse ten, "But you, why do you judge your brother?" And, "You again, why do you regard your brother with contempt? For we will all stand before the judgment seat of God. For it is written, 'As I live, says the Lord, every knee shall bow to me, and every tongue shall give praise to God.'"

We will all have to give an account for ourselves and the way that we treat other believers. That should remind us not to judge our fellow believers who are within the perimeters of God's will. These are not sin issues we are discussing here, but instead issues of conscience, issues where one believer thinks that something is wrong when it is in fact not wrong Biblically.

Paul says accept one another because God has accepted you and realize other believers are pleasing the Lord through their convictions. Each person will give an account before God.

In the second half of chapter fourteen, Paul launches into a discussion about the attitudes that believers should have towards each other. He emphasizes that we must be committed to live in consideration for others. You can make this relevant to whatever setting in which you find yourself. I teach at a Bible college that has students from diverse backgrounds, some from conservative backgrounds and others not. When you put these students in the same dormitory it can become an issue. Some watch movies or listen to music that they feel they are free to listen to or watch. Other students are offended by those things and struggle, wondering whether it is okay.

Committed to Care

Of course Paul is not saying that everything believers do is acceptable. We are discussing issues where there is legitimate Christian freedom and we have to learn how to live together in unity. We need to be committed to live in consideration for others. Paul says, "Let us not judge one another anymore but rather determine this" (Romans 14:13). The word for judge and determine is a play on words in Greek. Paul is saying do not judge one another, instead make a judgment call to never put a stumbling block in front of another believer. That means changing the way we live and forgoing the liberties we might enjoy for the sake of ministering to other believers. We lay aside our privileges and become living sacrifices, once again for the sake of the body.

I'll give you an analogy. When I used to walk with my youngest (who was three years old at the time) I would have to dramatically slow down my pace and reach down low to hold her hand. In the same way, we are sometimes called to alter the pace at which we are walking with other believers. We need to be considerate of them, perceiving what may or may not be a stumbling block for them so that we can ultimately serve them. Putting a stumbling block in front of someone is to somehow put pressure on them to violate their conscience, to do something they are not convinced that they have freedom to do.

Back to the first century context, let's say a Gentile believer is having a bacon, lettuce and tomato sandwich (we know the Jews could not eat pork). The Gentile believer is about to enjoy a bacon sandwich, and a stumbling block would be to place that sandwich in front a Jewish believer and to say, "Man, do you smell that bacon? Crispy, fried, this is so good, you have got to have some of this." A stumbling block is to put pressure on people to violate their conscience, and Paul says we need to determine not to pressure others to sin against their conscience. He elaborates on this, "I know and I am convinced in the Lord Jesus that nothing is unclean in itself" (Romans 14:14). Again, Paul is not saying that there are no moral absolutes. He is very clear that certain things are sin, but in this context he is talking about things that are not sinful, things that are issues of Christian liberty.

Paul is convinced that nothing is unclean in and of itself, however notice what he says, "To him who thinks anything to be unclean, to him it is unclean." Think back to the first century again. We know eating meat or pork could not defile believers. In fact, Jesus declared that all foods are clean, and so for a Jew to eat pork, he would not be sinning against the Lord as it was no longer forbidden. However, if that person thinks that God does not want them to eat pork and they eat it anyway, then even though it is not inherently sinful, they are actually sinning. If they think they are violating God's standard, then in their heart they are going through that same process. In essence they are dethroning Christ in their hearts and choosing to walk in what they think is rebellion against God. That rebellion is the sin, not the actual eating of the meat.

Valuing our freedom

Paul says that nothing is unclean, but to the one who thinks it is unclean, then for him it is unclean. If we value our liberties more than we value others, we are not living consistently with God's purposes. Paul goes on to say, "For if because of food your brother is hurt, you are no longer walking according to love. Do not destroy with your food him for whom Christ died." I love how Paul puts this into perspective for us. If we are using our liberty in such a way that pressures other believers to violate their consciences then we are doing a number of things. We are being a stumbling block, no longer walking in love, and have forgotten Romans twelve, about being a living sacrifice and preferring others in love. Paul says do not destroy with food him for whom Christ died. Our value of our freedom can sometimes be so high that we value it more than people. God values people so much that He died for them.

If that is how much God valued people, then we should value them as well and be willing to lay aside our liberties for the sake of others. Paul says in verse sixteen, "Do not let what is for you a good thing be spoken of as evil." Christian freedom can be a good thing. It is good that Christ declared all food clean and it is good Sabbath laws are no longer binding. However these good things could become spoken of as evil if we do not exercise wisdom. We should not pursue liberty at all costs, instead we should be pursuing edification within the body. Look at verse seventeen, "For the kingdom of God is not eating and drinking, but righteousness and peace and joy in the holy spirit." Valuing others is more important than our liberty.

This is what God is about, righteousness and peace and joy in the Spirit, not about how much liberty we can have. If that is what God is all about, then that is what we should be all about too. Look at verse eighteen, "He who in this way serves Christ is acceptable to God and approved by men so then we pursue the things which make for peace and the building up of one another." That means that as servants of Christ we want to be sensitive to issues of conscience in the lives of others so that we can ultimately serve them and that by pursuing those things, make peace.

Here's another analogy from Papua New Guinea. My wife and I spent the summer in Papua New Guinea back in 2006 along with our son. Before we went over, we were told by the missionaries that my wife would need to wear a dress that touched the ground, because anything that would show her ankles would be offensive to the culture we were serving in. Well, that is a case where we laid aside our liberty for the sake of ministry. That is what Paul is talking about here, pursuing things that make for peace.

It would not have been wrong for my wife to wear different clothing besides a dress that drags the ground, but that was a choice that we made for the sake of building up other believers, and that is what Paul speaks of here. He says in verse twenty not to tear down the work of God for the sake of food. God is trying to mature believers and we could actually interfere with that process with careless use of our Christian liberty.

Laying aside our freedom

Paul says, "It is good not to eat meat or to drink wine or to do anything by which your brother stumbles." We recognise that God has given us liberty in certain areas and He actually wants us to enjoy these freedoms, but not in a way that is hurtful to other believers and the work that God is doing amongst the body of Christ. Look at verse twenty-two, "The faith which you have, have as your own conviction before God. Happy is he who does not condemn himself in what he approves." Paul is saying that there are times when you may only get to enjoy your Christian liberty between you and God. This does not mean that we are secretly going around indulging ourselves in liberties and lying to other people. If somebody asks us about our liberty then we should be honest about it, but it does mean that sometimes we have to limit the use of our liberty because we do not want to offend others.

Note verse twenty-three, "But he who doubts is condemned if he eats, because his eating is not from faith; and whatever is not from faith is sin." Even though it is not sinful for believers to eat pork, if they think God disapproves of it and do it anyway, then it is sin. Paul is not teaching moral relativism, he is simply stating that if believers do not think they have liberty to do something and yet do it anyway, in essence they are disregarding what they think is God's authority and that would be the sin. Paul brings it then to a point of application here in chapter fifteen, "We who are strong ought to bear the weaknesses of those without strength." He puts the responsibility on the shoulders of those who are strong in faith to please themselves but to please others for their good edification.

Others first

Paul says be thinking of others first and then he gives us a memorable example, "For even Christ did not please himself; but as it is written, 'The reproaches of those who reproached you fell on me'" (Romans 15:3). Consider Christ, He is God in the flesh and He gave up certain rights and privileges that come with being God when He became a man and lived among us. Maybe that will help us put things into perspective. We give up certain liberties but Christ clothed Himself in humanity too. If He would do that for the sake of others, surely we can lay aside the exercise of our liberty for building up other believers. The purpose of this in in verse six, "So that with one accord you may with one voice glorify the God and Father of our Lord Jesus Christ." If in Paul's context Jewish and Gentile believers were not unified, then they could not glorify God together.

If we are not unified with the believers in our community, we cannot glorify God together. Paul should endeavor to arrive at a place where we are one unified voice, glorifying God together and serving each other for the glory of God.

Jews and Gentiles included

Finally Paul says Christian ministry is inclusive of Jews and Gentiles. This gets to the heart of the Christian liberty issues in Romans fourteen and fifteen because the issues of conscience were ultimately issues of culture. Paul brings this out and he talks about Christian being inclusive of both. Look at verse seven, "Accept one another, just as Christ also accepted us to the glory of God." Remember that when Jesus accepted us, he accepted us just as we were, not on the condition of us giving up or keeping our liberties, but just as we were. That is how Paul wants us to accept one another.

Christ's ministry is inclusive of Jews and Gentiles, look at verse eight, "Christ has become a servant to the circumcision on behalf of the truth of God to confirm the promises given to the fathers." So Jesus came as the Jewish Savior but not only did He come for the Jews, verse nine, "And for the Gentiles to glorify God for his mercy." He quotes from the Psalms and from the Law and from the Prophets (three sections of the Hebrew Scriptures) to back up this point that God had always designed for Christ's ministry to go beyond the Jews to the Gentiles. Paul's ultimate argument on why Jewish and Gentile believers should live together in unity is because Christ came for both of them. If Christ can accept Jews and Gentiles with their differing backgrounds and convictions, then we should be able to accept one another as well. He concludes this discussion with a benediction, "Now may the God of hope fill you with all joy and peace in believing, so that you will abound in hope by the power of the holy spirit." God reminds us that the ministry He is calling us to (serving one another in the body of Christ) is ultimately accomplished by the power of the Spirit.

CHRISTIAN LIBERTY

? DISCUSSION POINTS

1. Who are the "weak" in faith?

2. Who are the "strong" in faith?

3. How were the strong supposed to relate to the weak?

4. How were the weak to relate to the strong?

5. A stumbling block is...?

6. According to 15:1, upon which person does the bulk of responsibility rest, the strong or the weak?

7. 15:1-7, what reason does Paul give for each of us to please his neighbor and to accept one another?

8. Are you allowing this reality to effect the way you view yourself and the way you live?

9. Have you presented yourself to God as a living sacrifice? If not, on a separate sheet of paper, write down the reasons for not doing so, and think about the validity of your reasoning.

10. In what ways have you been conformed to the world?

➤ ACTIVITIES

1. A man was invited to a men's fellowship at the home of an elder in the church. Once he arrived, the elder offered everyone a beer as they waited for the food to cook. After supper, the guys planned on having a poker game (small amounts of money). As two of the guys drove home together, one believer was shocked and disappointed that this was happening at an elders home.

2. Taking the perspective of a weaker brother;

a. How do you feel about the strong brother in this situation?

b. How does his exercise of liberty make you feel?

c. How could it possibly effect what you do?

d. If the stronger brother puts pressure on you to do what he/she is doing, what are some practical ways to respond?

e. How is it sin for the weak brother to do something that is scripturally permissible?

3. Later that evening, the elder told his wife that he saw the disheartened look on the faces of his visitors. He knew he had probably offended them. Taking the perspective of a stronger brother (the elder in this scenario);

    a. How do you feel about the weak brother in this situation?

    b. How do his convictions make you feel about him?

    c. How do his convictions make you feel about yourself?

    d. How do you know when you have been a stumbling block?

    e. If there is a difference between offending someone and being a stumbling block, is there a place for setting aside the exercise of my liberty even if it is just offending the other person (vs. pressuring them to conform)?

    f. If I am exercising my liberty at the expense of another, what scriptural principles have I violated (things that we have learned in Romans thus far)

        i. I am not being a living sacrifice (12:1-2)

        ii. If I say I am loving my brother, I am loving with hypocrisy (12:9)

        iii. I am not preferring someone above myself (12:10)

        iv. I am not being of the same mind toward one another (12:16) v. I am being proud (12:16)

        vi. I am not living in peace with others (12:18)

        vii. I am not walking in love (13:8)

        viii. I am putting my own desires above the good of my brother (14:15)

4. How might the principles of Romans 14:1 – 15:13 impact your ministry?

3.18 Paul's Ministry Plans

 OBJECTIVES OF THIS TUTORIAL

Bible presenter Scot Keen concludes our study on the book of Romans in this tutorial. He discusses Paul's ministry plans and his final comments to the church in Rome.

Introduction

In this tutorial, we come to the conclusion of our study of the book of Romans. We will be looking at Romans 15:14 to 16:27, and the first part of this is Paul's ministry plans as he communicates his plans to the church in Rome.

Purpose in ministry

Over Look at Romans 15:14. Paul says, "And concerning you, my brethren, I myself also am convinced that you yourselves are full of goodness, filled with all knowledge and able also to admonish one another." Paul recognizes that the believers in the church in Rome were able to teach and to build each other up in the faith. Paul acknowledges that they were not without teaching. However, his desire was to take them further in their growth in the Lord. "But I have written very boldly to you on some points so as to remind you again, because of the grace that was given me from God" (Romans 15:15). When Paul speaks about the grace that was given to him in this context, he is not talking about grace for salvation but rather grace for ministry. He is talking about his ministry as an apostle and the gifts he was given to carry out his role.

Paul continues, "The grace … was given me from God, to be a minister of Christ Jesus to the Gentiles, ministering as a priest the gospel of God." The Gentiles were Paul's target audience. The book of Galatians reveals that Peter was an apostle to the Jews, whereas Paul was an apostle to the Gentiles. They were his primary target audience. He was given this grace to be a minister to the Gentiles, ministering as a priest the Gospel of God. There are a few beautiful images there. First of all, Paul ministers the Gospel. But his ministry of the Gospel was more than, "Christ died for your sins and rose again." He is speaking about a Gospel that has the power to build up believers.

I especially want to call attention to the figurative speech that Paul uses when he says ministers as a priest of the Gospel. He is using Old Testament imagery. Priests would represent God to the Israelites and lead them in worship to God. They would bring a sacrifice and give it to God as an act of worship. Paul pictures himself as a priest. He is a minister of the Gospel on God's behalf and he presents a gift to the Lord as a priest, and that gift being the Gentile churches.

Paul beautifully illustrates this concept for us. He sees himself bringing the Gentile church to maturity and then presenting it as his gift to God, an act of worship. In other words, Paul's ministry of discipleship was ultimately doxological. It was an act of worship towards God to be able to present these believers to the Lord. In verse fifteen Paul says, "So that my offering of the Gentiles may become acceptable, sanctified by the holy spirit." Note the sacrificial language he uses there.

Paul wants to see Gentile churches become mature so he can present them to God, and yet he recognizes that with all of his efforts, it is going to be the Spirit of God that ultimately matures believers, as he says, "sanctified by the holy spirit." That was his goal: to worship God by presenting sanctified churches to God. And we know his goal was met because he says, "Therefore in Christ Jesus I have found reason for boasting in things pertaining to God" (Romans 15:17). His goal was met. There are grounds for rejoicing, but he wants to make it very clear that he is not the one who met his goal. "I will not presume to speak of anything except what Christ has accomplished through me, resulting in the obedience of the Gentiles by word and deed" (Romans 15:18). Paul saw Gentiles become obedient by word and deed to the living God as he went about his ministry.

This illustration mirrors an event that took place in Ephesus. The believers there came forward confessing their magical practices and burned all the books of their incantations, an act which communicated that they were making a clean break from their idolatry. Although Paul was involved in this, he says that the credit did not go to him but to the glorified Christ who accomplished it, "I will not presume to speak of anything except what Christ accomplished through me." Paul knew that Christ was the one who accomplished this momentous event through Paul's ministry.

The same thing took place in Thessalonica. Paul says the believers there turned from idols to serve the living and true God. As you consider how God might use you to reach the nations with the Gospel, be encouraged that it is ultimately the living Christ who is working through you to accomplish His purposes in history. We can step out in faith and obedience to obey the Great Commission, knowing that God is going to be there, working through us frail instruments. And this is not limited to the first century, but even today the Gentiles (the nations) are becoming obedient to the faith. I could tell you story after story. I recently heard a testimony of a man who used to be a cannibal in an isolated people group in Papua New Guinea, and now he follows God. And that happened because of what the living Christ is doing through people who are faithful to take the Gospel Message to others.

And so Paul was excited about the Gentiles coming to Christ because it came about by God's power. The miracles that the apostles performed were called wonders, which speaks of the impact they had on those who observed them. Remember that they were accomplished by power of the Spirit. So Paul went about performing apostolic signs which accomplished several things, such as validating his apostolic message and gaining an ear for the Gospel, which in turn led to people coming to faith in Christ. And Paul fully preached the Gospel of Christ, he says, from Jerusalem round about Illyricum.

Paul's focus was on the unreached people groups. He preached the Gospel fully all around Illyricum. When we look at a map, we can see the impact that the Gospel had through Paul, all the way from Jerusalem and Damascus into Syria and Antioch, and then all the way up to Illyricum. We would not even know that Paul was there, were it not for Romans chapter fifteen. The Gospel spread in vast regions because of Paul's ministry, and ultimately because of what Christ did through him.

As I mentioned, Paul's focus was on unreached people groups. His desire was to reach out to them. In Romans 15:20, he tells us that he aspired to preach the Gospel where Christ was not named so that he would not build on another man's foundation. Paul focused on places where Christ had not been named, and his goal and heart's desire was to see them reached with the Gospel. He backs up his unique focus using an Old Testament passage, "As it is written, they who had no news of him shall see, and they who have not heard shall understand" (Isaiah 52). Paul knew that it was God's desire for him to take the Gospel to the unreached, and that is exactly what he did.

Intent to visit Rome

Paul explains that it was for that reason that he has not made it to Rome yet. He shares his intention to visit Rome in this next section, and discloses that his intent was previously unrealized because of his focus on the unreached. In verse twenty-two he says for this reason. For what reason? Well, for the reason that he was focusing on places where Christ had not been named. "For that reason," Paul says, "I have often been prevented from coming to you." Paul could not justify in his mind going to Rome (where there were believers) when there were other places where no one had heard the Gospel. And so that had prevented him from getting to Rome up until the point of writing this. But now Paul says, "With no further place for me in these regions, and since I have had for many years a longing to come to you whenever I go to Spain- for I hope to see you in passing."

Paul has reached the world with the Gospel in the places where he has traveled. He is not saying that every village has heard the Gospel, but that he had planted churches in key locations and is now ready to move to the regions beyond to see those places reached. And so he tells the Roman believers that he wants to see them on his way to Spain. We can deduce from this that he had further regions in mind. He had preached the Gospel in many parts of the world, but he wanted to go further and he wanted the church in Rome to partner with him in this. He wanted them to send him on his way, "I hope to see you in passing, and to be helped on my way there by you" (Romans 15:24). Paul wants them to partner with him (probably financially) and help him get to Spain, and in that way, they too would be a part of that ministry. But he first wants to enjoy their company for a while.

Paul also mentions an excursion that he is going to take. He wants to go to Rome, followed by Spain, but will stop at Jerusalem first, "But now, I am going to Jerusalem serving the saints. For Macedonia and Achaia have been pleased to make a contribution for the poor among the saints in Jerusalem" (Romans 15:25). We read about this particularly in 2 Corinthians. Paul has been collecting a generous offering from the saints throughout the world, Gentile churches, to take to the poor believers in Jerusalem. This is an amazing thing that Paul is doing.

Paul gives the reason that the Gentile churches gave for giving, "They were pleased to do this, and they are indebted to them. For if the Gentiles have shared in their spiritual things, they are indebted to minister to them also in material things" (Romans 15:27). Paul says that the Gentiles have shared in the Jewish salvation, the Jewish Messiah. And because they have shared in that, they should share back with the home church where it all began, in Jerusalem.

And Paul wants to be a part of this. Look at verse twenty-eight, "Therefore, when I have finished this, and have put my seal on this fruit of theirs," the fruit meaning their love offering, "I will go on by way of you to Spain." Paul will take this love offering to the believers in Jerusalem. Now, this would have been a fearful thing for Paul because he would not have known how this gift would be received.

Request for prayer

Look at the prayer request that Paul gives in verse Romans 15:30. He says, "I urge you, brethren, by our Lord Jesus Christ and by the love of the Spirit, to strive together with me in your prayers to God for me." He says pray for me. And specifically, pray "that I may be rescued from those who are disobedient in Judea, and that my service for Jerusalem may prove acceptable to the saints." He has two prayer requests. He wants to be rescued from attackers on his way to Jerusalem. Paul will tell us in the books of Acts that the Spirit testifies that bonds and afflictions await him in Jerusalem. God had revealed to Paul that he would be persecuted there. And so he asks prayer that he would be rescued from them so that he could continue his ministry.

He also prays that the church in Jerusalem would receive the financial gift he wants to give them. That might seem like an odd prayer request. Usually we do not pray that someone will accept the money we give them, as it is generally a given that they will. Paul knows that this could be an issue because, if Jewish Christians accept money from Gentile Christians, it might make it hard for the Jewish Christians to reach out to Jewish unbelievers. But if they reject this gift, then it would be an insult to the sacrificial giving of the Gentile believers. And so Paul is bathing this in prayer and asking others to pray about it as well.

Paul's ultimate desire is found in verse thirty-two, that he might, "Come to you in joy by the will of God and find refreshing rest in your company." He prays that he will get to Rome to be with them. Now, if you have read the book of Acts you will know that Paul did make it to Rome, but he did so in a way probably not expected by him. He went there as a prisoner. And yet, everywhere Paul went there were death plots, and he escaped them. Have you considered before that God could have used the prayers of the Roman believers to contribute to rescuing Paul in Jerusalem? So, they indeed had a part of Paul's ministry there.

Personal greetings and benediction

Let's turn now to chapter sixteen and look at Paul's personal greetings and benediction, which will wrap up the letter. As an aside, Romans sixteen in unique firstly in that Paul mentions many individual names. And secondly, it is unique because Paul gives attention to house churches. Paul talks about the church that is in the house of Priscilla and Aquila. He talks about the household of Aristobulus and the household of Narcissus. He speaks about Olympus and the saints who were there. It appears that the house churches collectively made up the church in Rome.

Another interesting thing in this section is Paul's mention of females. In the first century world, females were not given the same status in society that is ascribed to females in our modern cultures, and yet Christianity elevated the role that women could play. And the final thing that I find unique is that Paul recognizes the labor and the contribution of different individuals within the body. That is encouraging because it shows us that sometimes we may think that nobody knows or cares how we are serving the Lord, but God does know, and he does care, and that is important for us to remember.

Walk through chapter sixteen with me. Look at verses one and two, "I commend to you our sister Phoebe, who is a servant of the church which is at Cenchrea; that you receive her in the Lord in a manner worthy of the saints, and that you help her in whatever matter she may have need of you; for she herself has also been a helper of many, and of myself as well." Phoebe lived in Cenchrea, the eastern seaport of Corinth. Paul was in Corinth when he wrote the book of Romans, probably about nine miles away, and so it is likely that Phoebe carried the letter to the church in Rome. Then we see a reference to Priscilla and Aquila, Paul's fellow workers in the Lord. He talks about the sacrifices they had made. In other places in the New Testament we find that they had a church in their house in Ephesus. And now they have a church in their house in Rome. They were obviously very mobile in their ministry and would go where the needs were.

For the sake of time, I am not going to touch on each individual mentioned in Romans chapter sixteen, other than to point out the instances where Paul mentions the word work. Look at verse six, "Greet Mary, who has worked hard for you…Greet Urbanus, our fellow worker" (verse nine). Then down in verse twelve, "Tryphena and Tryphosa, workers in the Lord…Perseus, the blood, who has worked hard in the Lord." The fact that Paul mentions the labor of these individuals shows that he values their labor. Often in ministry we can get discouraged when it feels like no one appreciates our effort. Firstly, remember that we are ministering ultimately for the Lord, and that should be our motive. And secondly, when people do not seem to appreciate what we are doing, be encouraged that Christ does notice our labor.

You are likely aware that the Wright brothers were the first to fly an airplane. What you may not know is the other individuals who were a part of their adventure, and I am fairly confident that you do not know their names. Their names are Adam Etheridge, Will Dough, and John Daniels. The reason I mention them is because even though no one knows their names, they too were very much a part of the Wright brothers flight.

In the same way, there are many individuals in the body of Christ, and although we may not know their names, they are still equally a part of the work that God is doing. Paul singles out some individuals that he knows, although he probably leaves out many people that he could have mentioned. But understand this, God knows who you are, He knows your labor for the Lord and He takes note of it. Let that encourage you as you seek to serve the Lord as well.

To wrap this up, let's look at Paul's warning against malicious teachers, "Now I urge you, brethren, keep your eye on those who cause dissensions and hindrances contrary to the teaching which you learned, and turn away from them" (Romans 16:17). Paul is not talking about teachers who may have a different opinion on some detail of Scripture. Paul is talking about malicious false teachers who have an intent to deceive. Notice his explanation, "For such men are slaves, not of our Lord Christ but of their own appetites; and by their smooth and flattering speech they deceive the hearts of the unsuspecting." These teachers focus on the gullible, the unsuspecting. And they use flattering speech to deceive them and draw them towards their false teaching. Paul's answer to that is, "Mark those men, and stay away from those that teach contrary to what you have been taught." The idea here is that Apostolic Doctrine is the standard, and if people differ from that, mark them and stay away from them.

Paul finishes with greetings from certain of his associates. "Timothy, my fellow worker, greets you, and so do Lucius and Jason and Sosipater" (Romans 16:21). Tertius then says, "I, Tertius, who write this letter, greet you in the Lord." Tertius was Paul's scribe, and Paul allowed him to give his greeting as well. Tertius then proceeds to write more greetings from Paul's various associates.

And now we come to the benediction. This is the capstone of the book of Romans as it includes a declaration that God is able to establish believers in the faith. Look at Romans 16:25, "Now to him who is able to establish you according to my gospel and the preaching of Jesus Christ, according to the revelation of the mystery which has been kept secret for long ages past, but now is manifested, and by the Scriptures of the prophets, according to the commandment of the eternal God, has been made known to all the nations, leading to obedience of faith; to the only wise God, through Jesus Christ, be the glory forever." We sense Paul's excitement that the mystery is unfolded and that the Message is now going to the nations. What God intended all the way back with Abraham (that the nations would be blessed through him) is now being fulfilled in history. We are living in God's narrative. And in this narrative, God is maturing us as believers and using us to reach out to new people. And the capstone in the book, again, is the declaration that God is able to establish believers in the faith.

I must add that when I first studied the book of Romans, I felt so discouraged because I saw how far away I was from the maturity that I should have. But we see here that God is the One who is able to establish us. He is the One who started the work in us, who justified us, and who will also glorify us. He is leading us as sons and daughters of God, by His Spirit, into maturity. As we close this book, let's be confident that God is at work in us to make us like Christ, and remember that He will be faithful to accomplish His work.

When we hear these wonderful truths of Romans, the only appropriate response is that of Paul in Romans 16:27, "To the only wise God, through Jesus Christ, be the glory forever." In other words, we praise God for the wonderful Truths that He has given us. And then we say with Paul, "Amen, it is true." We worship God for His Truth, and we take Him at His Word. And on that note, we come to the end of our study on the book of Romans.

? DISCUSSION POINTS

1. What was Paul's goal in ministry according to 15:14-21?

2. Where did he focus his missionary efforts?

3. What was the standard by which the believers' were to measure the teaching they heard?

4. Paul says that the Lord will soon crush Satan. When will that happen according to God's Narrative?

5. Who is able to establish us in the faith according to 16:25? Are you trusting Him to do this? Are you walking in such a way that would further His work in you?

3.19 The Church in Thessalonica

 OBJECTIVES OF THIS TUTORIAL

Bible presenter Scot Keen commences our study on the book of 1 and 2 Thessalonians in this tutorial. He explains the history of the first church plant in the city of Thessalonica.

Introduction

In this tutorial we commence our study of 1 and 2 Thessalonians, the next section in module three. The books of 1 and 2 Thessalonians are very challenging for our walk with God as they remind us of the importance of being faithful in our walk with God.

Before we dive into the text I want to give you some background and history of the city of Thessaloniki, as it is now called. Thessaloniki, or Thessalonica, is a city that goes back to the 300's BC, and it was founded by Cassander, one of Alexander the Great's four generals. He actually founded the city in honor of his wife Thessaloniki.

In Paul's day there were approximately 100,000 living in this city, whereas now its population is roughly one million people. Thessalonica has a rich history with a sea port and also the Roman road, the Via Egnatia, coming through there. With the sea port and the Roman Road it was a very active city, making it an excellent place for a church plant, which is probably one of the reasons why Paul was there. Paul traveled on the Via Egnatia when he left Philippi and made his way towards Thessalonica.

The Ottoman Turks took control of Thessalonica in 1430 and basically dominated the city until the 1900's. The Greek culture and language were preserved in Thessalonica by the schools which operated there. So it has a rich history and of course now it is a modern metropolis. The most important day that ever took place in this city was not the day that Cassander presented this city to his lovely bride, and it is not the days in which the Greek language and culture were preserved. From God's perspective the most important day in this city is the day that Paul, Silas and Timothy took the Gospel of God's grace to this city.

We can read about this in Acts chapter seventeen. Paul was on his second missionary journey and he and Silas were arrested in Philippi, where they were imprisoned overnight until God sent an earthquake and they were ultimately released. They traveled from there on the Via Egnatia to Thessalonica where they preached the Gospel in a synagogue.

Acts 17

Let's look at Acts chapter seventeen to see the background of this church plant, "When they traveled through Amphipolis and Apollonia, they came to Thessalonica, where there was a synagogue of the Jews" (Acts 17:1). Look at verse two, "And according to Paul's custom, he went to them, and for three Sabbaths reasoned with them from the Scriptures, explaining and giving evidence that the Christ had to suffer and rise again from the dead, and saying, 'This Jesus whom I am proclaiming to you is the Christ.'" Paul's custom was to go to the synagogue, probably because it was a place where people had deep respect for the Scriptures, believing it to be the Word of God. They also lived in anticipation and expectation that the Christ would come. Paul was able to go in to synagogues well versed from his training by Gamaliel. He would often be given an opportunity to speak and he would use their Scriptures, our Old Testament Scriptures, to proclaim Christ.

Now those of you who have studied previous modules will know that the Old Testament spoke of the coming of Christ, and so this was an easy platform for Paul to proclaim the Gospel. Notice verse three where Paul is explaining and giving evidence that Jesus is the Messiah. Paul's methodology was explaining and giving evidence. Think about this for a moment, we explain things because we want others to understand. If we give evidence it is because we want others to believe.

We can gather from Paul's methodology that he desired a response of faith. To state the obvious, often when we evangelize we articulate our belief that people are saved by grace through faith in God's Word. We know people are justified by faith, as we saw in the book of Romans. So it is very odd that sometimes when Christians do evangelism, after they have shared the Good News, they try to get people to do something, like pray a prayer, or make a commitment. Notice that Paul's theology, that people are justified by faith, was consistent with his methodology. Paul's theology said that we believe and we are therefore justified, and so when he sought to see people come to faith, he explained and gave evidence. His method was consistent with his message.

I think that is a challenge for all of us. When we are sharing the Scriptures, we should be trying to see people come to faith in Christ by explaining and giving evidence, as Paul did. Now Paul knew that one of the biggest hurdles for the Jewish mind for trusting in Christ was the expectation that the Christ would reign in victory and defeat God's enemy and establish the glorious kingdom.

So Paul had to explain that Christ's suffering was also a Biblical concept. He explained and gave evidence that the Christ had to suffer. As an example, think about it from John chapter twelve. The question is asked, "How can the son of man be lifted up? We thought that the son of man would live forever." People had a hard time reconciling the sufferings of Christ and Christ reigning forever.

So Paul would give evidence from the Old Testament. When he explained and gave evidence that the Christ had to suffer, he would probably go to places like Isaiah fifty-three or Psalm twenty-two. He would talk about the suffering servant of God, the Messiah, who would suffer on behalf of Israel and by extension on behalf of man.

Paul gave evidence that the Christ had to suffer and rise again from the dead, saying, "This Jesus whom I am proclaiming to you, is the Christ or is the Messiah." He would describe the person of Christ, compared to the prophecies about the Christ, and show that there was a perfect match. The result? Some people were persuaded.

Look at Acts 17:4, "And some of them were persuaded," which means they were convinced. The author of Acts and Luke is using the word persuaded as synonymous with belief. "Some were persuaded and joined Paul and Silas, along with a large number of God fearing Greeks, and a number of leading women. But the Jews becoming jealous took along some wicked men from the market place, formed a mob and set the city in an uproar." We find that some were persuaded whereas others responded in hostility, to the point that Paul and Silas were sent away.

In verse seven we find that Jason and other believers in Thessalonica were accused of harboring criminals, "Jason has welcomed them, they act contrary to the decrees of Caesar, saying that there's another king, Jesus. They stirred up the crowd and the city authorities who heard these things, and when they had received a pledge from Jason and the others they released them." Jason and some of the other believers were arrested and then released. After this, the believers choose to send Paul and Silas away to protect them from further danger.

Impact of initial church plant

This initial church plant impacted the world in several ways. First of all Paul was able to ground the believers in many Biblical truths. For example, he taught that the church would be delivered from the wrath of God and he taught believers how to live consistently with their standing in Christ. He also taught believers that they would suffer persecution and how to walk in a way that is pleasing to God. He taught them about the events surrounding the day of the Lord, and we could go on and on. Paul was in Thessalonica for roughly three weeks, as we read in Acts chapter seventeen.

First Thessalonians

Now, I want to make a comment about this because many of you are training for ministry. Paul was able to ground these believers in many Biblical truths although he was only there for a short time. I want to challenge you to redeem the time, to use your time well in whatever ministry God gives you, because we have no promise of tomorrow. In the people groups that we may have the privilege of working with, the only Word of God that they will ever hear in their language is what we will tell them. Take this as a challenge to be faithful with the task that God gives you. The believers faced persecution, and because of that Paul wrote 1 Thessalonians. He wrote this letter from Corinth in 51 A.D, and it was written out of a deep concern for the believers' well-being.

Timothy's Report

Paul knew that they were being persecuted because of their faith. Many of them would have been separated from their families, excluded from the synagogue and feeling the weight of that. So Paul wrote 1 Thessalonians to encourage them, and also as a response to a report given by Timothy. We read about this in 1 Thessalonians 3:5, "For this reason when I could endure it no longer, I sent to find out about your faith, for fear that the tempter might have tempted you and our labor would be in vain." So he sent Timothy to find out how the believers were doing and Timothy brought back a good report of their faith and love.

It is likely that the problems that Paul corrects in 1 Thessalonians were those problems that he discovered through Timothy's report. Timothy would have informed Paul of the persecution that the believers were enduring. Timothy would have also revealed that Paul's character was under attack. When we read 1 Thessalonians chapter two, Paul defends his character, which implies that some people were attacking Paul's character. Timothy also identified several problems that the believers there had which threatened their walk with God.

For example, Paul talks about a resistance to church leadership in 1 Thessalonians chapter five. He talks about sexual immorality in 1 Thessalonians chapter four, and he also talks about confusion regarding those who have died. Paul wants to address these problems so that the believers can walk in truth.

Purpose & structure of the letter

So the purpose of 1 Thessalonians is to encourage the believers to persevere. I will develop that argument as we study this book, but for now I just want to give you a little taste of that.

Paul was concerned about their faith. He was concerned that the tempter would have tempted them and that his labor would have been in vain. He was afraid the believers were no longer living by faith, and we know from Scripture that God calls us to walk by faith, not by sight. So Paul wanted to encourage them and he accomplishes this by first of all reminding them of what God has already done in their lives. He does this in 1 Thessalonians chapter one, he defends his integrity in chapter two and he lifts their focus towards the return of Christ and away from temporal distress in chapters three, four and five. He also addresses the major problems which threaten their perseverance in chapters four and five as well.

Perseverance

Paul wants to motivate the believers to keep going, to keep living by faith and to keep growing in the Lord. If you are familiar with Paul's epistles, you will know that they typically address doctrine in the first half and application in the second. The book of Romans is a little longer than Paul's typical epistle in that it contains eleven chapters of doctrine and before the application. The first three chapters of Thessalonians focus on the relationship that Paul had with the believers there and the ministry in Thessalonica. It is largely a reminder of the good things that God did. Chapters four and five are then heavy with encouragement and exaltation. Before Paul teaches new things to the believers, he gives reassurance of the validity of his ministry and his message.

This is most likely because people were attacking his character and so he needed to do that to remind them of his credibility. The purpose of the epistle then is perseverance, and in chapter one Paul will encourage the believers to keep going because they had a great start. In chapter two he will tell them to keep going because the apostles have proved their genuineness. In chapter three he will tell them to keep going because he loves them, and that he sent Timothy to strengthen them so they would not give up or loose heart. In chapter four he tells them to keep going because Jesus is coming back, and in chapter five he says to keep going because we will be delivered from the day of the Lord, so hang in there. That, in essence, is what Paul wants to accomplish in this letter.

The return of Christ

The way Paul does this is by drawing attention to the return of Christ. It is very interesting that every chapter in 1 and 2 Thessalonians (with the exception of second

Thessalonians chapter three), ends with the return of Christ. In chapter one of 1 Thessalonians, they are waiting on God's son from heaven to deliver them from the coming wrath. The return of Christ in chapter two is a major driver in Paul's missionary endeavors. In chapter three Christ's return is mentioned as it relates to the judgment of believers and in chapter four as it relates to our glorification. In chapter five Christ's return is mentioned again as it relates to the day of the Lord and our deliverance from it as the church.

We will look at these chapters in detail as we move through 1 Thessalonians, but keep in mind that Paul's primary goal is to encourage the believers to keep walking with God. The chances are, if you are ever involved in a church planning ministry, that you are going to need these principles as well, not only for your own sake, but much more for the sake of the believers that you are investing in. I hope that God challenges you to look back at 1 Thessalonians in your ministry and apply the principles that we will find there.

DISCUSSION POINTS

1. For what purpose did Paul write 1st Thessalonians?
2. What are the major points that contribute towards that purpose?

3.20 A Call to Persevere

 OBJECTIVES OF THIS TUTORIAL

Bible presenter Scot Keen continues our study on the books of 1 and 2 Thessalonians in this tutorial. He encourages an exemplary church plant, the church in Thessalonica, to persevere after beginning well.

Introduction

In this tutorial, we will begin in 1 Thessalonians chapter one with Paul's challenge to believers to persevere because of the great beginning that they had. Chapter one emphasizes the good things that God did in the lives of the believers and that is supposed to motivate them to keep pressing on. We, too, would do well to remember the great things God has done in our lives when we get discouraged in our walk with God, as this encourages us to keep living by faith.

Thanksgiving

Paul begins the letter by giving thanks for their great beginning as believers, "Paul and Silvanus and Timothy, to the church of the Thessalonians in God the Father and the Lord Jesus Christ: Grace to you and peace. We give thanks to God always for all of you, making mention of you in our prayers."

Pause here for a moment and notice that Paul is giving thanks to God, which gives us an indication that Paul recognizes that God is ultimately responsible for anything good he sees in their lives. As you read Paul's letters you will notice that he is constantly in prayer for the believers.

You can read his prayers in the books of Philippians, Colossians, Ephesians and Thessalonians. Paul is always praying for believers and, in turn, asking them to pray for him. I think it is a wonderful reminder that part of Paul's church planning ministry involved intersession for the believers.

Response to God's word

Look at 1 Thessalonians 1:3, "Constantly bearing in mind your work of faith and labor of love and steadfastness of hope in our Lord Jesus Christ in the presence of our God and Father." What is it that Paul remembers? He first remembers their work of faith (because it says Paul remembers this, it means that he was present in person during that initial church plant), right out of the gates we find that the believers were living by faith and acting on it.

When Paul says work of faith, he is making mention of the works they did that were prompted by their faith in the Lord Jesus, and so from the beginning they were active in their faith. Not only that, but Paul also remembers their labor of love.

The Spirit of God was producing love in these brand-new Christians and they were acting on that love. They were laboring out of a sense of love. This is important for our walk with God. Sometimes we can labor out of a sense of obligation, hoping that maybe somehow our labor will help us please God. We know better than that after studying the book of Romans, but nevertheless, I think it serves as an important reminder that we should avoid laboring out obligation or legalism.

By implication, Paul's challenge to us (when he remembers this from the believers in Thessalonica) is that our labor should be prompted by love. It's the fruit of the Spirit that motivates us to reach out to others in love, and so we are referring to work that is produced by faith, we are talking about labor that is produced by love.

Paul then says that steadfastness, or perseverance, is produced by hope. In Greek, this is a genitive construction and can have a lot of different uses, but many people think that when Paul says perseverance of hope, he is alluding to perseverance that is produced by hope, and that means we need to understand what hope is because hope is an essential ingredient in producing perseverance. In Paul's letters hope is not something that may or may not happen, it refers to a certainty and an expectation of what God will do in the future, primarily our hope of the return of Christ.

Paul talks about our blessed hope, the glorious appearing of our great God and Saviour Jesus Christ. Paul is saying here that these believers are persevering and able to endure difficulties because of Christ's promised return. Hope produces perseverance.

Sometimes we can either become absorbed in eschatology or end times, or we can react in the opposite way and almost avoid it entirely because of how controversial it can be. Eschatology, or hope, is important for our perseverance and so we should not avoid it. It actually encourages us to continue walking with God.

People of God

Look at 1 Thessalonians 1:4, "Knowing your election of God." Paul is calling these believers in Thessalonica the elect of God. That is significant as well. It is significant firstly because Paul does not doubt their salvation, he calls them the elect of God, and yet he is concerned that they may not continue to walk by faith.

So in Paul's theology genuine believers either may or may not keep walking by faith and so need to be challenged to do so. Consider the context in which Paul states these words. Many of these people had come to faith in Jesus as Messiah from the synagogues, as we saw in our last tutorial. These Jewish believers (possibly some may have been proselytes to Judaism but primarily Jewish believers) would have been ostracized from their families and rejected from their homes, and Paul lets them know that they are actually the elect of God. What an encouragement to them.

The Jews are God's chosen people, which is something in which they took pride. Paul says actually, you believers in Thessalonica are the elect of God. This alludes to more than just Jews because there were also Gentile believers in Thessalonica. We learn about that later in verse nine when Paul says that they turned from idolatry to believe in the living God, which means that some of them came from Pagan backgrounds. Some of the believers were Gentiles and in spite of this Paul says that they are elect of God, and look at his reason why.

See in verse five, "For our gospel did not come to you in word only, but also in power." He is talking about apostolic signs there. That begs the question, how can we know that these believers are elect based on the signs that took place there? Once again, we need to think of the big picture. If you read the book of Galatians and Act chapter fifteen, you will discover that Paul was convinced that God was reaching out to Gentiles because God was validating apostolic signs at Paul's hands. This convinced not only Paul that God wanted the Gentiles to be saved, but also the Jerusalem council.

So we have this body of believers in Thessalonica, some from Jewish backgrounds, and others from Gentile backgrounds, and Paul says they are God's chosen people. We know that God granted Paul apostolic signs to convince them of this. The Gentiles not rejected of God, as their Jewish friends would say, they are actually God's people and that is a huge thing. The Gentile believers are the people of God. Paul is thankful for their initial response to God's word, he is thankful that they are God's people and finally, Paul is thankful for their example to others.

Example to others

Notice in verse six that Paul says, "You became imitators of us and of the Lord." Usually when we think about imitating Christ, this is not what comes to mind, but observe how he explains this imitation. They do so in much tribulation with the joy of the Holy Spirit.

Now, when Jesus accomplished the mission God gave him, it came with much affliction. It came with suffering; however, it was also accomplished by joy. The book of Hebrews says that Jesus endured the cross for the joy that was set before Him. Paul's obedience also cost him tribulation, but he also did so with joy. And now the believers in Thessalonica have become imitators. Walking in obedience to God's Word brought them persecution, and yet they did so with the joy from the Holy Spirit.

Paul continues talk about their example. Look at 1 Thessalonians 1:8, "For the word of the Lord has sounded forth from you, not only in Macedonia and Achaia, but also in every place your faith toward God has gone forth, so that we have no need to say anything." When Paul says that their testimony is going forth in Macedonia and Achaia, the idea is that wherever Paul goes he does not have to tell people about the Thessalonian church plant, rather they tell him about it. We see this again in verses eight through ten. He says, "For we have no need to say anything. For they themselves report about us what kind of a reception we had with you, and how you turned to God from idols to serve a living and true God, and to wait for his son from heaven, whom he raised from the dead, that is Jesus, who rescues us from the wrath to come."

Paul doesn't tell other people about the Thessalonian church plant, they tell him about it. When they tell Paul the story of what God did there, they talk about the fact that these people, now believers, turned to God from idolatry. That was their background, and they rejected it to serve the living and the true God. This imagery is wonderful. Often when a church plant takes place, especially among an unreached or least-reached people groups, it takes years for the people to leave the practices that they have had up until this point completely behind.

So it is an amazing testimony of what happened in Thessalonica because, in essence, they made a clean break with their idolatry. We do not always read about this happening, even in the New Testament. Acts chapter nineteen speaks about the fact that the people there had been believers for some time before they stopped their magical practices, but not so in Thessalonica. They were serving a living and true God, and they were waiting for God's Son from heaven whom He raised from the dead.

The believers had this posture of anticipation, an expectancy. They were expecting Jesus to come from heaven and deliver them from the wrath that was coming. We do not learn much about this wrath in the text here, but Paul will touch on it again later in the book. I believe that the wrath of God talked about in 1 Thessalonians 1:10, as we will see later on in the book, is not the wrath that someone might go to after they die, but instead is a wrath that is coming to the earth in the Day of the Lord, as Paul mentions in 1 Thessalonians chapter five and 2 Thessalonians chapter two.

These believers were waiting for Christ to rescue them from that wrath is coming. I love the play on words here. There were waiting on Jesus (which means Yahweh delivers) to deliver them from the coming wrath. The Savior is going to do what the Savior does and that is rescue. Paul encourages these believers to keep going because they had a great beginning. They were an example to other believers, they were lived by faith, they labored with love and worked with faith and they persevered because of their hope. This was an exemplary church plant, and Paul wanted to that encourage these believers to keep going in their walk with God.

? DISCUSSION POINTS

1. In 1st Thessalonians 1:3, Paul wrote about 'perseverance of hope.' What is the correlation between hope and the believer's perseverance?

2. As Paul reflected on his time in Thessalonica (when he planted the church) in 1st Thessalonians 1, he mentions the good things that he observed in their life (e.g., work of faith, labor of love, perseverance of hope, how they turned to God from idols, and their expectation to be delivered from the coming wrath). Are these things characteristic of your life as well? How would these qualities be expressed in your context?

3. In 1st Thessalonians 1, Paul said that the believers in Thessalonica became an example to other believers in Macedonia. In what way did they serve as an example to others?

3.21 A Reason to Continue

 OBJECTIVES OF THIS TUTORIAL

Bible presenter Scot Keen analyses the apostle Paul's credibility as a Gospel messenger in this tutorial. We learn that Paul motivates the Thessalonian church to keep going, assuring them that they can trust the Message he gave them.

Introduction

In our previous tutorial, we looked at what some would call the ideal church plant. The Thessalonians believers had welcomed the Word of God, they had a healthy walk with God from the beginning and they became an example to others. If 1 Thessalonians chapter one is the standard for the ideal church plant, then 1 Thessalonians chapter two is the standard for the ideal church planters.

So hopefully this portion of Scripture challenges us to consider serving others with the Gospel of Christ. Paul is still developing his theme of perseverance in 1 Thessalonians chapter two. In essence Paul has two main goals in this chapter (1) motivating the church to keep going and (2) establishing his credibility as a messenger of the Gospel. We can gather from this that most likely people were attacking Paul's character. It is not hard to see how this could happen. Paul planted a church and then was sent away by the believers to protect him, and possibly even to protect them.

After Paul is sent away, it is easy to imagine how some people could ask questions like, "If this man loved them so much, if he was such a great guy, why did he leave when things got tough?" Paul defends his character and he does it not for his own sake, but I believe Paul defends his character so that the believers will continue to trust in the Message that they heard from him. Paul begins his defense with the claim that he is a faithful steward of the Gospel.

Paul's defense

Look with me at 1 Thessalonians 2:1. Paul says, "You yourselves know, brethren, that our coming to you was not in vain." They had a purpose in coming to Thessalonica. Now look at verse two, "After we had already suffered and been mistreated in Philippi, as you know, we had the boldness in our God to speak to you the gospel of God amid much opposition." Paul is basically saying, "Guys you know that we're genuine because why else would we suffer and still come to you and do the same thing that got us in trouble in Philippi?"

The fact that Paul preached the Gospel in Thessalonica in the midst of opposition shows that he was not trying to take advantage of them, but rather that he had was genuinely concerned for them. This opposition establishes his credibility. He says that they had suffered and been mistreated in Philippi, and we can read about this in Acts chapter sixteen. They were stripped of their clothing and Paul and Silas were beaten with rods.

After they had been beaten, they were placed in stocks and imprisoned. This is severe treatment to endure, and Paul is able to remind the Thessalonians that this happened. Somehow they knew that Paul had suffered for the sake of Gospel ministry when he turned up in Thessalonica, possibly by the scars on his back. Paul was bold to speak the Gospel in the midst of opposition. He was sold out for Christ and had a genuine concern for these people in Thessalonica who became believers and, because of that, was bold to share the Gospel.

Faithful stewards

Notice Paul says boldness in our God, and it reminds us that his boldness was not necessarily a natural boldness. Some people are naturally timid, as was Timothy, and we can be encouraged by texts such as this to know that even if we are not naturally bold, our boldness should not be coming from us anyway. Paul's boldness is in God, and so he could share the Gospel in the midst of opposition.

Now J. Vernon McGee, who has long since been with the Lord, said this, "If I were to pick the greatest sermon of Paul, I would choose his life in Thessalonica. It was not an exposition but an experience. He made his points on the pavement of the streets of Thessalonica." Of course if Paul had not used words, then there would have been no church in Thessalonica, but I don't think that is what McGee is trying to say. He is just making the point that Paul has a beautiful testimony. He proclaimed the value of the Gospel just by virtue of being in Thessalonica after he had suffered in Philippi, and by persisting in preaching the Gospel, the very thing that got him in trouble in Philippi.

Paul gives the reason for his boldness in verse three, "Our exhortation does not come from error or impurity or by way of deceit," which seems like an odd statement. Douglas Moo and D. A. Carson (in their intro to the New Testament) talk about people who traveled in the first century who would raise a following after presenting a certain message. They would then collect money and leave town.

Paul is defending himself against accusations like that. He was not in Thessalonica by error or deceit or impurity, in fact he says he was there because he was approved by God to be entrusted with the Gospel. Now sometimes people are skeptical when you reach out to them, wondering what you hope to gain from them.

It is hard for people to believe that someone might be motivated simply out of a genuine concern for others. F.F. Bruce says this, "There are cynics who cannot believe that public or private action involving sacrifice is ever undertaken purely with a view to the well-being of others." I remember years ago when my wife and I were living in Kentucky, I was pastoring a church while we were preparing to leave for missions training. I met a man who I knew from years before when I was not a believer, and he found out that I was now a Christian. This was a shock enough to him, and then I told him, "Yeah, my wife and I are getting ready to sell everything and move to Papua New Guinea." When I said that he was absolutely shocked and stood there in silence for a few minutes. "How much are they paying you to do that?" he asked. I told him, "Well, I'm not being paid anything. I actually have to raise my own money to go." He stood in disbelief for a while and then said, "Are they making you do that?" He thought I was being forced somehow to go to another country with the Gospel of Christ.

People have a hard time believing that Christians do things because we genuinely care about others. So Paul defends himself and says his reason for doing this was because God had entrusted him with the Gospel. Paul saw the Gospel as a sacred trust that God had given him and so he wanted to be faithful with it.

The image that comes to my mind is that of a football player who is running with the ball close to his body. When I played football in high school the coach would say, "Cradle the ball and squeeze it is tight as you can and never let it go." He taught us to lower our shoulders and keep gigging our legs if we hit opposition, and that is what I see in Paul.

He had been entrusted with the Gospel, and whenever he faces opposition, he keeps going. Paul simply wants to be faithful because he is a steward of the precious Gospel of God's grace. What a challenge this is for us as servants of Christ to remember that we, too, have been entrusted with this Gospel of God's grace. So Paul says, "We speak not as pleasing men, but God who examines our hearts." Ultimately Paul's ministry is for God.

Paul wants to please God who had entrusted him with his ministry, and if we have that same mind-set (that our ministry is ultimately for God), then we will not be discouraged if people do not appreciate the sacrifices we make. We are ultimately doing it to please God who examines our hearts. Look at verse five, "We never came with flattering speech as you know, nor with the pretext for greed, God is witness." Paul was not there to take from these people.

Further on we will find that Paul actually worked while he was in Thessalonica. He was not trying to take from them, he was just wanting to give them the Gospel of God's grace. Notice verse six, "Nor did we seek glory or honor from men either from you or from others, even though as apostles we have a right to assert our authority." When Paul speaks about this right to assert his authority and about receiving honor, he is referring to financial compensation.

Those who preach the Word should be able to live by the Word, but Paul lays aside the right that he has as an apostle because he wants to serve the Thessalonian church and to set an example, which he will tell us more about this later on. Paul says that they were gentle among them as a nursing mother tenderly cares for her own children. This brings us to this next subsection, living sacrificially for the sake of the Gospel.

Living sacrificially

When I think about living sacrificially, I think about all the hours during the night my wife sacrificed to look after our first child. A nursing mother tenderly caring for her own children; this phrase also shows us that when Paul discipled these believers, he was aware of their maturity in the Lord and he treated them accordingly. In other words, he knew that they were just babies in Christ and so he was tender with them.

Paul is aware of their maturity and he responded accordingly. I think that is an important principle for us in ministry. We should know where people are at so we can disciple them based on where they are and move them to the next level. Paul was sacrificial like a nursing mother caring for her children. Look at verse eight, "Having so fond an affection for you, we were well-pleased to impart to you not only the gospel of God but also our own lives, because you had become very dear to us."

Catch this. Paul says they had a fond affection for the Thessalonian believers, to the point that they were willing to give their lives for them. Sometimes we can look at ministry as either-or instead of both-and. Here's what I mean. Some people emphasize that our ministry should have a God-ward focus, that we should ultimately be focused on pleasing him, and in fact Paul just said that in verse four. But other people talk about being focused on those we are serving.

A God-focused ministry and a genuine love for others are not mutually exclusive. Paul was serving to please God, but in the doing so he also had a fond affection for the people he was serving. Let me challenge you to have a genuine love for the people you are serving. Your love for them will not get you to the mission field, and it probably will not keep you on there either. It will be a God-ward focus which gets you there and keeps you there. But I believe it is Biblical to trust God to give us a love for the people we are serving, as He did with Paul.

Notice verse nine, "For you recall, brethren, our labor and hardship, how working night and day so as not to be a burden to any of you, we proclaimed to you the gospel of God."

Paul will talk more about this later on in 2 Thessalonians. He was actually bi-vocational while he was ministering to the Thessalonians because he wanted to set them an example of hard work and serving others. So he says here that he worked night and day so he would not be a burden to them and could minister to them free of charge.

Contrary to those who would attack Paul's character, Paul actually was sacrificial. He was not trying to take from the believers, all he did was give to them. Look at verse ten, "You are witnesses, and so is God, how devoutly and uprightly and blamelessly we behaved toward you believers; just as you know how we were exhorting and encouraging and imploring each one of you as a father would his own children."

Understand what Paul is saying here. Paul says they were gentle like a nursing mother, they had a fond affection for the people, they gave their own lives, they labored night and day, they lived devoutly, uprightly and blamelessly and they exhorted and encouraged.

Keep going

Paul did all of that so that because he had a goal in mind. Look at 1 Thessalonians 2:12, "So that you would walk in a manner worthy of the God who calls you into his own kingdom and glory." Everything Paul did was for the purpose of helping believers walk worthy of God. Paul's labor was for their maturity and a healthy walk with God. Paul is laboring so that they would keep going, so that they would live in a healthy way.

Now verse twelve is pivotal because it shows us that ministry and church planning is not just sharing the Gospel; it is not just about evangelism. Paul still was not satisfied even when these people came to faith. He was not satisfied until they were walking worthy of God. That shows us that Paul is focused on the entire Great Commission. Not just the going, not just the preaching of the Gospel, but he was also focused on seeing believers walk in a manner that pleases God.

So I want to challenge both myself and you to not to be content with our discipleship efforts until believers are living in such a way that is consistent with who God has called them to be. Paul tells the believers to keep going because everything he had done so far was for the purpose that they would walk worthy of God.

God is at work

Now Paul tells the Thessalonian believers to keep going because God is presently at work in them. Look at how God's Word was having an impact even when Paul wrote, "For this reason we also constantly thank God that when you received the word of God which you heard from us, you accepted it not as the word of men, but for what it really is, the word of God, which also performs its work in you who believe." Paul says that they accepted his teaching as the Word of God. The apostolic message is considered God's Word, for which they were God's representatives.

Notice Paul's comment in verse thirteen, "His word which performs (present tense) its work in you who believe." What Paul is saying is, "Yes, I remember God was active in your past, and now God's word is active in your present." His Word is actually working in you even now, and so that was reason enough to keep walking with God.

Paul also wants them to know that persecution is to be accepted. He says, "For you, brethren, became imitators of the churches of God in Christ Jesus that are in Judea, for you also endured the same sufferings at the hands of your own countrymen, even as they did from the Jews" (1 Thessalonians 2:14-16). Just like the churches in Judea were persecuted by the Jews, even so the Thessalonians were persecuted by their own surrounding countrymen. These Jews who persecuted the Christians in Jerusalem, Paul says in verse fifteen, "Killed the Lord Jesus and the prophets, and drove us out. They are not pleasing to God, but hostile to all men." They were hostile to all men because they were hindering the Gospel from going out.

Read verse sixteen, "Hindering us from speaking to the Gentiles or the nations so that they may be saved." Now, please don't miss this very important verse. The Jews hindered Paul from speaking to the Gentiles, and because of that he says, "So that they may be saved." In other words, Paul says if the Gospel does not go to the nations, then the nations cannot be saved. There is no other way. It has to be through the Gospel Message or not at all, and as long as the Jews kept the Gospel from going to the nations, the nations could not be saved. People have to hear the Gospel in order to be saved.

Paul says (speaking about the Jews) because of that, they fill up the measure of their sins and wrath has come upon them to the utmost. Now the way this wrath has come upon them to the utmost is going to be firstly their experience of a judicial hardening from God (as we saw previously in Romans). Another avenue of wrath may also be something that not even Paul was anticipating, but what Jesus said in Luke's Gospel that took place in 70 AD. Jesus said that the Jews would face destruction from the hands of the Romans, which indeed they did.

❓ DISCUSSION POINTS

1. In 1st Thessalonians 2, Paul talks about his ministry among the Thessalonians. As you read through the chapter, what do you identify as the primary goal(s) of his ministry?

2. Why was Paul so determined to faithfully preach the gospel in spite of the sufferings he endured? Are there principles that relate to your stewardship of the gospel? How might these principles impact your life choices?

➡ ACTIVITIES

1. Read 1st Thessalonians 2:5-11 and take note of the price that Paul paid as a servant of Christ.

a) According to 2:12, why did he do all of the things mentioned in 2:5-11?

b) How does this impact your view of discipleship and the time commitment involved in seeing a church brought to maturity?

2. Ask a cross-cultural church planter to describe the labor and time involved in establishing mature believers. Discuss this with a friend or mentor.

3.22 Blameless at the Judgment Seat

 OBJECTIVES OF THIS TUTORIAL

In this tutorial, Bible presenter Scot Keen examines whether the apostle Paul's labor among the Thessalonians was in vain. Paul longs for the Thessalonian church to be found blameless at the judgment seat of Christ.

Introduction

In this tutorial, we come into a very important section of verse Thessalonians as Paul challenges the believers to live in such a way that they will be blameless before Christ at his coming. Paul is encouraging the believers to keep going, in order to be blameless at the BEMA, or the judgment seat of Christ. Paul begins by explaining his absence and defending his love for the believers.

Explaining an absence

Look at 1 Thessalonians 2:17, "But we, brethren, having been taken away from you for a short while- in person, not in spirit- were all the more eager with great desire to see your face." Again we see Paul making statements like this, defending his reason for not being in Thessalonica. Evidently people were attacking Paul's character, saying he should have been there and that maybe he did not love them after all. So this is a defense of Paul's love. Notice that Paul says, "Having been taken away from you." Literally, "We were orphaned from you." Paul is using terminology that expresses being ripped apart from those who he saw as his children in the faith.

Recently some friends of mine who are foster parents looked after a child for several months. It was heart wrenching for them to have to give that child up when the time came for adoption. Paul is speaking in similar language here; he is talking about the grief of having to leave behind an infant church. These were new believers, and Paul had discipled them as much as he could, while present, but he was separated from them and he longed to go back. So he says in verse eighteen, "We wanted to come to you- I, Paul, more than once- and yet Satan hindered us." For some reason Paul could not make it back to Thessalonica to minister to these believers. Now he talks about how dear they are to him saying, "For who is our hope or joy or crown of exultation? Is it not even you, in the presence of our Lord Jesus at his coming? For you are our glory and joy" (1 Thessalonians 2:19). Paul's grounds for rejoicing at Christ's coming is the church. Paul is extremely thankful for these believers, and he loves them, and because of his love he has sent Timothy to check on them. He is concerned for their faith.

Look at 1 Thessalonians 3:1, "Therefore when we could endure it no longer." When life gets tough, we can all identify with the feeling that we can't take it anymore. Paul felt that way too, and what bothered him was that he did not know how the believers were doing. So he says, "When we could endure it no longer, we thought it best to be left behind at Athens alone." If you read about Athens and Paul's ministry there in Act chapter seventeen, Paul was grieved in his spirit when he saw that the city was given over to adultery. Paul needed companionship, but he would rather do without his companions than not know how the Thessalonian church was doing. So Paul sent Timothy to check on these believers.

So Paul says in verse two, "We sent Timothy, our brother and God's fellow worker in the gospel of Christ, to strengthen and encourage you as to your faith." Paul sent Timothy to build them up in the faith, to strengthen them and to encourage them. They had already accepted the Gospel. They were in the faith, but they were young and immature and movable. Paul wanted them to be strong and immovable. So Timothy was sent there to disciple them, to invest in these new believers, and to encourage them in their faith. And again, what is emphasized is that Paul was worried about their faith and so sent Timothy to strengthen them in their faith.

We know Timothy was sent to find out about their faith because Paul was concerned that they were not standing firm in the Lord. This alludes to a fear that Paul had that these believers were not living by faith. That's why I say that it is possible that the very elect of God may not be living by faith. Paul was concerned about that. So he said in verse three, "Timothy was sent to strengthen them, so that no one would be disturbed by these afflictions." It was the afflictions, the persecution, that Paul was concerned might be the thing that caused them to stop living by faith.

The Thessalonian believers could react to persecution in several different ways. First of all, they could simply hide their faith in order to avoid persecution. That would be a step backwards, because so far they were a testimony to other people. They could also have started doubting the character and the goodness of God. After all, that is where our minds naturally go when we suffer. We ask God, "If you love me, why are you letting me go through this difficulty?" Paul knows that they could be shaken because of these afflictions. So he reminds them this persecution is normal for Christians.

In verse three, Paul says, "You yourselves know that we have been destined for this." Our identification with Christ is going to result in persecution. That is the way it is in this broken world where Satan is the god of this world. Persecution will be our lot until Jesus comes back and turns the tables.

So Paul reminds them, "You know that we're destined for this?" If we know that persecution is to be expected, then we will not be shaken up when it takes place. Paul says in 1 Thessalonians 3:4, "Indeed when we were with you, we kept telling you in advance that we were going to suffer affliction; and so it came to pass, as you know."

When I was about ten years old, my dad and I went on a fishing trip in southern Canada. One day we were on a lake at sun down and a terrible commotion came on the water. It got so violent that we looked for a place to get out of the water and pull the boat up to shore. The undergrowth was so thick that there was no place to get out of the boat. We basically fought our way through the storm until we made it back to the boat dock. Then we spoke to owner of the fishing lodge on the lake and he said, "Oh yeah, I wish I would have told you ahead of time. That happens every evening about sun down." Well, my point in sharing that story is that if you know that things are going to get rough, then you don't get surprised when it happens. But if you are not expecting it to be that way, it can really shake you up.

Paul says here, "When we were with you, we kept telling you in advance that you were going to suffer, and so it came to pass." If we know that we are going to suffer and it happens, then instead of shaking our faith, it can actually strengthen our faith because we are reminded that things are happening exactly as God said.

Was Paul's labor in vain?

Paul was concerned about the faith of the believers because they were being persecuted. They needed to be encouraged to lift their eyes away from this difficulty. So in verse five we read, "For this reason, when I could endure it no longer, I also sent to find out about your faith, for fear that the tempter might have tempted you, and our labor would be in vain." Paul's concern is that his labor might be in vain. That begs the question, what does it mean that Paul's labor might be in vain?

Some people interpret this to mean that a believer can lose their salvation. From what we have seen in Romans so far, we know that this simply cannot be the case. Those whom God justified, He also glorified. Their salvation was not at stake. What was at stake was firstly their testimony before a watching world, and secondly, their blamelessness at the judgment seat of Christ. To really understand what Paul was meant when he said that his labor might be in vain, we need to know why he was laboring. What was the purpose? We actually already saw the purpose for which Paul was laboring in 1 Thessalonians 2:1-12. To summarize, Paul is basically saying, "We were gentle among you. We had a fond affection for you. We gave you our lives, we worked night and day.

We behaved devoutly and uprightly, and blamelessly. We exhorted and encouraged you, and implored you, like a father with his children." All of Paul's labor was done so that they would walk in a manner worthy of God. So that means, if Paul is afraid that his labor would be in vain, that he is afraid that they were not walking worthy of God. His concern was not their salvation, it was for their sanctification. It was their godly life as believers that Paul had a genuine concern about.

Now, this is an aspect of the New Testament that we really need to grasp. I'll explain it this way; some truths are positional truths. We have been justified. We died under sin. We are alive under God. We are reconciled. These are things that are true of us, regardless of our experience. They are positional truths. Then we have conditional truths; things that may or may not take place our lives. Paul challenges us to live in such a way that we can get a full reward, that we might be pleasing to God, things of that nature.

Jesus told the believers in Philadelphia (in Revelations chapter three) to hold on to what they had so that no one would take their crown. There are some rewards that believers can actually loose if they are not faithful till the end. Those are the sort of things that Paul is concerned about when he says that he is afraid his labor might be in vain.

And Paul sent Timothy to check on the believers because of this concern, and thankfully Timothy came back with a refreshing report. Look at 1 Thessalonians 3:6, "Now… Timothy has come to us from you, and has brought us good news of your faith and love." Timothy comes back and says, "Paul, they're still living by faith and they still love you," which was something else that Paul was concerned about. So Paul says in verse seven, "For this reason, brethren, in all our distress and affliction we were comforted about you through your faith." It keeps coming up, over and over again, that Paul was concerned about their faith. And so he is relieved to hear that they are still living by faith.

Look at 1 Thessalonians 3:8, "Now we really live, if you stand firm in the Lord." This implies that it is possible for a genuine believer to not stand firm in the Lord. Paul was very concerned that they would not stand firm and so he was praying for their growth. He sent Timothy to invest in their growth. He wrote them the letter of first Thessalonians to build them up in their faith. Paul was encouraged to receive Timothy's good report of the Thessalonians believers.

Read verse nine, "For what thanks can we render to God for you in return for all the joy with which we rejoice before our God on your account, as we night and day keep praying most earnestly that we may see your face, and may complete what is lacking in your faith?" Here is Paul's prayer for their continued growth; and hand in hand is Paul's prayer that he would return and complete what is lacking in their faith. The idea here is that he wanted to give them more of God's Word.

Think about this: is it a guarantee, if we have a certain amount of God's word, that we will continue in the faith? Of course not. It is not the volume of God's Word that somehow guarantees that we will continue in the faith. But here is what we can guarantee; that if a believer does not have the Word of God, they cannot be mature in the faith. We discover this elsewhere in Scripture. For example, Ephesians chapter four says that it is children who are tossed back and forth by every wind of doctrine. It is the mature who can handle the Word of God. The book of 1 John talks about young men who are strong because the Word of God abides in them. Paul wanted to give them more of the Word of God to complete what is lacking in their faith, to fill in the gaps, so to speak.

Then we come across a prayer for their growth in 1 Thessalonians 3:11-13. Paul says, "May our God and Father himself, and Jesus our Lord direct our way to you." Whenever Paul says, "May our God do such and such," he's praying. He is praying that God would open up a door for him to go back to Thessalonica.

Paul's prayer does not stop there. Look at verse twelve, "May the Lord cause you to increase and abound in love for one another, and for all people, just as we also do for you." Paul is praying that God would cause them to abound in love. Ponder this for a moment. Where does love come from in the life of a believer? We know this from our previous study in Romans. Love is the fulfillment of the Law, and love comes by means of the Spirit of God. The Holy Spirit produces love in the life of a believer. Paul's prayer is that God would cause them to abound in love, that God would produce love in them by His Holy Spirit.

Look a 1 Thessalonians 3:12 again, "May the Lord cause you to increase and abound in love for one another, and for all people, just as we also do for you; so that he may establish your hearts without blame in holiness before our God and Father at the coming of our Lord Jesus with all his saints." Look at the reason why. There was an end in mind in this prayer. Paul prayed that God would cause them to abound in love, with the goal in mind that God would, "Establish your hearts without blame in holiness before our God and Father at the coming of our Lord Jesus with all his saints."

Blameless at the BEMA

This has nothing to do with heaven or hell. It has everything to do with well done good and faithful servant, or as 1 John chapter two puts it, "Shrinking back in shame before him and his coming." It has everything to do with the way a believer is received by Christ at his coming.

That is why I call this blameless at the BEMA, which is the Greek word for the judgment seat. Now, blamelessness in this passage is not a given. It comes as a result of God causing them to abound in love. It is not a given. It is something that either may or may not happen in the life of a believer and so we are responsible. We are told elsewhere in Scripture to walk according to the Spirit, so that the fruit of the Spirit would be manifested in our lives.

Today you can see the ruins of a judgment seat (or the BEMA seat) in Corinth. This is where soldiers were awarded after victorious battles. This is where athletes were given a crown after they had won an athletic competition. This is also where cases were tried. Paul is picturing believers before Christ at His coming and either being rewarded for their faithfulness to the Lord or being ashamed because of their failure to walk with Him.

Blamelessness is not a given. I also want you to see that blamelessness does not equal perfection. Paul is not saying that they would be painfully perfect. His prayer is that they would abound in love. We know from Romans that if believers walk according to the Spirit (walk in love), then they are fulfilling that which God desires in their lives. They are utilizing God's means for God's end.

So Paul's prayer is that God would cause them to abound in love. If we only had that one verse, we would get a picture of God perhaps zapping us with love and somehow making us go live the Christian life. But we know from elsewhere that we are responsible for the way we live. Yet we are ultimately dependent upon God. I believe Paul has in mind the balance between these truths as he prays. In fact, the structure in 1 Thessalonians indicates the nature of the Christian life; it is a divine human endeavor. It is empowered by God, but it is lived out by us. If we sacrificed either one of those aspects, we end up in a ditch and ultimately an unhealthy walk with God.

A recipe for perseverance

Look at 1 Thessalonians 3:11-13 and you will find a prayer for God's enablement, that God would cause them to abound in love, and the result of that prayer is that God would establish their hearts without blame. Look also at 1 Thessalonians 5:23 - 24. We get the same concept. "May the God of peace, sanctify you entirely, and may your spirit, soul and body, be preserved complete," listen to this, "without blame, before Christ at his coming."

In verse twenty-four Paul prays, "Faithful as he who calls you, who will bring it to pass." He prays that God will make them blameless before Christ at His coming, and he says God is the One who is going to bring it to pass. This is a prayer for blamelessness with God's enablement.

You may notice that 1 Thessalonians 4:1 - 5:22 is all about what the believers are supposed to do. For example, Paul talks about love in 1 Thessalonians 4:10, "You practice it towards all the brothers but we urge you to excel still the more." In chapter four Paul tells the believers to abound in love. In chapter three he prays that God would cause them to abound in love. You see that? If it were up to me, I would just tell people to abound in love, without the prayer for God's enablement. On the other hand, if it was all God's activity, and we did not have to respond to Him, we would just have the prayer for enablement but no exhortations.

We find Paul telling the believers how to live and what to do, but that is sandwiched between a reminder of God's enablement. It gives our hearts confidence before God, that as we choose to walk with God and take responsibility for the Christian life, we are doing it in utter dependence upon Him. It is a divine human endeavor. It is also a life that is lived by us. We choose not to let sin reign. We choose to walk according to the Spirit, as we saw in Romans. As we choose to walk with Him, we do so as people who are entirely dependent upon God's Spirit to cause us to abound in love, so that we can ultimately live pleasing to Him. God's activity is what makes our obedience possible.

A recipe for perseverance is remembering God's faithfulness in the past. Paul remembers their work of love and their perseverance of hope, as well as their dependence upon God's enablement, as we just saw. There is a recognition in 1 Thessalonians of the fact that our choices are real and they have consequences. There is a focus too on the invisible and eternal things of God. Perseverance is produced by hope. The Word of God brings maturity. These are things that are very necessary, not only in our lives, but also in the life of the church, as we seek to be faithful disciple-makers in planting churches among those without the Gospel.

BLAMELESS AT THE JUDGMENT SEAT

? DISCUSSION POINTS

1. What was Paul's primary concern in 2:17 – 3:13?

2. What was at stake if the believers failed to persevere?

3. What does Paul mean by blameless in 3:13? Is this speaking of acceptance into heaven or something else?

4. In what way does the structure of 1st Thessalonians impact our understanding of the Christian life?

➡ ACTIVITIES

1. In 1st Thessalonians 3, Paul was concerned that the believers may not continue living by faith (persevere). Read through 1st and 2nd Thessalonians and identify the factors that can impact – those things that contribute towards or detract from – perseverance. How do these factors relate to you in your walk with God?

3.23 Living in Light of our Hope

 OBJECTIVES OF THIS TUTORIAL

In this tutorial, Bible presenter Scot Keen discusses 1 Thessalonians chapter four. In it Paul encourages the Thessalonian believers to persevere in their walk with God. He tells them to do so by avoiding sin and by anticipating Christ's return.

Introduction

In this tutorial, we will cover several important topics. One is the threat that the believers faced in their walk with God, in that some of them were involved in sexual immorality. The other is confusion about what happens to believers when they die. We begin, first of all, with Paul's encouragement to walk in a way that pleases God.

Don't get tangled in sin

Paul begins chapter four of 1 Thessalonians with an exhortation, "Finally then, brethren, we request and exhort you in the Lord Jesus, that as you received from us instruction as to how you ought to walk and please God (just as you actually do walk), that you excel still more." Notice that when Paul says, "We exhort you in the Lord Jesus," he is bringing to their attention that this is not just his opinion, it comes with the authority of Christ. He is an apostle and so he comes with apostolic authority. His challenge here is for them to excel in what they were taught. Paul recognizes that they actually do walk with God, but he does not want them to become complacent. He wants them to excel in it.

Even in just the little that we have covered so far in this chapter, there is a challenge and a lesson for us. God does not want us to become stagnant or complacent in our walk with Him. If we become stagnant or complacent, we are one step closer to losing ground. We are not going anywhere. Paul wants the trajectory of a believer to be that of moving forward, excelling, abounding and advancing in the walk with God. If we are always advancing, then our trajectory is headed in the right direction. The Thessalonian believers were, for the most part, walking with God, but Paul wants them to keep excelling in it.

Look at 1 Thessalonians 5:2, "You know what commandments we gave you by the authority of the Lord Jesus," so Paul, once again, talks about his apostolic authority. Then he gives us an example in verse three. He says, "This is the will of God, your sanctification; that is, that you abstain from sexual immorality." Paul speaks about a problem that was very common in the first century world, and that is sexual immorality. This is something that took place not only in their everyday culture but also in their pagan worship. There were temple prostitutes and also pagan worship rights that involved sexual immorality.

I'll give you some examples of this. There were 3,000 temple harlots in Corinth, and often there were also priestesses in the temple for the sexual service of the men who came. F.F. Bruce said that in Thessalonica, sexual immorality was sanctioned by the cult of Cabiri. The reason I think this is relevant is that some of the believers in Thessalonica had turned to God from idols. They had come out of these pagan backgrounds, and Paul is evidently aware of a problem with sexual immorality among the believers there. Paul says, "They need to know that as God's will, their sanctification (being set apart for God), that they would abstain from sexual immorality." Paul is turning them away from this problem.

Paul then tells the believers to possess their own vessels in sanctification and honor. He is telling them to treat their bodies as set apart for God. We know from Scripture God's design for sex is for it to be between a husband and wife. We read in Hebrews chapter thirteen that, "Marriage is honorable in all, and the bed is undefiled." That confines sex to marriage and any sex outside of would be considered immorality and would be met with the disapproval of God.

Then Paul gives a contrast, "Not in lustful passion, like the Gentiles who do not know God." It seems that Paul is referring to the background of some of these believers, for example to the background of those who came out of the cult of Cabiri, as F.F. Bruce mentioned. This would deal with these temple prostitutes that were in Corinth, and most likely in Thessalonica as well. Paul is saying, "Don't act like the Gentiles. You're different." God has made these believers new in Christ and so they should now live differently.

Paul goes on to say, "No man transgress and defraud his brother in the matter because the Lord is the avenger in all these things, just as we also told you before and solemnly warned you. For God has not called us for the purpose of impurity, but in sanctification." When Paul says not to defraud a brother, he is probably talking about believers who were having sex outside of marriage, and in doing so, were robbing from what God intended for that person and their spouse when they do get married. Paul is warning against this, and in fact, he says that the Lord is the avenger in all these things. This adds a note of sobriety. God will respond to the believer's sin of sexual immorality because it is a real issue. We do not get the definition of what it means that God is an Avenger, but we do feel the note of seriousness and sobriety, and so should be turned away from this sin.

God has not called us for impurity but for sanctification. Paul says in verse eight, "He who rejects this is not rejecting man but the God who gives his Holy Spirit to you." Think about this; whatever the sexual sin might be, whether it is pornography and the sins of the mind, or adultery, or any sort of immorality, Paul says that it is a serious thing. He says that God is the Avenger of these things, and that if we reject this, we are ultimately rejecting God.

I love Paul's statement at the end of this verse, "God who gives his holy spirit to you." Why do you think Paul throws that in at the end of this section? I think the reason is because believers are indwelt by the Spirit of God, and believers who are struggling with a sexual sin need to know, first of all, that God wants them to live in purity. They need to know, secondly, that God the Spirit lives in them, and by means of the indwelling Spirit they can live a new life. This is God's provision to walk in purity.

Now, in verse nine, Paul goes on to call believers to walk in love. He says, "As to the love of the brethren, you have no need for anyone to write to you, for you yourselves are taught by God to love one another." Obviously, Paul does not mean what he says in a literal sense, because after all he is writing to them and telling them to love each other. I think he is simply saying that love comes naturally for those who are new creatures in Christ and are indwelt by the Spirit. However, Paul adds in verse ten, "You ... practice it toward all the brethren who are in all Macedonia. But we urge you, brethren, to excel still more." Although love is natural and it is happening here, they are told to keep going, to advance, to excel and to abound in love.

I believe we get hints here of a problem that took place in Thessalonica. Paul says, "Make it your ambition to lead a quiet life and attend to your own business and work with your hands, just as we commanded you, so that you will behave properly toward outsiders and not be in any need." Evidently there were believers in Thessalonica who were not working, and they were actually becoming a nuisance to other people, probably because they were trying to borrow from them, or to take from them. Paul says, "Walk in love, to lead a quiet life, to work with your own hands." It's a Biblical thing to work and earn your bread by your own hands. Not only that, but Paul also says that in doing so, they will behave properly towards outsiders and not be in any need.

To give you an example from the little community where I grew up, there was a store owner who would let people come in and take groceries, and if they did not have the money to pay, he would write it down on a notepad, and at the beginning of every month the customers would pay him back. One time when the store owner was invited to come to church, he said, "Why would I want to come to your church? Half of the people in your church owe me money and they won't come back to my store because they're too embarrassed to be around me." That is an example of behaving improperly towards outsiders. Paul says to, "Work with your hands," and I think we could say, to live in such a way that we are a good testimony in front of unbelievers. That is Paul's challenge to these believers.

Don't lose sight of hope

Now Paul moves discusses another aspect of perseverance. He challenges the believers to keep going by saying, "Don't lose sight of your hope." We saw back in chapter one that perseverance is born out of hope. There needs to be this blessed hope, this eschatology, that encourages us to keep walking with God. We see this in 1 Thessalonians 4:13-18. Some people refer to this passage as the rapture passage, and others will say that there is no such thing as a rapture in the Bible, and they would contend, for good reason, that the world rapture does not appear in Scripture. By way of introduction, I'll make a few comments about this. When Paul talks about being caught up to meet the Lord in the air, the word he used in Greek is harpadzo, which was translated as rapturo in Latin. That is where we get the word rapture.

Paul never offers us a term to refer to the rapture, and I don't believe that the New Testament as a whole uses a single term to refer to this event. Now, I will present an argument to show that this event is different to the second advent. But you will have to come to your own conclusions on this. To begin with, Jesus said, "I will receive you unto myself, that where I am, there you may be also." In 1 Thessalonians 4:17, Paul says we will be caught up. In first Corinthians chapter fifteen, Paul says we will be changed, so there are different phrases and words that refer to some event, that some take to be the rapture. As I said, you will have to make your own conclusion about that, but Paul is talking here specifically to people who are sorrowing over loved ones who have died before Jesus comes back.

Look at 1 Thessalonians 4:13, "We do not want you to be uninformed, brethren, about those who are asleep (this is a euphemism for death), so that you will not grieve as do the rest who have no hope." There are those who grieve without hope. Paul says we are not those people. It is okay for us to be sorrowful when we lose a loved one, but we are not to grieve as if we have no hope. Here is the reason we have hope, "If we believe that Jesus died and rose again, even so God will bring with him those who have fallen asleep in Jesus" (1 Thessalonians 4:14). This concept of falling asleep in Jesus is another way of speaking about those who have died in Christ.

Paul says, "God will bring with him those who have fallen asleep in Jesus." Now, he lets us know that this is apostolic authority and so is God's word. He says, "This we say to you by the word of the Lord, that we who are alive and remain until the coming of the Lord, will not precede those who have fallen asleep." They were concerned about those who die before Jesus comes back. Paul says, actually, those are the ones who get to go first; "We who are alive and remain will not precede those who have fallen asleep."

He adds in verse sixteen, "The Lord himself will descend from heaven with a shout, with the voice of the archangel and with the trumpet of God." What we have are three descriptions about this attention-getting event: a shout, the voice of the archangel, and the trumpet of God, and it will be so arresting that the dead in Christ will rise first. It will not be something that anyone will miss. It will be the unmistakable call of God, and he says, "Then we who are alive and remain will be caught up together with them in the clouds to meet the Lord in the air, and so we shall always be with the Lord. Therefore comfort one another with these words."

The rapture and second advent

Notice in verse fourteen, "God will bring with him those who have fallen asleep in Jesus," and then in verse sixteen, "The dead in Christ will rise first." So what will happen first; will they rise, or will they come with Jesus? The way most theologians reconcile this is to say that to be absent from the body is to be present with the Lord. When believers die, they go to be with the Lord and they come back with him, but their bodies are in the grave. Evidently, at this event that I am calling the rapture, the dead in Christ will rise first and their bodies will be glorified, which means that they will be reunited with their original bodies, and now have a glorified body.

This is a lot to think through, so feel free to continue pondering this at leisure, but for now we have one way of reconciling that apparent contradiction. Paul says again, "We who are alive and remain will be caught up together with him in the clouds to meet the Lord in the air." Some people hear this and say, "Man, I hope that I'm alive when this happens. Wouldn't it be wonderful to experience this?" Please understand that this event is not just for believers who are alive when it happens, it is for every believer as this is when every Christian will receive a glorified body. This is for every believer in the church age; our glorification is connected to this event. In Philippians chapter three, for example, we discover that we are waiting for our Savior, the One who is going to change our bodies. In 1 John chapter three we learn that when we see Him, we will be like Him, so our glorification is connected to this event. So this event is for every believer in this age.

Look at 1 Thessalonians 4:18, "Therefore, comfort one another with these words." Paul is assuring the Thessalonians that they do not have to worry about those who have died before Christ returns. They will not miss out. They are, in fact, going to be the first ones to go. Let me just bring a few contrasts here to talk about this event. Granted, this is an event that is very debatable among theologians, and I do not want you to come to a premature conclusion. I believe that the Bible teaches a pre-tribulational rapture, but I do not think you can conclude that from this passage. I think we will have to go further in the text to find this mentioned. For now, let me show you a few contrasts between this event and the second advent.

There is no reason why the rapture could not happen at any time. In other words, we believe that the rapture is imminent, and we gather that, among other reasons, because Paul says, "We who are alive and remain." It is not that Paul was wrong about this, it just means that he saw the rapture as a possibility that could happen in his lifetime. It is something that could happen at any time; it is imminent. The second advent, on the other hand, cannot happen unless it is first preceded by certain signs. Jesus said, "There will be signs in the sun, the moon, and the stars, men fainting from fear and expectation of the things that will come. Then they will see the son of man coming in a cloud." There have to be specific signs that precede the second advent, which seems to be different than this other event that we are calling the rapture.

I believe that the rapture will take place before the tribulation, which I will explain in more detail in our next tutorial. For now, let me say that based on 1 Thessalonians 1:10, the Thessalonians were waiting for God's Son to deliver them from the coming wrath. If the coming wrath is the tribulation, then this verse would argue for a pre-tribulation rapture. The second advent is after the tribulation. Immediately after the tribulation of those days, then the sign of the Son of Man will appear in the sky. With this rapture event, believers will be caught up to meet the Lord in the air, whereas at the second advent, Jesus will come to the Mount of Olives.

For the rapture, the Lord Himself comes for the Church. He will descend from heaven; whereas with the second advent, He will send His angels to gather together His elect. With the rapture, there is a resurrection of the dead in Christ, those fallen asleep in Jesus; whereas with the second advent, believing Israelites would be rescued. With the rapture, we find that wickedness increases; whereas when the second advent takes place, it brings an end to wickedness on the earth as God destroys the wicked.

Paul calls the rapture a mystery. It is something that is not revealed in the Old Testament, whereas the second advent and the day of the Lord are talked about in the Old Testament. These are just a few examples of arguments that are typically given to indicate that these two events are different. Paul speaks about the rapture with joyful anticipation. We will be caught up to meet the Lord in the air, so we are to comfort one another with these words of blessed hope; whereas the second advent is great and terrible, and not something to be looked forward to because of the judgment that it will bring.

> **? DISCUSSION POINTS**
>
> **1.** In 1st Thessalonians 4, Paul deals with issues that could impact the believer's walk with God. What were they? Are these things a threat to your walk and ministry?

3.24 The Day of the Lord

> **OBJECTIVES OF THIS TUTORIAL**
>
> In this tutorial, Bible presenter Scot Keen explains his view on the day of the Lord, which is mentioned in chapter five of first Thessalonians.

Introduction

In this tutorial, we will look at Paul's challenge to the believers in Thessalonica to have a proper perspective of the day of the Lord. Paul encourages the believers to keep going by living in light of their hope. Let's look at 1 Thessalonians 5:1, "Now as to the times and the epochs, brethren, you have no need of anything to be written to you. For you yourselves know full well that the day of the Lord will come just like a thief in the night."

A contrast

Paul seems to change topics after chapter four (in which Paul discusses an event which I call the rapture). In chapter four verse thirteen, Paul says, "We don't want you to be uninformed." Then he goes on to talk about this event that I call the rapture. In chapter five, Paul says, "You yourselves know full well," and then he talks about the day of the Lord. Now, this seems to imply that they were ignorant of the material in 1 Thessalonians 4:13-18, but that they were aware of the content in chapter five. So, it does set these passages in a bit of a contrast and lets us know that Paul is changing topics at some level here.

He says again, "As to the times and seasons you have no need of anything to be written to you. You know full well that the day of the Lord will come just like a thief in the night." This raises the question, "What is the day of the Lord?" Now, those familiar with the Old Testament would know that the day of the Lord is a major theme which appears in books such as Joel, Amos and Zephaniah. It has its roots in the book of Deuteronomy where God begins to talk about a day of visitation. The day of the Lord is a time period of judgment on earth which is unparalleled in its severity. Jesus talked about this day in Matthew chapter twenty-four. He said that this great tribulation will be unparalleled in its severity. So, we are talking about a time period that is extremely severe. It will be the time of God's judgment on the earth and it has a particular purpose. In Isaiah chapter twenty-six, God says that He is going to punish the inhabitants of the earth for their iniquity. Think of it like this; God's posture right now is one of mercy. He is holding out His hand, as 2 Peter says, "Not willing that any should perish but that all would come to repentance."

But God is not going to extend His arm of salvation forever. At some point in the future, there will be a time when God no longer shows forbearance and brings judgment instead. He will punish the nations for their iniquity (Isaiah 26). This time period is so specifically designed for Israel, that in Jeremiah chapter thirty, it is called the time of Jacob's trouble. God is going to use this great tribulation, this day of the Lord, to bring Israel to her knees. Remember we saw in the tutorials on Romans that there will be a future salvation for the nation of Israel? This day of the Lord is part of the picture; it is how God is going to bring them to the point of recognizing their need, repenting for their sin of crucifying Messiah and ultimately placing their faith in Him.

Hopefully that gives you some background on the day of the Lord. God's purpose in it, then, is to bring Israel to repentance. Paul says that this day of the Lord will come like a thief in the night. Then he explains himself further, "While they are saying, 'Peace and safety!' then destruction will come upon them suddenly like labor pains upon a woman with child, and they will not escape." The day of the Lord is a time of judgment that is inescapable. The passages in Zephaniah, Joel, and Amos all echo the same thing. As far as it being inescapable, Zephaniah says their silver and their gold cannot deliver them. In Joel we find that it is so severe that he asks the question, "Who can abide it?" Then Amos says it is like a man who is running from a bear. He runs into his house, puts his hand on the wall in relief and then a snake bites him on the hand. You cannot get away from the day of the Lord.

Taken by surprise

That is the picture that Paul paints in the book of 1 Thessalonians as well. He says sudden destruction will come like labor pains upon a pregnant woman and they will not escape. God's judgment will be inescapable. It is interesting that Paul says it comes like a thief in the night. It is obviously unexpected, but not because there was no warning. We know that there are many warnings, specifically in the Old Testament, concerning the day of the Lord. So it will not be a surprise in the sense that there was no warning. It will be a surprise because no one listened to the warnings. Think about the days of Noah as an example. Noah warned the people that the flood was coming.

Even though the people were warned, it still took them by surprise. As Jesus said, they were getting married right up until the time that the flood came. It surprised people because they did not believe God's warning. Likewise, Paul says the day of the Lord come suddenly like labor pains for a pregnant woman. This is a comical picture to me because when I think about something that comes unexpectedly, I wouldn't typically think about labor pains for a woman. The labor pains obviously indicate that a woman is getting closer to giving birth to her child. Speaking from experience with our first born, we were over eight months into the pregnancy. And suddenly one night my wife woke me to tell me her water had broken. I was shocked. Looking back, I don't know why I was shocked. She was supposed to have a baby. But again, I wasn't expecting it at that time. What Paul says here is that the day of the Lord will come like a thief in the night. People will be predicting peace and safety at the time. I think this is the time alluded to in Daniel chapter nine. It mentions a peace treaty that is signed with Israel for seven years. The antichrist evidently breaks the peace treaty in the midst of this seven-year period. So, people will be anticipating peace and safety, but in the meantime, destruction will come suddenly and they will not escape.

I see the same picture in first Thessalonians chapter five. But first, please know that the reason they do not escape is not that the lake of fire overtakes them suddenly. It is the day of the Lord that comes upon people unexpectedly. So, people will be predicting peace and safety but then sudden destruction will come and they will not escape. Listen to what Paul is saying. Sudden destruction. Day of the Lord. Thief in the night. The idea of sudden parallels with thief in the night. Destruction parallels day of the Lord. Paul is using different terminology to speak about the same event. He is saying that what comes suddenly is destruction. The day of the Lord will take people unawares.

A distinction

Notice Paul's choice of words here. Who is it who are overtaken by the day of the Lord? Paul puts a distinction between us and them. He says that the day of the Lord will come like a thief in the night. Some people will be predicting peace and safety, and destruction will come upon them. I do not think that is an accidental reference, rather, it is intentional on Paul's part. Paul is saying that the ones who predict peace and safety are the ones who will face sudden destruction. They are the ones who will not escape.

Then Paul brings us to what I understand is a contrast. He begins talking about believers in relation to the day of the Lord. This is significant in the book of first Thessalonians as a whole. I take the position, as I said earlier, that these believers are waiting for God's Son from heaven to deliver them from the wrath to come, which is wrath that is coming to the earth. While chapter one verse ten is not enough to convince us of that, chapter five tells us that the wrath that is coming is the day of the Lord. Paul says that they have been waiting to be rescued from the wrath to come. Now he explains why they will be rescued from it.

Let's look at the contrast in verse four, "But you, brethren, are not in darkness, that the day would overtake you like a thief; for you are all sons of light and sons of day." Paul talks firstly about their identity. He does not mention their understanding or the way that they are living their lives. He will talk about that later in verses six and following, challenging them to live like who they already are. But here Paul is talking about their identity as sons of the day. Paul says, "You are not in darkness that that day would overtake you. You are sons of the light and sons of the day."

We could either read this in one of two ways. When Paul says they are not in darkness, we could think of darkness as ignorance. If we read it that way, Paul would be saying that others will be surprised but the believers won't because they are not ignorant. In other words, Paul could be saying that the believers will not be surprised by the day of the Lord. They will be ready for it.

However, that is not what I think Paul is saying here. When Paul says, "You are not in darkness," I think he is talking about their identity and standing before God. They are not in darkness because they are saved. They are in the light. They are sons of the day and they should live that way. Let me give some examples of this concept from the first century world. In John 12:36, Jesus talks about this concept, "While you have the light," he calls himself the light of the world, "while you have the light, believe in the light." Look at the result, "So that you may become sons of the light." We are talking about an issue of identity, not about how much we understand or our lack of awareness. Paul says, "Believe in the light and then you become sons of the light."

Another clue that Paul is referring to identity is found in Colossians chapter one. Paul says that the believers have been translated out of the kingdom of darkness, "He has rescued us from the domain of darkness and transferred us into the kingdom of his beloved son." I take this to be a statement of identity. Jesus uses this terminology in John chapter twelve and Paul uses it in Colossians chapter one. We can also find it in Ephesians 5:6-8, "Let no one deceive you with empty words. Because of these things, the wrath of God comes upon the sons of disobedience." Paul is talking about unbelievers here. Sons of disobedience. "Therefore, do not be partakers with them." Don't live like unbelievers. And Paul explains why.

He says, "You formerly were darkness but now you are light in the Lord." He is not talking about the way they live, he is talking about their identity. I know that because he says, "You are light in the Lord." That is their identity. "Walk as children of the light." That's the way they live. In other words, Paul is saying, "This is who you are, a child of light, so live that way. Walk as children of the light." Well, that is my understanding of Paul's contrast here. So, I take Paul to be saying, "They say peace and safety. Sudden destruction comes upon them. They will not escape, but brothers, this is not what you'll face." That is the way I read this. They are sons of the light. They are not in darkness.

Applying doctrine

Now that Paul has distinguished the believers from unbelievers, he gives an application of that doctrine. He challenges them to live like who they are. Look at how he does this. In Ephesians 5:6 he says, "So then," which signifies that he is about to apply doctrine, "So then, let us not sleep as others do but let us be alert and sober." It would make sense for an unbeliever to be checked out and unaware and living a clueless life, but Paul says that is not who we are, so we should not live that way. "Let us not sleep as others do, but let's be alert and sober. Those who sleep do their sleeping at night. Those who get drunk get drunk at night."

If someone has a habit of getting drunk, it is not a surprise if they get drunk at night. That is typical for them at that time of day. If someone sleeps at night, we don't say, "Wow, how unusual. They're sleeping at night time." No. It is normal to sleep at night; that is when we sleep. So, Paul is saying let's be consistent with who we are, "Since we are of the day, let us be sober" (Ephesians 5:8). Let's live like who God has made us to be. And how do we do that? By doing the daytime things that he speaks of, "Having put on the breastplate of faith and love and as a helmet, the hope of salvation."

These are pieces of armor that Roman soldiers would wear. Paul says we need to arm ourselves with faith and love and hope. Do you remember how we defined hope at the beginning of our study on Thessalonians? Hope produces perseverance. Hope, in Pauline theology, is eschatological hope. It is the coming of Christ. It is, in my understanding, the rapture which gets us out of here. So Paul is saying that we have this hope of salvation and we need to live with it in mind. If I am correct in saying the hope of salvation is the hope of deliverance, then it completely ties in with verse nine.

Paul explains why we have the hope of salvation. He says, "for," which means he is explaining what he just said. "For God has not destined us for wrath, but for obtaining salvation through our Lord Jesus Christ who died for us so that whether we are awake or asleep, we will live together with him." This is a beautiful thing here. When Paul says God has not destined us for wrath, here are the questions I believe we need to be asking. First of all, what is wrath in context? Secondly, what is salvation in context? The wrath in context, I believe, is the great tribulation or the day of the Lord. Notice how Paul does not stick with one phrase here.

The wrath of God

In verse two, he calls this event the day of the Lord. Then he says it comes like a thief in the night. In verse three he calls it destruction and he tells us that it will come suddenly. Then in verse nine he names it wrath. The wrath in the context of first Thessalonians, especially chapter five, is the wrath of the day of the Lord. That is what he is talking about in those paragraphs. If that is the case, Paul is saying we have a helmet, the hope of deliverance. He explains specifically that God has not destined us believers for wrath. He has not destined us to predict peace and safety and then have sudden destruction come upon us. He has destined us to obtain salvation through our Lord Jesus Christ.

Paul says salvation comes through Christ. I take this context to be the wrath of God on earth, the day of the Lord. Therefore the deliverance he is talking about is deliverance from the day of the Lord. Now, I think it is talking about a pre-tribulation rapture. Here's why. The day of the Lord is unparalleled in severity and so is the tribulation, so they must be the same thing. If that is the case and God has not destined us for that, but has destined to deliver us from it, then God has destined to deliver us from the tribulation or the day of the Lord.

Now, some take the position that God is going to deliver us through the day of the Lord, meaning He puts His hands around us and He keeps us safe through the tribulation. That does not fit with the book of Revelation when it speaks about all the people who are martyred during the tribulation. So that is why I take this position. Again, everyone has to come to their own conclusions.

Let's go now to verse ten, "He died for us so that whether we are awake or asleep, we will live together with him." At first glance, it looks like awake and asleep are dealing with being dead or alive, as we saw in chapter four. But in reality, the words that Paul uses here are actually different. Paul is probably saying that since we are sons of the day (since we are believers), we should be doing daytime things. He says we should be awake and not asleep. Yet, even if we are asleep or awake, we will live together with Him. I think the idea is simply this. Believers should live for the Lord, but even if they don't (God forbid), they will still live together with Him. Why is that? Because He died for us.

Our salvation is rooted in what He did and not how we live. It is similar to the difference between the Israelites and the Egyptians in the book of Exodus. God, too, puts a difference between the church and the unbelieving world. They predict peace and safety. They face sudden destruction, but God has destined us for salvation, which in context, I believe, is deliverance from the day of the Lord.

Encouraged to persevere
Finally Paul concludes the book by urging the believers to keep going. Paul encourages healthy interaction in the body of Christ as part of their continuing growth in the Lord. Look at Ephesians 5:12, "We request to you brothers, that you appreciate those who diligently labor among you and have charge or authority over you and the Lord and give you instruction. That you esteem them very highly in love because of their work. Live in peace with one another." Now, my approach to scripture is if Paul "corrects" a problem, then that means the problem likely already exists. For example in chapter four, when Paul says, "Avoid sexual immorality," the implication is that they were involved in sexual

immorality. Here in chapter five where Paul says to appreciate spiritual leadership and to esteem them with respect, we can gather that the church was not showing proper respect.

If you think about this practically, believers' continued growth in the Lord is going to be in jeopardy if they do not relate well to the spiritual leadership that God has given them. According to Hebrews chapter thirteen, spiritual leadership is given for the sake of the body. Church leadership are to watch over our souls. So, we want to relate well with the leadership in a local church because that is one of the ways in which God helps us become mature in the faith. Another way we become mature is by ministering to the needs of others. Look at verse fourteen, Paul says, "We urge you, brethren, admonish the unruly, encourage the fainthearted, help the weak, be patient with everyone."

I love this verse because Paul doesn't say to encourage the unruly or admonish the weak. His instructions are specific to how each person is living. It is the unruly who need to be warned and the faint hearted who need to be encouraged and the weak who need help. This means that for you and me to be able to minister to the spiritual needs of other believers, we have to know what their needs are. Their needs will determine the way in which we should build them up. That cannot happen apart from spending time with other believers.

As people in ministry, we need to be spending time with those we seek to disciple so we can recognise their needs. In verse fifteen Paul says, "See that no one repays another with evil for evil, but always seek after that which is good for one another and for all people." As we are interacting with one another and happen to discourage or hurt each other, we should not pay back evil for evil.

Then Paul tells us to trust God daily. Look at verses sixteen to eighteen, Paul says, "Rejoice always." He is saying this to a persecuted church and he is aware that they are persecuted. Yet, he is trying to lift their eyes away from the here and now towards their hope in Christ and their reason to rejoice. We can always trust God because we know He is not going to leave us here forever. So there is an encouragement for us there. Paul also says to pray without ceasing. This does not mean that believers are to literally pray for every second of the day, but that we are to be given to prayer, devoted to prayer. Our lives are to be characterized by dependence upon God. Look at verse eighteen, "In everything give thanks; for this is God's will for you in Christ Jesus."

Prophetic utterances

Now, Paul talks about proper attitudes towards the Spirit's ministry in verse nineteen. In the first century before the Scriptures were completed, there were people who gave prophetic utterances and during that time period it was important to learn from those. Paul says do not quench the Spirit and then proceeds to explain what He means by that.

He says we are not to despise prophetic utterances. At times God moved an individual to give a prophetic utterance.

We see this in the book of Acts; different people prophesied, like Agabus who warned of a coming famine. Paul says they were not to quench the Spirit by placing no value on prophetic utterances. The danger, though, is that prophetic utterances could lead to imitation. So notice how Paul gives a caveat here in verse twenty-one, "Examine everything carefully; hold fast to that which is good; abstain from every form of evil." They would test these prophetic utterances by comparing them to the Word of God. If the prophecy was consistent, then they could embrace it, but if it was not, they were supposed to recognise it for what it was: not the Truth of God's Word.

A conclusion

Finally, Paul concludes the book in 1 Thessalonians 5:23- 28, "Now may the God of peace himself sanctify you entirely; and may your spirit and soul and body be preserved complete, without blame at the coming of our Lord Jesus Christ." Paul is praying that God would continue His work of sanctification in them, and then he adds, "Faithful is he who calls you, and he also will bring it to pass."

I don't think we should take from this that it does not matter how we live our lives because God will sanctify us anyway. I think Paul is giving us note of confidence by assuring us that God is committed to this. It does not mean that our response is unimportant, but it does mean that he will ultimately be the one to establish us and bring us to maturity.

Then Paul moves on to a prayer request in 1 Thessalonians 5:25, "Brethren, pray for us. Greet all the brethren with a holy kiss". Some people take this to be a literal statement. It was obviously literal in Paul's day. It was a culturally appropriate way to show Christian love. In my culture, this translates to a good handshake or a warm pat on the back, or something like that. Paul then says, "I adjure you by the Lord to have this letter read to all the brethren." Now, this is significant because it shows the habit of the first century church to give attention to the public reading of Scripture and it also shows that Paul recognized His letters as having apostolic authority. That was why he wanted them read in the assemblies. It would be read and understood as an authoritative document having come from Paul the apostle. So, that explains why he adjured them by the Lord to have it read. Then finally, Paul closes in verse twenty-eight, "The grace of our Lord Jesus Christ be with you."

? DISCUSSION POINTS

1. In 1st Thessalonians 5, Paul makes distinctions between "us" and "them." Can you identify these distinctions?

2. Paul speaks about God's wrath in 1st Thessalonians 5. Based on the context, what is meant by "wrath"?

3. In 1st Thessalonians 5:12, Paul highlighted the importance of respecting church leadership. In what ways could their response to Paul's instruction impact their walk with God (if they respond positively... negatively...)?

3.25 God will bring Rest

 OBJECTIVES OF THIS TUTORIAL

In this tutorial, Bible presenter Scot Keen tackles Paul's second letter to the Thessalonians. In the first chapter of 2 Thessalonians, we find encouragement to persevere because God has promised us rest.

Introduction

In this tutorial, we look at Paul's second letter to the Thessalonians. Most people understand this to be written soon after Paul wrote first Thessalonians, for several reasons. First of all, we have the mention of Paul, Silas, and Timothy being together in both letters. When we follow their ministry in the book of Acts, it looks like there is approximately an eighteen-month window when these three men were all together. If that is the case, both letters had to be written within an eighteen-month time period. That is significant because Paul was thinking about these believers, and he did not wait years or move to write them the letters after the initial church plant. Paul almost immediately checked on them and reached out to them. And so, it seems that 2 Thessalonians was written soon after 1 Thessalonians.

Purpose of Second Thessalonians

The purpose of the letter is to encourage the church as they persevere through suffering. We find in 2 Thessalonians that their persecution is still taking place. In chapter one verse four, Paul thanks God for their perseverance in the midst of their persecutions which they endure. So, it was ongoing. Paul also wrote this letter to clear up confusion regarding the day of the Lord. We will look at that more closely in chapter two. But evidently somebody had previously written a letter to the church in Thessalonica. They had put Paul's name on that letter, and that letter said that they were currently in the day of the Lord. This letter caused great confusion for the believers. Also in this letter, Paul corrects a problem regarding work ethic which he had seen while present during the initial church plant, addressed in 1 Thessalonians chapter four, and by this point, it is a full-blown problem that Paul has to deal with pretty strongly.

GOD WILL BRING REST

Paul's basic message in chapter one is to keep going because someday God will bring rest. And I think of it this way. Years ago I was in the car with my family travelling to Kentucky. And we were going to see family and had about an eight-hour trip ahead of us. At this time, my daughter was roughly between six and nine months old. She cried for the last several hours of the trip. What I wanted to communicate with her was that we didn't have much farther to go. But it's hard to communicate to a young child, and obviously she wouldn't have understood me as she experienced time differently. My point to this illustration is that we know we are not going to be on earth forever, regardless of how intense the persecution gets, and this will encourage us to hang on and to be faithful because, after all, this is not the final chapter. And that is what Paul does here.

Paul begins the letter with an introduction and greeting, "Paul and Silvanus and Timothy, to the church of the Thessalonians in God our Father and the Lord Jesus Christ: grace to you and peace from God the Father and the Lord Jesus Christ" (2 Thessalonians 1:1). And then Paul praises God for the good things that he saw taking place in Thessalonica. Look at verse three. He says, "We ought always to give thanks to God for you, brethren, as is only fitting, because your faith is greatly enlarged, and the love of each one of you toward one another grows ever greater." Now, this is amazing, because in 1 Thessalonians, Paul was concerned about their faith. He does not seem to show that same concern in 2 Thessalonians. So far, Paul is encouraged. It seems like the Thessalonians are maturing and are stable which gives Paul a sense of relief. In 1 Thessalonians, Paul had exhorted them to grow in the faith, and he also prayed that they would abound in love.

Look again at verse three. Paul says their love towards one another grows increasingly greater. That means firstly that God answered Paul's prayer as he was causing the Thessalonians to bound in love. And it also shows that they took Paul's exhortation to excel in love in first Thessalonians seriously. No wonder Paul is giving thanks to God. They are responding to the Message that he gave them. He is so encouraged that God answered his prayer and that they responded in obedience to the Word of God. In verse four, Paul says, "Therefore, we ourselves speak proudly of you among the churches of God for your perseverance and faith in the midst of all your persecutions and afflictions which you endure." Not only were their afflictions ongoing, but so was their faith. They were still trusting God. They were living by faith.

And so you could say that 1 Thessalonians was successful. They responded to Paul's Message. For those of you who may be involved in a church plant someday, imagine how encouraging this would be to a church planter; to know that you have instructed a church, seen a need and spoken into that from God's Word, and they respond! No wonder Paul praised God. Paul talks about the afflictions that they endure in verse four, and then he says in verse five that their perseverance and persecution is a plain indication of God's righteous judgment. This is worded in a slightly obscure way, so let me explain it. Paul says, "You guys are trusting God in the midst of persecution, and that proves that God does the right thing." What does Paul mean by that? He says it proves God's righteous judgment. Here is his explanation: so that they will be considered worthy of the kingdom of God for which indeed they are suffering.

Looking at persecution biblically

Paul says when they find themselves in the kingdom of God, they will be worthy to be there because they have suffered faithfully for Christ, and therefore they deserve the honors that will be bestowed upon them in the kingdom. But God's righteous judgment is not just seen in rewarding the believers for their faithfulness. God's righteous judgment is also seen in the way in which He treats the unbelieving world. Look at verse six, "After all it is only just for God to repay with affliction those who afflict you." Now, this is interesting terminology here. Our translations do a great job, "Repay with afflictions those who afflict you."

Paul uses a play on words in Greek. Here is the concept: God pays back in kind. The law of the harvest rings true. People reap what they sow. Think about, for example, Mordecai and Solomon and Hamon in the Old Testament. Hamon wanted to have Mordecai hung on the gallows, but Hamon ended up being hung on the very gallows that he had prepared for Mordecai. Take for example the men who framed Daniel when they caught him praying to God in Jerusalem. They wanted Daniel thrown into the lion's den, which he was. And in the end, God spared Daniel in the lion's den, and his attackers were thrown into the lion's den. The idea here is that God pays back with trouble those who trouble us. And so we see that God is going to bring judgment on the unbelieving world.

Obviously Paul is talking about those who trouble the believers in the first century. But I believe he is looking more broadly than that. He seems to be looking as humanity as a whole who will face God's judgment in the tribulation or the day of the Lord. And so God will pay back with trouble those who trouble us. He will give relief to those who are afflicted. And He will do this when the Lord Jesus is revealed from heaven with His mighty angels in flaming fire, dealing out retribution to those who do not know God and those who do not obey the Gospel of our Lord Jesus.

We now come to a resolution that we have been waiting for since Genesis chapter four. Think about how righteous Abel was murdered by wicked Cain. And the cry of God's people down through the ages has been, "How long, oh Lord? When is God going to turn the tables and finally make things right again?" And Paul says he will give wrath to the wicked and rest to us ultimately when Jesus comes back in flaming fire. Now, this is not a reference to what I've been calling the rapture. This is a reference to the second advent of Christ. And I think you could argue that when a believer dies, they finally have rest. You could also argue that, if I'm correct on my order of events here, when the rapture happens, all Christians will have rest. But when are things going to ultimately change, never to be messed up again? It will be when Jesus comes back at the second advent. I believe it was as if Paul was looking through a telescope and could see ahead to the final event. He did this to encourage believers that it will not be like this forever. God will give relief to those of us who are afflicted when the Lord Jesus is revealed from heaven in flaming fire, dealing out retribution to those who do not know Him.

When I consider this passage, a comical image comes to my mind which takes me back to first grade in the little town that I grew up in, Hyden, Kentucky. And I remember there was a young man in our class, which is strange, because it was first grade and so he should have been a small boy. I don't know how many times he'd had to repeat first grade. When the teacher would leave the room, this young man would look around to be sure no teachers were there, and literally would grab the tables and start flipping them over, terrorizing all the children in the classroom. We were scared to death of this guy. And he would continue doing that until the door opened and Ms. Roahr came back into the room. And then he would become as docile as a lamb.

In the same way, the world is under the sway of the Prince of the Power of the Air. Satan is the god of this world, and he wreaks havoc across the globe. But when Jesus comes back, he will be brought to a sudden and screeching halt. And so there will be relief when Jesus comes back. We can anticipate this with confidence and also with a sense of joy as we wait for it to take place. For the sake of time, I will not discuss this further expect to say that when this takes place, our world will be dramatically different. Evolution will not be taught in schools anymore. Abortion clinics will not be open anymore. Christians won't be persecuted. It will be radically different; things will finally be right on planet earth.

And so, Christ is coming back, and notice that He deals out retribution to those who do not know God and do not obey His Gospel. And if you look in Romans at the phrase obey the Gospel, it is referring to obedience of faith. Paul is saying that those who do not know the Lord will face eternal destruction. It is not that the wicked are consumed with fire and annihilated, they will face eternal destruction away from the presence of the Lord and from the glory of His power.

Remembering back to 1 Thessalonians chapter five, I argued that Paul contrasted believers with unbelievers. Unbelievers face sudden destruction and will not escape. But we who believe are not in darkness. God has destined us for salvation. Well, Paul does a similar thing here. He talks about what will face the unbelieving world. But then look at what He says about believers in verse ten, "When he comes to be glorified in his saints on that day, and to be marveled at among all who have believed." On that day, the believers will glorify Him. It is not that we can somehow add something to the majesty of God's glory, but the fact that we will be there glorifying, knowing what we were and what He has made us, will ultimately bring Him glory. He will be marveled at by all who have believed. In the presence of the glorified Christ, we are going to be gripped and stunned in our hearts, marveling in His presence.

Here is the difference between eternal destruction and marveling in the presence of Christ. Look at verse ten, "Because our testimony to you was believed." The reason the Thessalonians will be marveling in the presence of Christ is because Paul, Silas and Timothy went into Thessalonica with the Gospel of God's grace. They proclaimed that Message, and these people believed. And I want to encourage you with a thought: maybe one day there will be an indigenous church marveling in the presence of Christ, instead of eternally separated from Him and enduring his wrath, all because you took the Gospel to them and they believed it.

Prayer for growth

Paul then prays for continued growth in 2 Thessalonians 1: 11-12, "To this end also we pray for you always, that our God will count you worthy of your calling." If God is going to count us worthy of our calling, then would have to be living consistently with our calling. So, in essence, Paul is praying that they would walk worthy of their calling, just like he did back in first Thessalonians chapter two. Not only that, but he also prays that they would fulfil every desire for goodness, and the work of faith with power. Imagine being this believer in Thessalonica. As a believer you have desires for goodness and desires to live for the Lord. And as we saw in Romans chapter seven, sometimes the willing is present, but the doing is not. Paul prayed that not only would they have the desire, but that God would also fulfil that work of faith with power.

Notice the purpose or the goal of that prayer request in verse twelve, "So that the name of our Lord Jesus will be glorified in you, and you in him." Paul is praying that God would answer both their prayers and his for them to live worthy of Christ and to fulfil their desires for goodness with the power of God's Spirit as they walk by faith. And as a result, Christ will be glorified. And how will this request be granted? Paul says, "According to the grace of our God, and the Lord Jesus Christ." Paul is praying for their continued growth so that they will ultimately live in a way that is pleasing to Christ. He is praying that they will keep going.

? DISCUSSION POINTS

1. According to 2nd Thessalonians 1:10, why will the Thessalonians be rejoicing in the presence of God?

2. How does the previous question impact your view of missions?

3.26 Don't Forget the Truth

 OBJECTIVES OF THIS TUTORIAL

In this tutorial, Bible presenter Scot Keen shows how Paul alleviates the fears of the Thessalonian believers. Paul does this by clarifying the day of the Lord.

Introduction

In this tutorial, we will look at chapter two of second Thessalonians, specifically honing in on Paul's response to the believers' confusion over a false letter they received. This letter claimed that they were already in the day of the Lord, and so Paul addresses this in 1 Thessalonians chapter two. First of all, he will alleviate their fears by giving clarification regarding the day of the Lord. Then he will remind them of their hope. Think of it this way. At one time, the Thessalonians were waiting for God's Son from heaven to deliver them from the wrath to come (1 Thessalonians 1:10). I think this means they were waiting on Jesus to come and rescue them, to deliver them before God's wrath comes to the earth. I take this to be a reference to a pre-tribulation rapture. In 1 Thessalonians chapter five, we found that the Thessalonians were not destined for wrath, the day of the Lord, but were destined to obtain salvation.

Clarification

In 2 Thessalonians, we find that they thought the wrath had already come, and this really upset them and confused them. So Paul wrote second Thessalonians to clarify that confusion. What were they confused about? We can find the answer in 2 Thessalonians 2:1, "Now we request you, brethren, with regard to the coming of our Lord Jesus Christ and our gathering together to him, that you not be quickly shaken from your composure or be disturbed either by a spirit or a message or a letter as if from us, to the effect that the day of the Lord has come." As I mentioned previously, evidently someone wrote a letter and placed Paul's signature on that letter, as if it were from him. And in the letter, they claimed the day of the Lord had come. This is significant. If Paul had taught that they would go through the day of the Lord, they obviously would not be surprised by a letter saying they were in the day of the Lord. The fact that they were surprised about this shows that they originally expected to be delivered from the coming wrath.

Alleviating fears

That is one of the major reasons why they were confused here. Paul will try to avoid being impersonated like this again in the future. When he closes 2 Thessalonians, he says, "I write this greeting with my own hand. This is a distinguishing mark in every letter." So Paul developed a trademark, if you will, to put on every one of his letters, so ensure that someone wouldn't forge his signature again. However in this case, someone had, and the believers were confused. Paul wants to alleviate their fears, "Let no one in any way deceive you, for it (meaning the day of the Lord) will not come unless the apostasy comes first, and the man of sin is revealed, the son of destruction." Paul says certain things must happen first. Before the day of the Lord can come, the apostasy has to have come, and not only the apostasy, but also the man of sin, who is the son of destruction. They could not say they were in the day of the Lord because these things had not happened yet.

Let me talk about some of the phrases here. Paul says that first of all will come the apostacy and there are different ways that people can take this. Some people take it to literally mean the rapture. Of course, you know whose view that would support. That view is highly debated, and perhaps not where we should put our weight. The other and major dominant view is that apostasy here refers to a religious falling away, a departure from the faith. We see this mentioned throughout the New Testament, so that is probably what Paul means here. There will be an apostasy, but not only that. The man of lawlessness, who is the son of destruction, will also be revealed.

The man of lawlessness will be characterized by rebellion; he will oppose God's Word. Not only that, but he is also called the son of perdition or destruction. That is a Hebrew idiom that expresses character and destiny. He is the son of destruction, meaning he came from hell, and he is going to hell. That is a rough but fairly accurate rendition of that. In verse four we find that this man will oppose and exalt himself above every so-called god. Many people refer to this same individual as the anti-Christ. The term anti-Christ is John's terminology. Paul tends to call him the man of lawlessness, and there are reasons to believe that they are referring to the same individual. The term anti- Christ alludes to being in opposition to, and when the anti-Christ comes, he will offer himself instead of, or in place of Christ, and he will also stand in opposition to God's Word.

The anti-Christ will exalt himself above every so-called god or object of worship. He will claim to be God. Notice that he takes his seat in the temple of God, proclaiming himself as God. When 1 and 2 Thessalonians were written, the temple still stood in Jerusalem.

Now the temple no longer stands, and so people today look at various individuals and call them the anti-Christ. The problem with that is no one can recognise the anti-Christ until he starts fulfilling the prophecy about himself. We see here that the anti-Christ will enter the temple of God, so the temple will have to be rebuilt before the anti-Christ can be identified. Let me take you back to Daniel chapter eleven briefly, which Paul is alluding to here. Daniel says, "The king will do as he pleases. He will exalt and magnify himself above every god. He will speak monstrous things against the God of gods, and he will prosper for a certain amount of time" (Daniel 11:36).

Notice how Paul uses the same terminology. The anti-Christ exalts himself above every so-called god or object of worship. He will enter the temple of God, displaying himself as God. Some people who have spent a lot of time looking into this would say the timing of this seems to be in the middle of the tribulation. However I won't go into that now for the sake of time. In his self-exaltation, the man of sin opposes any deity being worshiped other than himself (2 Thessalonians 2:4). He enters the temple, claims to be God, and according to Daniel chapters nine and twelve, he causes sacrificial worship to cease. He puts an end to the Jewish sacrificial system. Paul says in verse five, "Do you not remember while I was still with you, I was telling you these things?" Let's pause here briefly.

It shocks me that in the short time period in which Paul was in Thessalonica, he was able to teach them about eschatology to this extent. Paul didn't view eschatology as too debatable to mention. Neither did he see it as unnecessary. He saw it as a part of Christian teaching that was necessary, and for good reason. We saw in 1 Thessalonians chapter one that hope produces perseverance, and so eschatology was part of Paul's discipleship with the believers. He did not see it as too controversial or unnecessary to mention. Paul says, "I told you these things while I was with you." But what restrains the anti-Christ now? We get this picture that someone or something is restraining him from coming onto the scene. He is being held back. There have been different theories about who the anti-Christ is throughout church history, and one of the most common is that it must be human government. The question is asked, "Who or what was around in the first century that is still around to this day, that is restraining Satan's evil program?"

Of course, human government has been around since then. The problem with that view is that the anti-Christ doesn't work against human government. The anti-Christ works through human government. He exalts himself as being a god, and he is a political ruler, according to Daniel, and so that brings us to the best explanation of what is holding him back. It is probably God restraining Satan from his evil plan until God's timing is ready. If you remember from the book of Genesis, God restrained Abimelech from taking Sarah as his wife. God kept Abel for his purposes. That is probably the case here. If you want to picture what it is like when restraint is removed, just look at certain countries where riots have taken place, and things have deteriorated in a hurry. I remember when Hurricane Katrina came to New Orleans years ago, and there was an onslaught of rebellion, violence, looting and things like that. When restraint is removed, we see the true character of fallen man, and so that is what we will see in the time period of the anti-Christ. The restrainer then would have to be removed, as Paul says in verse seven, "The mystery of lawlessness is already at work; only he who now restrains will do so until he is taken out of the way," so the restrainer keeps working until he is removed, and then and only then, the lawless one will be revealed. Paul doesn't go into the career of the lawless one yet. He will get there shortly, but as soon as Paul says he will be revealed, Paul wants us to know how the story will end. "That lawless one will be revealed whom the Lord will slay with the breath of his mouth and bring to an end by the appearance of his coming." That terminology comes out of Isaiah chapter eleven, and it is speaking about the anti-Christ being bought to a screeching halt by the appearing of the true Christ at the end of the tribulation. Then Paul gives us more details about the anti-Christ in verse nine.

He says, "The one who is coming is in according with the activity of Satan." He will operate by Satanic power, and not only will he operate by Satanic power, but he also has all power, signs and wonders. This is very interesting, because that triplet, power, signs, and wonders, is used in reference to Jesus in Acts chapter two. It is also used to talk about Paul's apostolic signs and miracles in second Corinthians. This is significant because these signs and wonders were given by God to Christ and to the apostles to validate their claims of who they were. The anti-Christ comes, in the activity of Satan, and he mimics those things to validate his claims of being the Christ of God, and so he comes in the activity of Satan. Think about the magicians in Egypt who imitated the things that Moses did, to a certain degree. That is what the anti-Christ is going to do. This man of sin will perform miracles to validate his claims of being God.

I want to take you to a passage in Revelation chapter thirteen that speaks about this beast and the false prophet. The beast seems to be the same figure as the anti-Christ here. It describes the beast. His feet are like a bear's and his mouth is like a lion's. The dragon gives him his power, and his throne and great authority. John saw that one of his heads looked as if it had been slain, and his fatal wound was healed. It looks like there was a fatality and then a recovery from that fatality and notice the response. All the people worshiped the beast saying, "Who is like the beast? Who is able to wage war against him?" The reason I call attention to that is because these powers and signs that are accomplished by the anti-Christ, and through the beast and the false prophet, are so convincing that Jesus said they would deceive even the elect if possible, and so Satan is going to do everything in his power to deceive the unbelieving world. It will be very, very effective.

God is going to let the unbelieving world face judgment, which is the coming of the anti-Christ, because they rejected the Truth of His Word. He says, "They did not receive the love of the truth, so as to be saved," and that shows us that their damnation, or their eternity in the lake of fire, is due to their own refusal to believe the Gospel Message. He says in 2 Thessalonians 2:11, "For this reason God will send upon them a deluding influence so that they will believe what is false." I don't think that means God will simply drop a mist over the minds of people, and somehow cause them to be deluded in that way. I think the deluding influence is the anti-Christ and the false prophet that works in conjunction with him. In other words, because people rejected the Truth, God will let them embrace a lie.

In fact, God sends the liar. He allows the anti-Christ to come on the scene. This is similar to what we saw in Romans chapter one. People rejected the knowledge of God through creation. Therefore, God gave them over. It is the same concept here: God lets people believe the lies of the anti-Christ, and notice the result, "In order that they all might be judged who did not believe the truth, but took pleasure and wickedness." This is a fascinating verse because Paul is contrasting belief with having pleasure in wickedness. The idea is that these people had heard the Gospel message, but they were aware that embracing this Message could come with moral ramifications for their lives, and so they chose pleasure in wickedness instead. They would not believe the Message because of their pleasure in wickedness. Paul talks about what comes upon them. I want you to notice something interesting here.

We see that they do not love the truth. They chose the pleasure of unrighteousness. It is their own choice that brings about their condemnation, which is important to note. So what will happen to the anti-Christ? Revelation chapter fourteen talks about the beast and those who worship him. It says, "The smoke of their torment ascends up forever and ever, and they have no rest day and night who worship the beast and his image." We see a similar picture to 1 Thessalonians chapter five, but it is amplified in Revelation. The day of the Lord, the tribulation, will come and unbelievers will be predicting peace and safety. They will be worshiping the beast and his image. They will have completely bought into the lies of the anti-Christ and, because of that, they will be judged.

As a friend of mine says it will be hell on earth. Then it will be hell in hell, and then death and hell will be cast into the lake of fire. It will go from bad to worse because they rejected the Message of God's salvation. Interestingly, Paul turns the tables now, and he talks about the Christian in relation to the day of the Lord. Paul reminds them of their hope. Think back to the pattern we saw in 1 Thessalonians chapter five. First Paul talked about what the day of the Lord will mean for unbelievers, and then he contrasted it with what it will mean for believers. It was destruction for them, but God has not destined us for wrath, for day of the Lord, but to obtain salvation. There is a contrast. That is the Message that Paul taught them when he was with them. That is the Message that he wrote them in 1 Thessalonians. What do you do if somebody believes your message, and then they get confused about it? You write them the same message again, and that is exactly what second Thessalonians chapter two is.

A reminder of hope

It's a mirror of 1 Thessalonians chapter five. Paul says, "This is what will happen to them, but this is what God has planned for you." Look at 2 Thessalonians 2:13, "But we should always give thanks to God for you, brethren, beloved by the Lord, because God has chosen you from the beginning for salvation, through sanctification by the Spirit, and faith in the truth." Think about this, God has not destined you for wrath, but to obtain salvation (1 Thessalonians 5:9). See the similarity? They gave thanks to God for them, because God has chosen them from the beginning for salvation. God is not figuring out what he is going to do with people in the midst of tribulation. From the beginning, God had His plan. He chose us for salvation through sanctification by the Spirit, and faith in the Truth, and part of this package deal for believers in the church age is being delivered from this wrath.

In the context of 2 Thessalonians chapter two, that is a description of the wrath and salvation. Obviously, salvation includes sanctification by the Spirit, and we entered into that through faith in the truth, but look at the trajectory that he sets verse fourteen, "It was for this he called you, through our gospel." In other words, this is what God's plan is for you. God called us so that we may gain the glory of our Lord Jesus. Look at how the road between believers and unbelievers gets farther and farther apart. They rejected the Gospel. They love the pleasures of unrighteousness. The anti-Christ is going to come. They are going to follow his lies, and they are going to face the wrath of God when Jesus comes back. Then they are going to be thrown into the lake of fire. That is their trajectory. As for believers, we heard the Gospel Message (2 Thessalonians 1:10). We believe the Gospel, and as we believe it, we are set apart, and not only that, but as believers we are ultimately destined to obtain salvation from the day of the Lord, and ultimately to gain the glory of our Lord Jesus Christ.

A mirror-image

What I find here, then, is Paul is mirroring what he said in 1 Thessalonians. This is a strong literary feature. In fact, there are other places this happens in 1 and 2 Thessalonians. In 1 Thessalonians chapter five, the unsaved world thinks all is well and judgment comes upon them unexpectedly. That Is in the context of the day of the Lord. In 2 Thessalonians chapter two, the unsaved world embraces the lies of anti-Christ. They are unsuspecting of any threat of judgment. And again, this is in the context of the day of the Lord. See how Paul is saying the same thing? He says that the unsaved will not escape the judgment of God (2 Thessalonians 2:12). God's plan for believers is different from His plan for the unsaved world, and it's marked by the contrastive term but (1 Thessalonians 5:4). In 2 Thessalonians, we also see that God's plan for believers is different from His plan for the unsaved world, marked again by a contrastive but (2 Thessalonians 2:13).

In 1 Thessalonians chapter five, God has destined believers for salvation, which in context includes deliverance from the day of the Lord. The word salvation cannot be understood apart from its context in the day of the Lord. Think about this. When you read the book of James, for an example, we see that the prayer of faith will save the sick. Salvation, in this context, is deliverance from physical illness. When the disciples were on the boat and said, "Lord, save us," in this context, salvation meant being saved from the storm. The word salvation has to be understood in its context, and here it means salvation from the day of the Lord. In 2 Thessalonians chapter two, we see that God has chosen believers for salvation, which in context includes deliverance from the coming wrath. Salvation cannot be understood apart from its context of the day of the Lord. When you get to the end of 1 Thessalonians chapter five, Paul says, "Therefore encourage one another." And in 2 Thessalonians chapter two, Paul says, "Comfort one another," and so the beauty of this structure is a literary parallel.

This shows us that Paul taught something that they previously believed. Then they got a false letter that confused their thinking, and then he wrote them 2 Thessalonians to teach them the same thing again, and so the two books help us understand each another. Paul is imploring the believers to continue to believe what he originally told them. They should be expecting God's Son to deliver them from the coming wrath. Look at verse fifteen, "So then brothers, stand firm and hold to the traditions which you were taught," traditions here not meaning like something handed down by human minds. He is talking about apostolic doctrine. He says, "Hold to the traditions which you were taught." Paul is saying, "Keep believing what we taught you," and then he prays for them, "Now may our Lord Jesus Christ Himself and God our Father, who has loved us and given us eternal comfort and good hope by grace, comfort and strengthen your hearts in every good work and word."

Paul tells them to comfort one another with these truths, and when we look at it in context, he clarifies that it is in regards to the day of the Lord. First Paul says, "You are not in the day of the Lord, because it is impossible for it to be that time yet. None of this is happening," and then he says, "By the way, you're not going to be there for the day of the Lord anyway, just like I told you in first Thessalonians." So Paul is telling them to keep going and to not forget the Truth.

DON'T FORGET THE TRUTH

One last word of encouragement here. When you work in church planting ministries, you will find that the people you teach get confused at times, and you will have to teach them over and over and over again. I want to encourage you to be patient and faithful and remember all the times you have had to come back to those same basic truths that you were once taught. Keep teaching God's Word and trust Him to strengthen the hearts of those whom you serve.

DISCUSSION POINTS

1. According to 2nd Thessalonians 2, why will the unbelievers perish under God's wrath in the Day of the Lord?

2. How does the previous question impact your view of missions?

3. According to 2nd Thessalonians 2, the believers had been led astray by a letter claiming to be from Paul. This passage shows us how important it is for believers to have the written word of God to cling to. How does this impact the way you view translation in a church planting effort?

ACTIVITIES

1. Read 2nd Thessalonians 1 and 2 and make a list of those things that God has planned for believers and a contrasting list of those things that God says will happen to unbelievers.

2. Discuss the ways in which God's plan for believers differs from His plan for unbelievers in 2nd Thessalonians 2

3.27 Focus on Christ

> **OBJECTIVES OF THIS TUTORIAL**
>
> In this tutorial, Bible presenter Scot Keen concludes our study on 2 Thessalonians and also on the module as a whole. We find that Paul leaves the Thessalonians with a resounding call to persevere and also an intriguing command to not be lazy.

Introduction

This tutorial brings us to the end of our study on 2 Thessalonians and also on this module as a whole. We have been talking about living in God's narrative. So let's look now at 2 Thessalonians chapter three.

Request for Prayer

Paul exhorts the believers to keep going by focusing on Christ. In 2 Thessalonians chapter three, Paul gives a prayer request. He says, "Finally, brethren, pray for us that the word of the Lord will spread rapidly and be glorified, just as it did also with you."

Now it is interesting that Paul is giving this prayer request and he is praying specifically that God's Word would spread, in other words not be inhibited, and that it would be glorified. We see in Acts chapter thirteen that God's Word is glorified when it is believed to be what it truly is, the Word of God. And so Paul is praying that the Word of God would spread and that it would be recognized for what it is, in the same way as it was in Thessalonica.

Paul also asked for prayer that he would, "Be rescued from perverse and evil men; for not all have faith." He is saying, in essence, that not everybody is a believer. Now this is an interesting prayer request because it shows us that Paul believed that his ministry could be furthered by the ministry of the Thessalonians in prayer. They could be part of the church plant in Corinth, which was where Paul was when he wrote this. They could be part of that church plant by praying for Paul right where they were.

This should motivate us to pray for the church plants that we are aware of and, in doing so, pray that God's word would have its way in the hearts of men. When you look at Paul's prayer request, he doesn't ask for prayer for material things. He is not praying about health or situations like that, not that they are bad things to pray about. But it shows that Paul's heart was focused on the advance of the Gospel and the building up of believers in the faith.

What is amazing about this is that when Paul wrote this, he faced a lot of opposition (Acts 18). And while he was there facing that opposition, the Lord appeared to him, telling him not to be afraid but to keep speaking. And God kept him there for eighteen months. Now could it be that God answered the prayer of the Thessalonian believers on Paul's behalf, and that was part of Paul's success in ministry in Corinth? I believe it was.

Paul says, "Not all have faith," which is another way of saying that some people are unbelievers. But then he uses a play on words and says, "But the Lord is faithful, and he will strengthen and protect you from the evil one." Paul wants the believers to know that God is faithful, that He will continue to be involved in their lives and that He will strengthen them and protect them from the evil one.

Now we come to Paul's statement of confidence about the believers. He says in verse four, "We have confidence in the Lord concerning you." I'm constantly amazed and appreciative of the language of Scripture. Paul is so specific in his wording. He is confident in the Lord about them. And specifically, he is confident in the Lord concerning them that they are doing and will continue to do what Paul commanded.

Let's elaborate on this briefly. When Paul wrote 1 Thessalonians, he did not seem to have the confidence that they were doing and continuing to do what he commanded. He was afraid that the tempter had tempted them, and his labor would be in vain. Well, Paul does not show that same concern in 2 Thessalonians. Now Paul is confident in the Lord concerning them that they are doing and continuing to do what he commanded. And the reason Paul had this confidence is because he had seen their obedience to the Word long enough to see a track record, to see a trajectory.

And yet, even then, Paul's confidence was ultimately in the Lord, but it was about them. And the idea here is that he was confident that they would keep walking with God, but his confidence was in God to make this happen, not necessarily in them. And this is not a blanket promise that he knows that there is nothing they could ever do to mess up, but it shows that he believes they are on the right trajectory. They are responding to the Word of God, and he trusts and knows that God will continue to be faithful, so he has every reason to be confident that they will keep maturing in the Lord and walking the path that God has for them.

Exhortation to persevere

Now Paul gives what I call the climactic exhortation to persevere. Remembering back to chapter one of 1 Thessalonians, Paul said, "Keep going. You had a great start. You turned to God from idols. You had work of faith, labor of love, perseverance of hope. You were an example to everybody else. Keep going. You had a great start." In chapter two Paul said, "Keep going. We are credible messengers and everything we did was so that you would walk worthy of God." In chapter three, Paul said, "Keep going in order to be blameless before Christ at his coming. May God cause you to abound in love so that you will be blameless before Christ." And so, keep moving ahead. Then in chapter four, he says, "We urge you excel still the more in your life. Watch out for sexual immorality. Don't be confused about what happens when believers die. Keep going." In chapter five Paul says, "Keep going because God has not destined us for the day of the Lord or for wrath, he's destined us for salvation. You have this hope, this helmet of salvation. Respect your church leadership. Listen to prophetic utterances and keep going."

Now we move on to 2 Thessalonians. In chapter one Paul says, "Keep going because we're not going to suffer forever. Christ comes back, and it will be wrath for them but rest for us." Then in chapter two, "Keep going because God has different plans for us than he has for the unsaved world." And now in chapter three Paul comes to a climactic exhortation. He says, "May the Lord direct your hearts into the love of God" (2 Thessalonians 3:5). And this is a beautiful image.

The picture that comes to my mind is of my son when he was a year old. He would stand in the glass doorway and he would watch for me to come home from work. And it was so funny because I could see him long before his little eyes could focus on me. And I would be walking towards the house and all of a sudden, I could see his look changed and he would get all excited and start shaking his fists. He was so glad to see his dad. He directed his gaze onto me and it changed his demeanor.

And Paul is praying that God would direct our hearts into the love of God. The idea is that we are so prone to be performance driven, to labor to earn God's love and to think of it in the wrong terms that Paul is praying that the believers that God would turn their attention towards God's perfect love. When God turns our attention towards His love in the midst of suffering, it has a way of bringing deep peace to us. We know that even though we are being persecuted, God loves us and has our best interests at heart. So may the Lord direct your hearts into the love of God. And then, look at this, into the steadfastness of Christ.

In Greek this translates to, "May God direct your hearts into the perseverance of Christ." And what we need to know when we are being challenged to persevere is that God loves us. Then we need to lift up our eyes towards the One who himself persevered, who endured the cross, despised the shame and sat down at the right hand of God. We look to Jesus and that is what sustains us in the difficult times. And so Paul is praying that God would turn their attention toward the love of God and towards Christ's perfect example of perseverance. We can be encouraged to be faithful knowing that one day we too, will be in the presence of the Lord.

Correcting the lazy

Now Paul gives a correction for those in the church who are lazy. He deals with some problems here as he wraps up the letter. I mentioned in a previous tutorial that when Paul was present among the church in Thessalonica, he saw a problem with their work ethic. He addressed that in 1 Thessalonians. By this point, it has grown into an epidemic and Paul has to deal with it, "We command you, brethren, in the name of our Lord Jesus Christ, that you keep away from every brother who leads an unruly life and not according to the tradition which you received from us" (2 Thessalonians 3:6).

Paul is telling the believers to separate fellowship from other believers who are walking out of God's will. And then, he lets us know what that problem is in verse seven, "You yourselves know how you ought to follow our example, because we did not act in an undisciplined manner among you, nor did we eat anyone's bread without paying for it." So evidently, even though Paul could have used his apostolic authority to receive finances from the Thessalonians, he refrained from doing so because he wanted to set an example. Perhaps Paul had early on already detected the potential, or even the actual problem, that was there.

And so Paul says, "With labor and hardship we kept working night and day so we would not be a burden to any of you." Paul paid for his own ministry expenses in order to be an example. Look at verse ten, "When we were with you, we used to give you this order: if anyone is not willing to work, then he is not to eat, either." And so, we could be fooled in thinking the Thessalonians had love feasts and communal meals as believers. But when Paul was there, he would notice that the same ones would come to the feasts. They would not contribute to this meal. They were taking from other people but never giving. And Paul recognized that it was not because they could not work but rather because they refused to work. Paul realized this was a problem and he addressed it even during the initial church plant. He said they should not eat if they are not willing to work.

Pauls adds, "We hear that some among you are leading an undisciplined life, doing no work at all, but acting like busybodies" (2 Thessalonians 3:11). This is appalling to me. Out of all the people on the face of this earth who have a purpose in life, it is believers. The last people who should be aimless in their lives and going around as busybodies are believers. We know why we exist: to

live in God's narrative. We exist to take the Gospel Message to the nations. We exist to see believers built up in the faith and, though not everyone goes to do that, those who don't go should be working with their hands in order to have something to give to those in need. They should be reaching out in their own communities and building up believers in their own local churches.

And so, Paul was bothered by the fact that they were busybodies. He says, "Such persons we command and exhort in the Lord Jesus Christ to work in quiet fashion and eat their own bread." How would the Message get across? Someone would have carried this letter to Thessalonica and would read it publicly to the assembly there. Imagine being the undisciplined person sitting in the congregation, hoping for somewhere to hide when these words were read, "Such persons we command and exhort in the Lord Jesus Christ to work in quiet fashion and eat their own bread." But for those who are being faithful, Paul says, "But as for you, brethren, do not grow weary of doing good."

It goes without saying that working in a benevolent ministry, where you are trying to care for those who are in need, lends itself to being taken advantage of. So Paul said, "Do not grow weary in doing good." Correct the problem, yes, but don't stop doing good. And he also says, "If anyone does not obey our instruction in this letter (meaning to get a job and to work with their hands) take special note of that person and do not associate with them so that he would be put to shame." This was a shame culture, after all, and church discipline involved shaming the person into seeing the gravity of their wrong choices so they would function in a healthy way in the body.

Some people feel this was severe church discipline, but realize Paul had addressed this problem several times already, first when he was planting the church and then again in 1 Thessalonians, and so far they have not responded. Now it is time for corporate action and so he says to for the church to disassociate with these people, but he also adds that they are not to be regarded as enemies but admonished as brothers. This correction is done because they are fellow believers in the Lord and the goal is for them to be restored to a healthy walk with God. And so the church discipline is not punishment but an act of loving correction. And that was Paul's intent.

A conclusion

Well, Paul concludes in verses sixteen to eighteen, "Now may the Lord of peace himself continually grant you peace in every circumstance. The Lord be with you all!" And as I mentioned in the last tutorial, Paul gives his personal signature so that no one could copy his letters again. "I, Paul, write this greeting with my own hand" (1 Thessalonians 3:17). This is a distinguishing mark in every letter. This is the way he writes. Paul wants to be very clear on this. And then he concludes by saying, " The grace of our Lord Jesus Christ be with you all."

Now just a few quick comments to wrap up this study about living in God's narrative. We started in Romans chapter one. We have ended in 2 Thessalonians chapter three. During this time period in history, God is visiting the nations with the Gospel. He has turned to the Gentiles, as we saw in the book of Romans. And we have this Gospel Message: people are justified by faith in Christ and sanctified through the Message that we are dead to sin and alive to God. We are secure in Christ. This is the teaching that we need to be preaching in local churches.

We learnt in Romans chapters nine through eleven that God has turned his attention towards the nations but will one day focus back on the Jewish people and fulfil the promises he made them. Then in Romans chapters twelve to sixteen, we found God desires for us to be living sacrifices, to submit to human government, to function with our gifts in the body of Christ, to live in unity together with one another and to be faithful with what he has entrusted to us. He will establish us in the faith.

We also discussed in 1 and 2 Thessalonians that as believers, we are secure in our salvation and so salvation is not at stake. But we are responsible to keep walking with God and to keep moving ahead with our growth in Him. And one of the key factors in that perseverance is hope. And 1 and 2 Thessalonians keep that hope in front of us.

My prayer and challenge for you is that you would live in light of God's narrative, believing and obeying the Word of God, knowing that one day God will accomplish His plan, as is hinted in the book of Romans and 1 and 2 Thessalonians. Thank you so much for being a part of this study.

❓ DISCUSSION POINTS

1. What major problem did Paul deal with in 2nd Thessalonians 3?

2. Have you ever seen church discipline practiced? How was the issue dealt with?

Training Resources for Making Truth *Accessible*.

RESOURCES FOR

> Discipleship > Evangelism > Church Planting
> Language Learning > Bible Translation > Cross-cultural work

Equipping God's people to be more effective as they serve in cross-cultural contexts, either locally or globally.

accesstruth.com

www.ingramcontent.com/pod-product-compliance
Lightning Source LLC
Chambersburg PA
CBHW061811290426
44110CB00026B/2846